Birnbaum's 95
Washington, DC

A BIRNBAUM TRAVEL GUIDE

Alexandra Mayes Birnbaum
EDITORIAL CONSULTANT

Lois Spritzer
Editorial Director

Laura L. Brengelman
Managing Editor

Mary Callahan
Senior Editor

David Appell
Patricia Canole
Gene Gold
Jill Kadetsky
Susan McClung
Associate Editors

HarperPerennial
A Division of HarperCollinsPublishers

To Stephen, who merely made all this possible.

BIRNBAUM'S WASHINGTON, DC 95. Copyright © 1995 by HarperCollins Publishers.
All rights reserved. Printed in the United States of America. No part of this
book may be used or reproduced in any manner whatsoever without written
permission except in the case of brief quotations embodied in critical articles
and reviews. For information address HarperCollins*Publishers*, 10 East 53rd
Street, New York, NY 10022.

FIRST EDITION

ISSN 0749-2561 (Birnbaum Travel Guides)
ISSN 1061-544X (Washington, DC)
ISBN 0-06-278176-6 (pbk.)

94 95 96 97 ❖/RRD 5 4 3 2 1

Cover design © Drenttel Doyle Partners
Cover photograph © Llewellyn
Cherry blossoms, Jefferson Memorial and Potomac River

BIRNBAUM TRAVEL GUIDES

Bahamas, and Turks & Caicos
Berlin
Bermuda
Boston
Canada
Cancun, Cozumel & Isla Mujeres
Caribbean
Chicago
Country Inns and Back Roads
Disneyland
Eastern Europe
Europe
Europe for Business Travelers
France
Germany
Great Britain
Hawaii
Ireland
Italy
London
Los Angeles
Mexico
Miami & Ft. Lauderdale
Montreal & Quebec City
New Orleans
New York
Paris
Portugal
Rome
San Francisco
Santa Fe & Taos
South America
Spain
United States
USA for Business Travelers
Walt Disney World
Walt Disney World for Kids, By Kids
Washington, DC

Contributing Editors

Brad Durham
Anita Peltonen
Elise Nakhnikian
Tom Wiener

Maps

Mark Carlson
Susan Carlson

Contents

Diversions

A selective guide to a variety of unexpected pleasures,
pinpointing the best places to pursue them.

Exceptional Pleasures and Treasures

Directions

Seven of the most delightful walks in and around
Washington, DC.

Foreword

I recall an early family vacation: My father was determined that his two daughters (then age about 10 and 11) were going to see our nation's capital. Come hell or high water—a distinct probability, given my recollection of the weather—we were dragged from monument to monument, from glimpses of one noble document to another, from museum to foot-fatiguing museum. See it we did. Or so my father insisted.

Flash forward: Washington was the site of choice for my high school senior class trip. The teacher in charge shepherded a herd of ungrateful 1950s teenage girls to the same monuments, museums, and must-sees. The only must-see on *our* list was to catch a glimpse of a very young and handsome senator from Massachusetts, John F. Kennedy.

By the time my husband, Steve Birnbaum, and I made our first trip together, to this—one of the most beautiful of American cities—I had absolutely no recollection of ever having seen anything other than the Washington Monument. And so we began the first of what turned into numerous pilgrimages to the capital, taking in and taking advantage of the history, beauty, and excitement of this city. Whether reading the Constitution or the names on the Vietnam Memorial; visiting the Library of Congress; seeing the cherry trees in bloom around the Tidal Basin; wandering around Georgetown, ice cream cone dripping in hand—we were the most dedicated of tourists, many a time hopping on the shuttle from New York just to see one or another of the extraordinary exhibits at the National Gallery. If youth was wasted on the young, later trips made up for it.

We have tried to create a guide to Washington that's specifically organized, written, and edited for today's demanding traveler, one for whom qualitative information is infinitely more desirable than mere quantities of unappraised data. We realize that it's impossible for any single travel writer to visit thousands of restaurants (and nearly as many hotels) in any given year and provide accurate appraisals of each. And even if it were physically possible for one human being to survive such an itinerary, it would of necessity have to be done at a dead sprint, and the perceptions derived therefrom would probably be less valid than those of any other intelligent individual visiting the same establishments. It is, therefore, both impractical and undesirable (especially in a large, annually revised and updated guidebook *series* such as we offer) to have only one person provide all the data on the entire world. Instead, we have chosen what we like to describe as the "thee and me" approach to restaurant and hotel evaluation and, to a somewhat more limited degree, to the sites and sights we have included in the other sections of our text. What this really reflects is a personal sampling tempered by intelligent counsel from informed local sources.

This guidebook is directed to the "visitor," and such elements as restaurants have been specifically picked to provide the visitor with a representative, enlightening, and, above all, pleasant experience. Since so many extraneous considerations can affect the reception and service accorded a regular restaurant patron, our choices can in no way be construed as an exhaustive guide to resident dining. We think we've listed all the best places, in various price ranges, but they were chosen with a visitor's enjoyment in mind.

Other evidence of how we've tried to tailor our text to reflect modern travel habits is apparent in the section we call DIVERSIONS. Where once it was common for travelers to spend an urban visit seeing only the obvious sights, today's traveler is more likely to want to pursue a special interest or to venture off the beaten path. In response to this trend, we have collected a series of special experiences so that it is no longer necessary to wade through a pound or two of superfluous prose just to find exceptional pleasures and treasures.

Finally, I also should point out that every good travel guide is a living enterprise; that is, no part of this text is carved in stone. In our annual revisions, we refine, expand, and further hone all our material to serve your travel needs better. To this end, no contribution is of greater value to us than your personal reaction to what we have written, as well as information reflecting your own experiences while using the book. Please write to us at 10 E. 53rd St., New York, NY 10022.

We sincerely hope to hear from you.

Alexandra Mayes Birnbaum

ALEXANDRA MAYES BIRNBAUM, editorial consultant to the *Birnbaum Travel Guides*, worked with her late husband, Stephen Birnbaum, as co-editor of the series. She has been a world traveler since childhood and is known for her travel reports on radio on what's hot and what's not.

Washington, DC

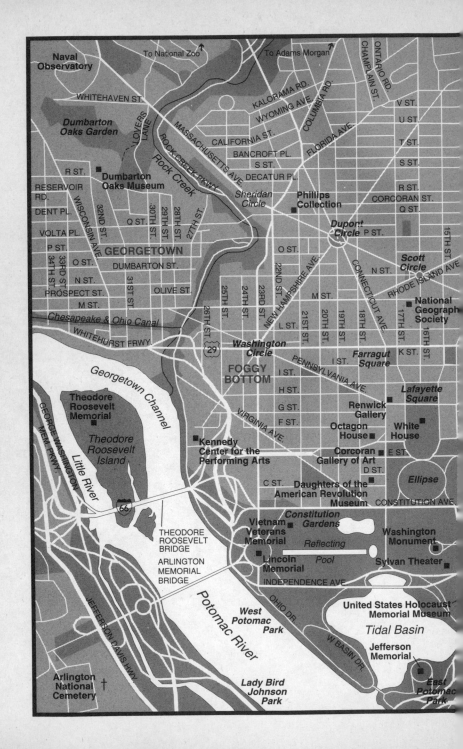

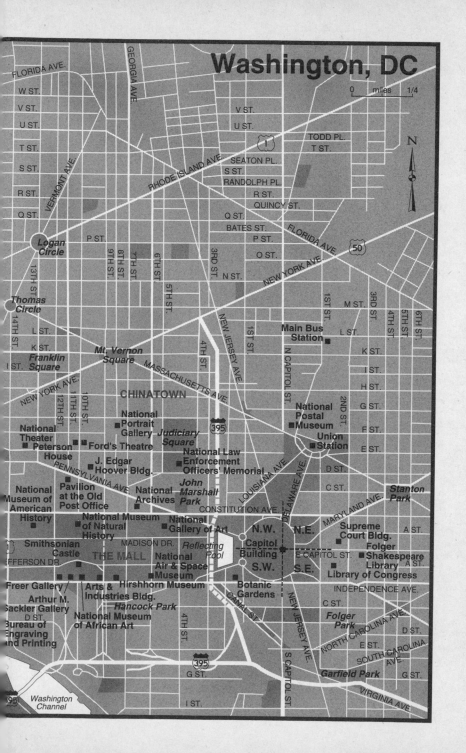

Washington, DC

How to Use This Guide

A great deal of care has gone into the special organization of this guidebook, and we believe it represents a real breakthrough in the presentation of travel material.

Our text is divided into four basic sections in order to present information in the best way on every aspect of a vacation to Washington, DC. Our aim is to highlight what's where and to provide basic information—how, when, where, how much, and what's best—to assist you in making intelligent choices. We believe that you will find both your travel planning and en route enjoyment enhanced by having this book at your side.

Here is a brief summary of what you can expect to find in each section:

GETTING READY TO GO

This mini-encyclopedia of practical travel facts includes all the precise data necessary to create a successful trip to Washington, DC. Here you will find how to get where you're going, plus selected resources—including useful publications, and companies and organizations specializing in discount and special-interest travel—providing a wealth of information and assistance useful both before and during your trip.

THE CITY

Our individual report on Washington, DC, offers a short-stay guide, including an essay introducing the city as a historic entity and as a contemporary place to visit; an *At-a-Glance* section that surveys the most important, interesting, and unique sights to see and things to do in the city; *Sources and Resources,* a concise listing of pertinent tourism information, such as the address of the local tourist office, which sightseeing tours to take, where to find the best nightspot or to hail a taxi, which shops have the finest merchandise and/or the most irresistible bargains, and where the best museums and theaters are to be found; and *Best in Town,* which lists our cost-and-quality choices of the best places to eat and sleep on a variety of budgets.

DIVERSIONS

This section is designed to help travelers find special places in which to engage in a variety of exceptional experiences, without having to wade through endless pages of unrelated text.

DIRECTIONS

Here are seven walks that cover Washington, DC, its main thoroughfares and side streets, and its most spectacular landmarks and outlying communities, including Old Town Alexandria, Virginia.

To use this book to full advantage, take a few minutes to read the table of contents and random entries in each section to get a firsthand feel for how it all fits together. You will find that the sections of this book are building blocks designed to help you put together the best possible trip. Use them selectively as a tool, a source of ideas, a reference work for accurate facts, and a guidebook to the best buys, the most exciting sights, the most pleasant accommodations, and the tastiest foods—*the best travel experience* that you can possibly have.

Getting Ready to Go

800-343-1991 elsewhere in the US; 24-hour hotline: 310-521-1060; fax: 310-521-1061).

Traveler's Advantage (3033 S. Parker Rd., Suite 900, Aurora, CO 80014; phone: 800-548-1116 or 800-835-8747; fax: 303-368-3985).

Vacations to Go (1502 Augusta Dr., Suite 415, Houston, TX 77057; phone: 713-974-2121 in Texas; 800-338-4962 elsewhere in the US; fax: 713-974-0445).

Worldwide Discount Travel Club (1674 Meridian Ave., Miami Beach, FL 33139; phone: 305-534-2082; fax: 305-534-2070).

GENERIC AIR TRAVEL These organizations operate much like an ordinary airline standby service, except that they offer seats on not one but several scheduled and charter airlines. One pioneer of generic flights is *Airhitch* (2790 Broadway, Suite 100, New York, NY 10025; phone: 212-864-2000).

BARTERED TRAVEL SOURCES Barter—the exchange of commodities or services in lieu of cash payment—is a common practice among travel suppliers. Companies that have obtained travel services through barter may sell these services at substantial discounts to travel clubs, who pass along the savings to members. One organization offering bartered travel opportunities is *Travel World Leisure Club* (225 W. 34th St., Suite 909, New York, NY 10122; phone: 800-444-TWLC or 212-239-4855; fax: 212-564-5158).

CONSUMER PROTECTION

Passengers whose complaints have not been satisfactorily addressed by the airline can contact the *US Department of Transportation* (*DOT;* Consumer Affairs Division, 400 Seventh St. SW, Room 10405, Washington, DC 20590; phone: 202-366-2220). Also see *Fly Rights* (Publication #050-000-00513-5; *US Government Printing Office*, PO Box 371954, Pittsburgh, PA 15250-7954; phone: 202-783-3238; fax: 202-512-2250). If you have safety-related questions or concerns, write to the *Federal Aviation Administration* (*FAA;* 800 Independence Ave. SW, Washington, DC 20591) or call the *FAA Consumer Hotline* (phone: 800-322-7873).

On Arrival

Of the three major airports serving the Washington, DC area, *Washington National Airport* is the city's primary facility. It is about 4½ miles from downtown, and the 15- to 20-minute ride by cab costs about $10. The *Washington Flyer* (phone: 703-685-1400) provides express bus and van service from *National* to 1517 K St. NW (at the rear of the *Capitol Hilton*) for $8 one way, $14 round trip; from there, the company provides free shuttle service to most downtown and Capitol Hill hotels. Washington's subway system, called *Metrorail* (or *Metro*), also operates between the airport and downtown. The "Blue Line" stops at the main terminal at

Getting Ready to Go

When to Go

There really isn't a best time to visit Washington, DC. The most popular vacation times traditionally are spring and summer, but autumn is cool and crisp, and winter temperatures usually do not drop much below freezing. Room rates are lowest from early August until mid-September, when Congress is in recess and business travel drops, although prices also routinely drop on weekends throughout the year. The notable exception is cherry blossom time in the spring, when hotels are packed, bargains disappear, and reservations are required months in advance.

If you have a touch-tone phone, you can call *The Weather Channel Connection* (phone: 900-WEATHER) for current weather forecasts. This service, available from *The Weather Channel* (2600 Cumberland Pkwy., Atlanta, GA 30339; phone: 404-434-6800), costs 95¢ per minute; the charge will appear on your phone bill.

Traveling by Plane

SCHEDULED FLIGHTS

There are three major airports in the Washington, DC area: *Washington National, Washington Dulles International,* and *Baltimore/Washington International.* Leading airlines offering flights to these airports include *America West, American, American Eagle, Continental, Continental Express, Delta, Delta Connection, Delta Shuttle, Midwest Express, Northwest, NW Airlink, TWA, TWA Express, United, United Express, USAir, USAir Express, USAir Shuttle,* and *ValueJet.*

FARES The great variety of airfares can be reduced to the following basic categories: first class, business class, coach (also called economy or tourist class), excursion or discount, and standby, as well as various promotional fares. For information on applicable fares and restrictions, contact the airlines listed above or ask your travel agent. Most airfares are offered for a limited time. Once you've found the lowest fare for which you can qualify, purchase your ticket as soon as possible.

RESERVATIONS Reconfirmation is not generally required on domestic flights, although it is wise to call ahead to make sure that the airline has your reservation and any special requests in its computer.

SEATING Airline seats usually are assigned on a first-come, first-served basis at check-in, although you may be able to reserve a seat when purchasing your ticket. Seating charts sometimes are available from airlines and also are included in the *Airline Seating Guide* (Carlson Publishing Co., 11132 Los Alamitos Blvd., Los Alamitos, CA 90720; phone: 310-493-4877).

SMOKING US law prohibits smoking on flights scheduled for six hours or less within the US and its territories on both domestic and international carriers. A free wallet-size guide that describes the rights of nonsmokers under current regulations is available from *ASH* (*Action on Smoking and Health;* DOT Card, 2013 H St. NW, Washington, DC 20006; phone: 202-659-4310).

SPECIAL MEALS When making your reservation, you can request one of the airline's alternate menu choices for no additional charge. Though not always required, it's a good idea to reconfirm your request the day before departure.

BAGGAGE On major airlines, passengers usually are allowed to carry on board one bag that will fit under a seat or in an overhead bin and to check two bags in the cargo hold. Specific regulations regarding dimensions and weight restrictions vary among airlines, but a checked bag usually cannot exceed 62 inches in combined dimensions (length, width, and depth), or weigh more than 70 pounds. There may be charges for additional, oversize, or overweight luggage, and for special equipment or sporting gear. Check that the tags the airline attaches are correctly coded for your destination.

CHARTER FLIGHTS

By booking a block of seats on a specially arranged flight, charter operators frequently can offer travelers bargain airfares. If you do fly on a charter, however, read the contract's fine print carefully. Federal regulations permit charter operators to cancel a flight or assess surcharges of as much as 10% of the airfare up to 10 days before departure. You usually must book in advance, and once booked, no changes are permitted, so buy trip cancellation insurance. Also, make your check out to the company's escrow account, which provides some protection for your investment in the event that the charter operator fails. For further information, consult the publication *Jax Fax* (397 Post Rd., Darien, CT 06820; phone: 203-655-8746; fax: 203-655-6257).

DISCOUNTS ON SCHEDULED FLIGHTS

COURIER TRAVEL In return for arranging to accompany some kind of freight, a traveler pays only a portion of the total airfare (and sometimes a small registration fee). One agency that matches up would-be couriers with courier companies is *Now Voyager* (74 Varick St., Suite 307, New York, NY 10013; phone: 212-431-1616; fax: 212-334-5243).

Courier Companies

Discount Travel International (169 W. 81st St., New York, NY 10024; phone: 212-362-3636; fax: 212-362-3236; and 801 Alton Rd., Suite 1, Miami Beach, FL 33139; phone: 305-538-1616; fax: 305-673-9376).

F.B. On Board Courier Club (10225 Ryan Ave., Suite 103, Dorval, Quebec H9P 1A2, Canada; phone: 514-633-0740; fax: 514-633-0735).

Halbart Express (147-05 176th St., Jamaica, NY 11434; phone: 718-656-8279; fax: 718-244-0559).

Midnite Express (925 W. Hyde Park Blvd., Inglewood, CA 90302; phone: 310-672-1100; fax: 310-671-0107).

Way to Go Travel (6679 Sunset Blvd., Hollywood, CA 90028; phone: 213-466-1126; fax: 213-466-8994).

Publications

Insiders Guide to Air Courier Bargains, by Kelly Monaghan (The Intrepid Traveler, PO Box 438, New York, NY 10034; phone: 212-569-1081 for information; 800-356-9315 for orders; fax: 212-942-6687).

Travel Unlimited (PO Box 1058, Allston, MA 02134-1058; no phone).

CONSOLIDATORS AND BUCKET SHOPS These companies buy blocks of tickets from airlines and sell them at a discount to travel agents or directly to consumers. Since many bucket shops operate on a thin margin, be sure to check a company's record with the *Better Business Bureau*—before parting with any money.

Council Charter (205 E. 42nd St., New York, NY 10017; phone: 80(800-8222 or 212-661-0311; fax: 212-972-0194).

International Adventures (60 E. 42nd St., Room 763, New York, 10165; phone: 212-599-0577; fax: 212-599-3288).

Travac Tours and Charters (989 Ave. of the Americas, New York 10018; phone: 800-872-8800 or 212-563-3303; fax: 212-563-3(

Unitravel (1177 N. Warson Rd., St. Louis, MO 63132; phone: 8(2222 or 314-569-0900; fax: 314-569-2503).

LAST-MINUTE TRAVEL CLUBS Members of such clubs receive informatior nent trips and other bargain travel opportunities. There usually i fee, although a few clubs offer free membership. Despite the na of the clubs listed below, you don't have to wait until literally th to make travel plans.

Discount Travel International (114 Forrest Ave., Suite PA 19072; phone: 215-668-7184; fax: 215-668-9182

FLY ASAP (PO Box 9808, Scottsdale, AZ 85252-3808; ASAP or 602-956-1987; fax: 602-956-6414).

Last Minute Travel (1249 Boylston St., Boston, MA LAST-MIN or 617-267-9800; fax: 617-424-194?

Moment's Notice (425 Madison Ave., New York, N 486-0500/1/2/3; fax: 212-486-0783).

Spur of the Moment Cruises (411 N. Harbor Blvd CA 90731; phone: 800-4-CRUISES or 310-

12

Getting Ready to Go

When to Go

There really isn't a best time to visit Washington, DC. The most popular vacation times traditionally are spring and summer, but autumn is cool and crisp, and winter temperatures usually do not drop much below freezing. Room rates are lowest from early August until mid-September, when Congress is in recess and business travel drops, although prices also routinely drop on weekends throughout the year. The notable exception is cherry blossom time in the spring, when hotels are packed, bargains disappear, and reservations are required months in advance.

If you have a touch-tone phone, you can call *The Weather Channel Connection* (phone: 900-WEATHER) for current weather forecasts. This service, available from *The Weather Channel* (2600 Cumberland Pkwy., Atlanta, GA 30339; phone: 404-434-6800), costs 95¢ per minute; the charge will appear on your phone bill.

Traveling by Plane

SCHEDULED FLIGHTS

There are three major airports in the Washington, DC area: *Washington National, Washington Dulles International,* and *Baltimore/Washington International.* Leading airlines offering flights to these airports include *America West, American, American Eagle, Continental, Continental Express, Delta, Delta Connection, Delta Shuttle, Midwest Express, Northwest, NW Airlink, TWA, TWA Express, United, United Express, USAir, USAir Express, USAir Shuttle,* and *ValueJet.*

FARES The great variety of airfares can be reduced to the following basic categories: first class, business class, coach (also called economy or tourist class), excursion or discount, and standby, as well as various promotional fares. For information on applicable fares and restrictions, contact the airlines listed above or ask your travel agent. Most airfares are offered for a limited time. Once you've found the lowest fare for which you can qualify, purchase your ticket as soon as possible.

RESERVATIONS Reconfirmation is not generally required on domestic flights, although it is wise to call ahead to make sure that the airline has your reservation and any special requests in its computer.

SEATING Airline seats usually are assigned on a first-come, first-served basis at check-in, although you may be able to reserve a seat when purchasing your ticket. Seating charts sometimes are available from airlines and also are included in the *Airline Seating Guide* (Carlson Publishing Co., 11132 Los Alamitos Blvd., Los Alamitos, CA 90720; phone: 310-493-4877).

SMOKING US law prohibits smoking on flights scheduled for six hours or less within the US and its territories on both domestic and international carriers. A free wallet-size guide that describes the rights of nonsmokers under current regulations is available from *ASH (Action on Smoking and Health;* DOT Card, 2013 H St. NW, Washington, DC 20006; phone: 202-659-4310).

SPECIAL MEALS When making your reservation, you can request one of the airline's alternate menu choices for no additional charge. Though not always required, it's a good idea to reconfirm your request the day before departure.

BAGGAGE On major airlines, passengers usually are allowed to carry on board one bag that will fit under a seat or in an overhead bin and to check two bags in the cargo hold. Specific regulations regarding dimensions and weight restrictions vary among airlines, but a checked bag usually cannot exceed 62 inches in combined dimensions (length, width, and depth), or weigh more than 70 pounds. There may be charges for additional, oversize, or overweight luggage, and for special equipment or sporting gear. Check that the tags the airline attaches are correctly coded for your destination.

CHARTER FLIGHTS

By booking a block of seats on a specially arranged flight, charter operators frequently can offer travelers bargain airfares. If you do fly on a charter, however, read the contract's fine print carefully. Federal regulations permit charter operators to cancel a flight or assess surcharges of as much as 10% of the airfare up to 10 days before departure. You usually must book in advance, and once booked, no changes are permitted, so buy trip cancellation insurance. Also, make your check out to the company's escrow account, which provides some protection for your investment in the event that the charter operator fails. For further information, consult the publication *Jax Fax* (397 Post Rd., Darien, CT 06820; phone: 203-655-8746; fax: 203-655-6257).

DISCOUNTS ON SCHEDULED FLIGHTS

COURIER TRAVEL In return for arranging to accompany some kind of freight, a traveler pays only a portion of the total airfare (and sometimes a small registration fee). One agency that matches up would-be couriers with courier companies is *Now Voyager* (74 Varick St., Suite 307, New York, NY 10013; phone: 212-431-1616; fax: 212-334-5243).

Courier Companies

Discount Travel International (169 W. 81st St., New York, NY 10024; phone: 212-362-3636; fax: 212-362-3236; and 801 Alton Rd., Suite 1, Miami Beach, FL 33139; phone: 305-538-1616; fax: 305-673-9376).

F.B. On Board Courier Club (10225 Ryan Ave., Suite 103, Dorval, Quebec H9P 1A2, Canada; phone: 514-633-0740; fax: 514-633-0735).

Halbart Express (147-05 176th St., Jamaica, NY 11434; phone: 718-656-8279; fax: 718-244-0559).

Midnite Express (925 W. Hyde Park Blvd., Inglewood, CA 90302; phone: 310-672-1100; fax: 310-671-0107).

Way to Go Travel (6679 Sunset Blvd., Hollywood, CA 90028; phone: 213-466-1126; fax: 213-466-8994).

Publications

Insiders Guide to Air Courier Bargains, by Kelly Monaghan (The Intrepid Traveler, PO Box 438, New York, NY 10034; phone: 212-569-1081 for information; 800-356-9315 for orders; fax: 212-942-6687).

Travel Unlimited (PO Box 1058, Allston, MA 02134-1058; no phone).

CONSOLIDATORS AND BUCKET SHOPS These companies buy blocks of tickets from airlines and sell them at a discount to travel agents or directly to consumers. Since many bucket shops operate on a thin margin, be sure to check a company's record with the *Better Business Bureau*—before parting with any money.

Council Charter (205 E. 42nd St., New York, NY 10017; phone: 800-800-8222 or 212-661-0311; fax: 212-972-0194).

International Adventures (60 E. 42nd St., Room 763, New York, NY 10165; phone: 212-599-0577; fax: 212-599-3288).

Travac Tours and Charters (989 Ave. of the Americas, New York, NY 10018; phone: 800-872-8800 or 212-563-3303; fax: 212-563-3631).

Unitravel (1177 N. Warson Rd., St. Louis, MO 63132; phone: 800-325-2222 or 314-569-0900; fax: 314-569-2503).

LAST-MINUTE TRAVEL CLUBS Members of such clubs receive information on imminent trips and other bargain travel opportunities. There usually is an annual fee, although a few clubs offer free membership. Despite the names of some of the clubs listed below, you don't have to wait until literally the last minute to make travel plans.

Discount Travel International (114 Forrest Ave., Suite 203, Narberth, PA 19072; phone: 215-668-7184; fax: 215-668-9182).

FLY ASAP (PO Box 9808, Scottsdale, AZ 85252-3808; phone: 800-FLY-ASAP or 602-956-1987; fax: 602-956-6414).

Last Minute Travel (1249 Boylston St., Boston, MA 02215; phone: 800-LAST-MIN or 617-267-9800; fax: 617-424-1943).

Moment's Notice (425 Madison Ave., New York, NY 10017; phone: 212-486-0500/1/2/3; fax: 212-486-0783).

Spur of the Moment Cruises (411 N. Harbor Blvd., Suite 302, San Pedro, CA 90731; phone: 800-4-CRUISES or 310-521-1070 in California;

800-343-1991 elsewhere in the US; 24-hour hotline: 310-521-1060; fax: 310-521-1061).

Traveler's Advantage (3033 S. Parker Rd., Suite 900, Aurora, CO 80014; phone: 800-548-1116 or 800-835-8747; fax: 303-368-3985).

Vacations to Go (1502 Augusta Dr., Suite 415, Houston, TX 77057; phone: 713-974-2121 in Texas; 800-338-4962 elsewhere in the US; fax: 713-974-0445).

Worldwide Discount Travel Club (1674 Meridian Ave., Miami Beach, FL 33139; phone: 305-534-2082; fax: 305-534-2070).

GENERIC AIR TRAVEL These organizations operate much like an ordinary airline standby service, except that they offer seats on not one but several scheduled and charter airlines. One pioneer of generic flights is *Airhitch* (2790 Broadway, Suite 100, New York, NY 10025; phone: 212-864-2000).

BARTERED TRAVEL SOURCES Barter—the exchange of commodities or services in lieu of cash payment—is a common practice among travel suppliers. Companies that have obtained travel services through barter may sell these services at substantial discounts to travel clubs, who pass along the savings to members. One organization offering bartered travel opportunities is *Travel World Leisure Club* (225 W. 34th St., Suite 909, New York, NY 10122; phone: 800-444-TWLC or 212-239-4855; fax: 212-564-5158).

CONSUMER PROTECTION

Passengers whose complaints have not been satisfactorily addressed by the airline can contact the *US Department of Transportation* (*DOT;* Consumer Affairs Division, 400 Seventh St. SW, Room 10405, Washington, DC 20590; phone: 202-366-2220). Also see *Fly Rights* (Publication #050-000-00513-5; *US Government Printing Office,* PO Box 371954, Pittsburgh, PA 15250-7954; phone: 202-783-3238; fax: 202-512-2250). If you have safety-related questions or concerns, write to the *Federal Aviation Administration* (*FAA;* 800 Independence Ave. SW, Washington, DC 20591) or call the *FAA Consumer Hotline* (phone: 800-322-7873).

On Arrival

Of the three major airports serving the Washington, DC area, *Washington National Airport* is the city's primary facility. It is about 4½ miles from downtown, and the 15- to 20-minute ride by cab costs about $10. The *Washington Flyer* (phone: 703-685-1400) provides express bus and van service from *National* to 1517 K St. NW (at the rear of the *Capitol Hilton*) for $8 one way, $14 round trip; from there, the company provides free shuttle service to most downtown and Capitol Hill hotels. Washington's subway system, called *Metrorail* (or *Metro*), also operates between the airport and downtown. The "Blue Line" stops at the main terminal at

Metro Center (11th and G Sts. NW), and the "Yellow Line" stops at Gallery Place (Seventh and G Sts.). Note that the *Washington Metropolitan Area Transit Authority* (600 Fifth St. NW, Washington, DC 20001; phone: 202-637-7000), which operates the *Metrorail* system, offers a one-day pass for $5 that permits unlimited travel on all subway lines (good after 9:30 AM on weekdays; no restrictions on weekends). It can be purchased (in person only; no mail orders) at the central office (address above), the Metro Center and Pentagon stations, and at some *Safeway* supermarkets in the city.

Washington Dulles International Airport is about 26 miles west of downtown Washington, DC. The trip takes 45 minutes to an hour by cab and costs between $40 and $45. The *Washington Flyer* also provides service between *Dulles* and 1517 K St. NW ($16 one way, $26 round trip), including free shuttle service from there to downtown and Capitol Hill hotels.

Baltimore/Washington International Airport (BWI) is approximately 28 miles from downtown Washington, DC; cab fare and transit time are about the same as from *Dulles*. *BWI Airport Connection* (phone: 301-441-2345) provides bus service to downtown for $14 one way and $25 round trip.

RENTING A CAR

You can rent a car through a travel agent or national rental firm before leaving home, or from a local company once in Washington, DC. Reserve in advance.

Most car rental companies require a credit card, although some will accept a substantial cash deposit. The minimum age to rent a car is set by the company; some also may impose special conditions on drivers above a certain age. Electing to pay for collision damage waiver (CDW) protection will add to the cost of renting a car, but releases you from financial liability for the vehicle. Additional costs include drop-off charges or one-way service fees.

Car Rental Companies

Alamo (phone: 800-327-9633).
Avis (phone: 800-331-1212).
Budget (phone: 800-527-0700).
Dollar Rent A Car (phone: 800-800-4000).
EASI Car Rentals (phone: 703-521-0188).
Enterprise Rent-A-Car (phone: 800-325-8007).
Hertz (phone: 800-654-3131).
National (phone: 800-CAR-RENT).
Sears (phone: 800-527-0770).
Snappy Car Rental (phone: 800-669-4802).
Thrifty (phone: 800-367-2277).

Package Tours

A package is a collection of travel services that can be purchased in a single transaction. Its principal advantages are convenience and economy— the cost usually is lower than that of the same services purchased separately. Tour programs generally can be divided into two categories: escorted or locally hosted (with a set itinerary), and independent (usually more flexible).

When considering a package tour, read the brochure *carefully* to determine exactly what is included and any conditions that may apply, and check the company's record with the *Better Business Bureau*. The *United States Tour Operators Association* (*USTOA;* 211 E. 51st St., Suite 12B, New York, NY 10022; phone: 212-750-7371; fax: 212-421-1285) also can be helpful in determining a package tour operator's reliability. As with charter flights, to safeguard your funds, always make your check out to the company's escrow account.

Many tour operators offer packages focused on special interests such as the arts, local history, sports, and other recreations. *All Adventure Travel* (5589 Arapahoe St., Suite 208, Boulder, CO 80303; phone: 800-537-4025 or 303-440-7924; fax: 303-440-4160) represents such specialized packagers. Many also are listed in the *Specialty Travel Index* (305 San Anselmo Ave., Suite 313, San Anselmo, CA 94960; phone: 415-459-4900 in California; 800-442-4922 elsewhere in the US; fax: 415-459-4974). In addition, a number of local companies offer half- or full-day sightseeing tours in and around Washington, DC.

Package Tour Operators

Adventure Tours (10612 Beaver Dam Rd., Hunt Valley, MD 21030-2205; phone: 410-785-3500 in the Baltimore area; 800-638-9040 elsewhere in the US; fax: 410-584-2771).

American Airlines FlyAAway Vacations (offices throughout the US; phone: 800-321-2121).

Capitol Reservations (1730 Rhode Island Ave. NW, Suite 506, Washington, DC 20036; phone: 800-VISIT-DC or 202-452-1270; fax: 202-452-0537).

Capitol Tours (PO Box 4241, Springfield, IL 62708; phone: 800-252-8924 for reservations; 217-529-8166 for information; fax: 217-529-5831).

Caravan Tours (401 N. Michigan Ave., Chicago, IL 60611; phone: 800-CARAVAN or 312-321-9800; fax: 312-321-9810).

Collette Tours (162 Middle St., Pawtucket, RI 02860; phone: 800-752-2655 in New England; 800-832-4656 elsewhere in the US; fax: 401-727-4745).

Contiki Holidays (300 Plaza Alicante, Suite 900, Garden Grove, CA 92640; phone: 800-266-8454 or 714-740-0808; fax: 714-740-0818).

Continental Grand Destinations (offices throughout the US; phone: 800-634-5555).

Corliss Tours (436 W. Foothill Blvd., Monrovia, CA 91016; phone: 800-456-5717 or 818-359-5358; fax: 818-359-0724).

Dailey-Thorp (330 W. 58th St., New York, NY 10019-1817; phone: 212-307-1555; fax: 212-974-1420).

Dan Dipert Tours (PO Box 580, Arlington, TX 76004-0580; phone: 800-433-5335 or 817-543-3710; fax: 817-543-3729).

Delta's Dream Vacations (PO Box 1525, Ft. Lauderdale, FL 33302; phone: 800-872-7786).

Domenico Tours (751 Broadway, Bayonne, NJ 07002; phone: 800-554-8687, 201-823-8687, or 212-757-8687; fax: 201-823-1527).

Globetrotters SuperCities (139 Main St., Cambridge, MA 02142; phone: 800-333-1234 or 617-621-0099; fax: 617-577-8380).

Globus/Cosmos (5301 S. Federal Circle, Littleton, CO 80123; phone: 800-221-0090, 800-556-5454, or 303-797-2800; fax: 303-347-2080).

GOGO Tours (69 Spring St., Ramsey, NJ 07446-0507; phone: 201-934-3759).

Gold Line/Gray Line (Gray Line Terminal, *Union Station,* 50 Massachusetts Ave. NE, Washington, DC 20002; phone: 202-289-1995; fax: 202-484-0573).

Jefferson Tours (1206 Currie Ave., Minneapolis, MN 55403; phone: 800-767-7433 or 612-338-4174; fax: 612-332-5532).

Kerrville Tours (PO Box 79, Shreveport, LA 71161-0079; phone: 800-442-8705 or 318-227-2882; fax: 318-227-2486).

Le Ob's Tours (4635 Touro St., New Orleans, LA 70122-3933; phone: 504-288-3478; fax: 504-288-8517).

Maupintour (PO Box 807, Lawrence, KS 66044; phone: 800-255-4266 or 913-843-1211; fax: 913-843-8351).

Mayflower (1225 Warren Ave., Downers Grove, IL 60515; phone: 800-323-7604 or 708-960-3430; fax: 708-960-3575).

MLT Vacations and Northwest World Vacations (c/o *MLT,* 5130 Hwy. 101, Minnetonka, MN 55345; phone: 800-328-0025 or 612-989-5000; fax: 612-474-0725).

New England Vacation Tours (PO Box 560, West Dover, VT 05356; phone: 800-742-7669 or 802-464-2076; fax: 802-464-2629).

Panorama Tours (600 N. Sprigg St., Cape Girardeau, MO 63701; phone: 800-962-8687 in Missouri and adjacent states; 314-335-7824 elsewhere in the US; fax: 314-335-7824).

Saga International Holidays (222 Berkeley St., Boston, MA 02116; phone: 800-343-0273 or 617-262-2262).

Smithsonian Study Tours and Seminars (1100 Jefferson Dr. SW, Room 3045, Washington, DC 20560; phone: 202-357-4700; fax: 202-786-2315).

Tauck Tours (PO Box 5027, Westport, CT 06881; phone: 800-468-2825 or 203-226-6911; fax: 203-221-6828).

Tours and Travel Odyssey (230 E. McClellan Ave., Livingston, NJ 07039; phone: 800-527-2989 or 201-992-5459; fax: 201-994-1618).

TravelTours International (250 W. 49th St., Suite 600, New York, NY 10019; phone: 800-767-8777 or 212-262-0700; fax: 212-944-5854).

Trek America (PO Box 470, Blairstown, NJ 07825; phone: 800-221-0596 or 908-362-9198; fax: 908-362-9313).

TWA Getaway Vacations (Getaway Vacation Center, 10 E. Stow Rd., Marlton, NJ 08053; phone: 800-GETAWAY; fax: 609-985-4125).

United Airlines Vacations (PO Box 24580, Milwaukee, WI 53224-0580; phone: 800-328-6877).

Yankee Holidays (435 Newbury St., Suite 210, Danvers, MA 01923-1065; phone: 800-225-2550 or 508-750-9688; fax: 508-750-9692).

Companies Offering Day Tours

All About Town (519 Sixth St. NW, Washington, DC 20001; phone: 202-393-3696; fax: 202-393-2006).

Gray Line Sightseeing (see *Gold Line/Gray Line,* above, for address).

National Fine Arts Associates (5301 Wisconsin Ave. NW, Washington, DC 20015; phone: 202-966-3800; fax: 202-362-7368).

Old Town Trolley Tours (*Union Station,* 50 Massachusetts Ave. NE, Washington, DC 20002; phone: 202-682-0079; and 5225 Kilmer Pl., Hyattsville, MD 20781; phone: 301-985-3021; fax: 301-927-7526).

Potomac Riverboat Company (205 The Strand, Alexandria, VA 22314; phone: 703-684-0580; fax: 703-548-9001).

Spirit Cruises (Pier 4, Sixth & Water Sts. SW, Washington, DC 20024; phone: 202-554-8000; fax: 202-484-9062).

Tourmobile Sightseeing (1000 Ohio Dr. SW, Washington, DC 20024; phone: 202-554-7950; fax: 202-488-5200).

Insurance

The first person with whom you should discuss travel insurance is your own insurance broker. You may discover that the insurance you already carry protects you adequately while traveling and that you need little additional coverage. If you charge travel services, the credit card company also may provide some insurance coverage (and other safeguards).

Types of Travel Insurance

Automobile insurance: Provides collision, theft, property damage, and personal liability protection while driving.

Baggage and personal effects insurance: Protects your bags and their contents in case of damage or theft at any point during your travels.

Default and/or bankruptcy insurance: Provides coverage in the event of default and/or bankruptcy on the part of the tour operator, airline, or other travel supplier.

Flight insurance: Covers accidental injury or death while flying.

Personal accident and sickness insurance: Covers cases of illness, injury, or death in an accident while traveling.

Trip cancellation and interruption insurance: Guarantees a refund if you must cancel a trip; may reimburse you for additional travel costs incurred in catching up with a tour or traveling home early.

Combination policies: Include any or all of the above.

Disabled Travelers

Make travel arrangements well in advance. Specify to all services involved the nature of your disability to determine if there are accommodations and facilities that meet your needs. For detailed information on Washington, DC, contact the *Information, Protection, and Advocacy Center for People with Disabilities (IPACHI;* 4455 Connecticut Ave. NW, Suite B-100, Washington, DC 20008; phone: 202-966-8081; TDD: 202-966-2500; fax: 202-966-6313), which publishes *Access Washington* and the *Directory of Services for Persons with Disabilities.*

Organizations

ACCENT on Living (PO Box 700, Bloomington, IL 61702; phone: 800-787-8444 or 309-378-2961; fax: 309-378-4420).

Access: The Foundation for Accessibility by the Disabled (PO Box 356, Malverne, NY 11565; phone/fax: 516-887-5798).

American Foundation for the Blind (15 W. 16th St., New York, NY 10011; phone: 800-232-5463 or 212-620-2147; fax: 212-727-7418).

Information Center for Individuals with Disabilities (Ft. Point Pl., 27-43 Wormwood St., Boston, MA 02210; phone: 800-462-5015 in Massachusetts; 617-727-5540 elsewhere in the US; TDD: 617-345-9743; fax: 617-345-5318).

Mobility International (main office: 228 Borough High St., London SE1 1JX, England; phone: 44-171-403-5688; fax: 44-171-378-1292; US office: *MIUSA,* PO Box 10767, Eugene, OR 97440; phone/TDD: 503-343-1284; fax: 503-343-6812).

Moss Rehabilitation Hospital Travel Information Service (telephone referrals only; phone: 215-456-9600; TDD: 215-456-9602).

National Rehabilitation Information Center (8455 Colesville Rd., Suite 935, Silver Spring, MD 20910; phone: 301-588-9284; fax: 301-587-1967).

Paralyzed Veterans of America (*PVA;* PVA/ATTS Program, 801 18th St. NW, Washington, DC 20006; phone: 202-872-1300 in Washington, DC; 800-424-8200 elsewhere in the US; fax: 202-785-4452).

Royal Association for Disability and Rehabilitation (*RADAR;* 12 City Forum, 250 City Rd., London EC1V 8AF, England; phone: 44-171-250-3222; fax: 44-171-250-0212).

Society for the Advancement of Travel for the Handicapped (*SATH;* 347 Fifth Ave., Suite 610, New York, NY 10016; phone: 212-447-7284; fax: 212-725-8253).

Travel Industry and Disabled Exchange (*TIDE;* 5435 Donna Ave., Tarzana, CA 91356; phone: 818-368-5648).

Publications

Access Travel: A Guide to the Accessibility of Airport Terminals (Consumer Information Center, Dept. 578Z, Pueblo, CO 81009; phone: 719-948-3334).

Air Transportation of Handicapped Persons (Publication #AC-120-32; *US Department of Transportation,* Distribution Unit, Publications Section, M-443-2, 400 Seventh St. SW, Washington, DC 20590; phone: 202-366-0039).

The Diabetic Traveler (PO Box 8223 RW, Stamford, CT 06905; phone: 203-327-5832; fax: 203-975-1748).

Directory of Travel Agencies for the Disabled and Travel for the Disabled, both by Helen Hecker (Twin Peaks Press, PO Box 129, Vancouver, WA 98666; phone: 800-637-CALM or 206-694-2462; fax: 206-696-3210).

Guide to Traveling with Arthritis (Upjohn Company, PO Box 989, Dearborn, MI 48121; phone: 800-253-9860).

The Handicapped Driver's Mobility Guide (*American Automobile Association,* 1000 AAA Dr., Heathrow, FL 32746-5080; phone: 407-444-7000; fax: 407-444-7380).

Handicapped Travel Newsletter (PO Box 269, Athens, TX 75751; phone/fax: 903-677-1260).

Handi-Travel: A Resource Book for Disabled and Elderly Travellers, by Cinnie Noble (*Canadian Rehabilitation Council for the Disabled,* 45 Sheppard Ave. E., Suite 801, Toronto, Ontario M2N 5W9, Canada; phone/TDD: 416-250-7490; fax: 416-229-1371).

Incapacitated Passengers Air Travel Guide (*International Air Transport Association,* Publications Sales Department, 2000 Peel St., Montreal, Quebec H3A 2R4, Canada; phone: 514-844-6311; fax: 514-844-5286).

Ticket to Safe Travel (*American Diabetes Association,* 1660 Duke St., Alexandria, VA 22314; phone: 800-232-3472 or 703-549-1500; fax: 703-836-7439).

Travel for the Patient with Chronic Obstructive Pulmonary Disease (Dr. Harold Silver, 1601 18th St. NW, Washington, DC 20009; phone: 202-667-0134; fax: 202-667-0148).

Travel Tips for Hearing-Impaired People (*American Academy of Otolaryngology,* 1 Prince St., Alexandria, VA 22314; phone: 703-836-4444; fax: 703-683-5100).

Travel Tips for People with Arthritis (*Arthritis Foundation,* 1314 Spring St. NW, Atlanta, GA 30309; phone: 800-283-7800 or 404-872-7100; fax: 404-872-0457).

Traveling Like Everybody Else: A Practical Guide for Disabled Travelers, by Jacqueline Freedman and Susan Gersten (Modan Publishing, PO Box 1202, Bellmore, NY 11710; phone: 516-679-1380; fax: 516-679-1448).

The Wheelchair Traveler, by Douglass R. Annand (123 Ball Hill Rd., Milford, NH 03055; phone: 603-673-4539).

Package Tour Operators

Accessible Journeys (35 W. Sellers Ave., Ridley Park, PA 19078; phone: 800-846-4537 or 215-521-0339; fax: 215-521-6959).

Accessible Tours/Directions Unlimited (Attn.: Lois Bonnani, 720 N. Bedford Rd., Bedford Hills, NY 10507; phone: 800-533-5343 or 914-241-1700; fax: 914-241-0243).

Beehive Business and Leisure Travel (1130 W. Center St., N. Salt Lake, UT 84054; phone: 800-777-5727 or 801-292-4445; fax: 801-298-9460).

Classic Travel Service (8 W. 40th St., New York, NY 10018; phone: 212-869-2560 in New York State; 800-247-0909 elsewhere in the US; fax: 212-944-4493).

Evergreen Travel Service (4114 198th St. SW, Suite 13, Lynnwood, WA 98036-6742; phone: 800-435-2288 or 206-776-1184; fax: 206-775-0728).

Flying Wheels Travel (143 W. Bridge St., PO Box 382, Owatonna, MN 55060; phone: 800-535-6790 or 507-451-5005; fax: 507-451-1685).

Good Neighbor Travel Service (124 S. Main St., Viroqua, WI 54665; phone: 800-338-3245 or 608-637-2128; fax: 608-637-3030).

The Guided Tour (7900 Old York Rd., Suite 114B, Elkins Park, PA 19117-2339; phone: 800-783-5841 or 215-782-1370; fax: 215-635-2637).

Hinsdale Travel (201 E. Ogden Ave., Hinsdale, IL 60521; phone: 708-325-1335 or 708-469-7349; fax: 708-325-1342).

MedEscort International (*ABE International Airport,* PO Box 8766, Allentown, PA 18105-8766; phone: 800-255-7182 or 215-791-3111; fax: 215-791-9189).

Prestige World Travel (5710-X High Point Rd., Greensboro, NC 27407; phone: 800-476-7737 or 910-292-6690; fax: 910-632-9404).

Sprout (893 Amsterdam Ave., New York, NY 10025; phone: 212-222-9575; fax: 212-222-9768).

Weston Travel Agency (134 N. Cass Ave., Westmont, IL 60559; phone: 708-968-2513 in Illinois; 800-633-3725 elsewhere in the US; fax: 708-968-2539).

SPECIAL SERVICES

Wheelchair Getaways (main office: PO Box 605, Versailles, KY 40383; phone: 800-642-2042; phone/fax: 606-873-4973; Washington, DC area office: PO Box 348, Jarrettsville, MD 21084-0348; phone: 800-438-8465 or 410-557-0125; fax: 410-692-2392) rents vans designed to accommodate wheelchairs.

Single Travelers

The travel industry is not very fair to people who vacation by themselves—they often end up paying more than those traveling in pairs. There are services catering to single travelers, however, that match travel companions, offer travel arrangements with shared accommodations, and provide information and discounts. Useful publications include *Going Solo* (Doerfer Communications, PO Box 123, Apalachicola, FL 32329; phone/fax: 904-653-8848) and *Traveling on Your Own,* by Eleanor Berman (Random House, Order Dept., 400 Hahn Rd., Westminster, MD 21157; phone: 800-733-3000; fax: 800-659-2436).

Organizations and Companies

Contiki Holidays (300 Plaza Alicante, Suite 900, Garden Grove, CA 92640; phone: 800-466-0610 or 714-740-0808; fax: 714-740-0818).

Gallivanting (515 E. 79th St., Suite 20F, New York, NY 10021; phone: 800-933-9699 or 212-988-0617; fax: 212-988-0144).

Globus/Cosmos (5301 S. Federal Circle, Littleton, CO 80123; phone: 800-221-0090, 800-556-5454, or 303-797-2800; fax: 303-347-2080).

Jane's International and Sophisticated Women Travelers (2603 Bath Ave., Brooklyn, NY 11214; phone: 718-266-2045; fax: 718-266-4062).

Marion Smith Singles (611 Prescott Pl., N. Woodmere, NY 11581; phone: 516-791-4852, 516-791-4865, or 212-944-2112; fax: 516-791-4879)

Partners-in-Travel (11660 Chenault St., Suite 119, Los Angeles, CA 90049; phone: 310-476-4869).

Singles in Motion (545 W. 236th St., Riverdale, NY 10463; phone/fax: 718-884-4464).

Singleworld (401 Theodore Fremd Ave., Rye, NY 10580; phone: 800-223-6490 or 914-967-3334; fax: 914-967-7395).

Solo Flights (63 High Noon Rd., Weston, CT 06883; phone: 800-266-1566 or 203-226-9993).

Suddenly Singles Tours (161 Dreiser Loop, Bronx, NY 10475; phone: 718-379-8800 in New York City; 800-859-8396 elsewhere in the US; fax: 718-379-8858).

Travel Companion Exchange (PO Box 833, Amityville, NY 11701; phone: 516-454-0880; fax: 516-454-0170).

Travel Companions (Atrium Financial Center, 1515 N. Federal Hwy., Suite 300, Boca Raton, FL 33432; phone: 800-383-7211 or 407-393-6448; fax: 407-451-8560).

Travel in Two's (239 N. Broadway, Suite 3, N. Tarrytown, NY 10591; phone: 914-631-8301 in New York State; 800-692-5252 elsewhere in the US).

Umbrella Singles (PO Box 157, Woodbourne, NY 12788; phone: 800-537-2797 or 914-434-6871; fax: 914-434-3532).

Older Travelers

Special discounts and more free time are just two factors that have given older travelers a chance to see the world at affordable prices. Many travel suppliers offer senior discounts—sometimes only to members of certain senior citizens organizations (which provide benefits of their own). When considering a particular package, make sure the facilities—and the pace of the tour—match your needs and physical condition.

Publications

The Mature Traveler (PO Box 50820, Reno, NV 89513-0820; phone: 702-786-7419).

The Senior Citizen's Guide to Budget Travel in the US and Canada, by Paige Palmer (Pilot Books, 103 Cooper St., Babylon, NY 11702; phone: 516-422-2225; fax: 516-422-2227).

Take a Camel to Lunch and Other Adventures for Mature Travelers, by Nancy O'Connell (Bristol Publishing Enterprises, PO Box 1737, San Leandro, CA 94577; phone: 510-895-4461 in California; 800-346-4889 elsewhere in the US; fax: 510-895-4459).

Unbelievably Good Deals & Great Adventures That You Absolutely Can't Get Unless You're Over 50, by Joan Rattner Heilman (Contemporary Books, 1200 Stetson Ave., Chicago, IL 60601; phone: 312-782-9181; fax: 312-540-4687).

Organizations

American Association of Retired Persons (*AARP;* 601 E St. NW, Washington, DC 20049; phone: 202-434-2277).

Golden Companions (PO Box 754, Pullman, WA 99163-0754; phone: 208-858-2183).

Mature Outlook (Customer Service Center, 6001 N. Clark St., Chicago, IL 60660; phone: 800-336-6330).

National Council of Senior Citizens (1331 F St. NW, Washington, DC 20004; phone: 202-347-8800; fax: 202-624-9595).

Package Tour Operators

Elderhostel (75 Federal St., Boston, MA 02110-1941; phone: 617-426-7788; fax: 617-426-8351).

Evergreen Travel Service (4114 198th St. SW, Suite 13, Lynnwood, WA 98036-6742; phone: 800-435-2288 or 206-776-1184; fax: 206-775-0728).

Gadabout Tours (700 E. Tahquitz Canyon Way, Palm Springs, CA 92262; phone: 800-952-5068 or 619-325-5556; fax: 619-325-5127).

Grand Circle Travel (347 Congress St., Boston, MA 02210; phone: 800-221-2610 or 617-350-7500; fax: 617-423-0445).

Grandtravel (6900 Wisconsin Ave., Suite 706, Chevy Chase, MD 20815; phone: 800-247-7651 or 301-986-0790; fax: 301-913-0166).

Interhostel (*University of New Hampshire,* Division of Continuing Education, 6 Garrison Ave., Durham, NH 03824; phone: 800-733-9753 or 603-862-1147; fax: 603-862-1113).

Mature Tours (c/o *Solo Flights,* 63 High Noon Rd., Weston, CT 06883; phone: 800-266-1566 or 203-226-9993).

OmniTours (104 Wilmot Rd., Deerfield, IL 60015; phone: 800-962-0060 or 708-374-0088; fax: 708-374-9515).

Saga International Holidays (222 Berkeley St., Boston, MA 02116; phone: 800-343-0273 or 617-262-2262; fax: 617-375-5950).

Money Matters

CREDIT CARDS AND TRAVELER'S CHECKS

Most major credit cards enjoy wide domestic and international acceptance; however, not every hotel, restaurant, or shop in Washington, DC accepts all (or in some cases any) credit cards. It's also wise to carry traveler's checks while on the road, since they are widely accepted and replaceable if stolen or lost. You can buy traveler's checks at banks and some are available by mail or phone. Keep a separate list of all traveler's checks (noting those that you have cashed) and the names and numbers of your credit cards. Both traveler's check and credit card companies have international numbers to call for information or in the event of loss or theft.

CASH MACHINES

Automated teller machines (ATMs) are increasingly common worldwide, and most banks participate in international ATM networks such as *CIRRUS* (phone: 800-4-CIRRUS) and *PLUS* (phone: 800-THE-PLUS). Cardholders can withdraw cash from any machine in the same network using either a "bank" card or, in some cases, a credit card. Additional information on ATMs and networks can be obtained from your bank or credit card company.

SENDING MONEY

Should the need arise, you can have money sent to you in Washington via the services provided by *American Express MoneyGram* (phone: 800-926-9400 for information; 800-866-8800 for money transfers) or *Western Union Financial Services* (phone: 800-325-6000 or 800-325-4176).

Time Zone

Washington, DC is in the eastern standard time zone. Daylight saving time is observed from the first Sunday in April until the last Sunday in October.

Business and Shopping Hours

The District of Columbia maintains business hours that are fairly standard throughout the US: 9 AM to 5 PM, Mondays through Fridays. Although banking hours generally are weekdays from 9 AM to 3 PM, many banks stay open later (as late as 8 PM) at least one day a week, and some also offer Saturday morning hours. Most stores are open Mondays through Saturdays from 9:30 or 10 AM to 5:30 or 6 PM; many also are open on Sundays, usually from around noon to 5 PM. Department stores and malls may stay open until 8 or 9 PM during the week.

Mail

Washington's main post office (900 Brentwood Rd. NE, Washington, DC 20066; phone: 202-636-1532) provides window service weekdays from 8 AM to 8 PM, Saturdays from 10 AM to 6 PM, and Sundays from noon to 6 PM; the lobby (with stamp machines and mail drops) is open 24 hours daily. The *National Capitol Station* (2 Massachusetts Ave., Washington, DC 20002; phone: 202-523-2628) is open weekdays from 7 AM to midnight, and weekends from 7 AM to 8 PM. For other branches, call the main post office or check the yellow pages.

Stamps also are available at most hotel desks, some supermarkets and other stores, and from public vending machines. For rapid, overnight delivery to other cities, use *Express Mail* (available at post offices), *Federal Express* (phone: 800-238-5355), or *DHL Worldwide Express* (phone: 800-225-5345).

You can have mail sent to you care of your hotel (marked "Guest Mail, Hold for Arrival") or to the main post office (sent "c/o General Delivery" to the address above). *American Express* offices in Washington also will hold mail for customers ("c/o Client Letter Service"); information is provided in their pamphlet *Travelers' Companion.*

Telephone

The area code for Washington, DC is 202. The area code for the adjoining Maryland suburbs is 301; in nearby Virginia, it is 703. To make a long-distance call, dial 1 + the area code + the local number. The nationwide number for information is 555-1212; you also can dial 411 for local information. If you need a number in another area code, dial 1 + the area code + 555-1212. (If you don't know an area code, dial 555-1212 or 411 for directory assistance.)

Although you can use a telephone company calling card number on any phone, pay phones that take major credit cards (*American Express, MasterCard, Visa,* and so on) are increasingly common. Also available are combined telephone calling/bank credit cards, such as the *AT&T Universal Card* (PO Box 44167, Jacksonville, FL 32231-4167; phone: 800-423-4343). Similarly, *Sprint* (8140 Ward Pkwy., Kansas City, MO 64114; phone: 800-THE-MOST or 800-800-USAA) offers the *VisaPhone* program, through which you can add phone card privileges to your existing *Visa* card. Companies offering long-distance phone cards without additional credit card privileges include *AT&T* (phone: 800-CALL-ATT), *Executive Telecard International* (4260 E. Evans Ave., Suite 6, Denver, CO 80222; phone: 800-950-3800), *MCI* (323 Third St. SE, Cedar Rapids, IA 52401; phone: 800-444-4444; and 12790 Merit Dr., Dallas, TX 75251; phone: 800-444-3333), *Metromedia Communications* (1 International Center, 100 NE Loop 410, San Antonio, TX 78216; phone: 800-275-0200), and *Sprint* (address above).

Hotels routinely add surcharges to the cost of phone calls made from their rooms. Long-distance telephone services that may help you avoid this added expense are provided by a number of companies, including *AT&T* (International Information Service, 635 Grant St., Pittsburgh, PA 15219; phone: 800-874-4000), *MCI* (address above), *Metromedia Communications* (address above), and *Sprint* (address above). Note that even when you use such long-distance services, some hotels still may charge a fee for line usage.

Useful resources for travelers include the *AT&T 800 Travel Directory* (phone: 800-426-8686 for orders), the *Toll-Free Travel & Vacation Information Directory* (Pilot Books, 103 Cooper St., Babylon, NY 11702; phone: 516-422-2225; fax: 516-422-2227), and *The Phone Booklet* (Scott American Corporation, PO Box 88, W. Redding, CT 06896; no phone).

Medical Aid

In an emergency: Dial 911 for assistance, 0 for an operator, or go directly to the emergency room of the nearest hospital.

Hospitals

Georgetown University Hospital (3800 Reservoir Rd. NW; phone: 202-784-2000).

George Washington University Medical Center (901 23rd St. NW; phone: 202-994-3884).

24-Hour Pharmacies

Peoples Drug Store (1121 Vermont Ave. NW; phone: 202-628-0720).
Peoples Drug Store (6-7 Dupont Circle NW; phone: 202-785-1466).

Additional Resources

International SOS Assistance (PO Box 11568, Philadelphia, PA 19116; phone: 800-523-8930 or 215-244-1500; fax: 215-244-2227).
Medic Alert Foundation (2323 Colorado Ave., Turlock, CA 95382; phone: 800-ID-ALERT or 209-668-3333; fax: 209-669-2495).
Travel Care International (*Eagle River Airport,* PO Box 846, Eagle River, WI 54521; phone: 800-5-AIR-MED or 715-479-8881; fax: 715-479-8178).

Legal Aid

Although most cities offer legal referral services for those who don't have, or cannot reach, their own attorneys, Washington—the seat of government—ironically, does not. Instead, the *DC Bar* (1250 H St. NW, Sixth floor, Washington, DC 20005; phone: 202-737-4700; 202-737-3499 for recorded information; fax: 202-626-3471) publishes the *Legal Service Sourcebook,* which lists local lawyers by specialty (no recommendations are given). If you must appear in court, you are entitled to court-appointed representation if you can't obtain a lawyer or can't afford one.

For Further Information

Tourist information is available from the *Washington, DC, Convention and Visitors Association* (*WCVA;* main office: 1212 New York Ave. NW, Suite 600, Washington, DC 20005; phone: 202-789-7000; fax: 202-789-7037; visitor information center: 1455 Pennsylvania Ave. NW, Washington, DC 20004; phone: 202-789-7038). For additional sources of tourist information for Washington, DC, see *Sources and Resources* in THE CITY.

The City

Washington, DC

Back in the 1950s, during one of the thaws in the Cold War, President Eisenhower was showing the visiting Nikita Khrushchev around Washington. Every time Eisenhower pointed out a government building, the Soviet leader would claim that the Russians had one bigger and better that had taken only half as long to build. Eisenhower, so the story goes, got pretty weary of this civic one-upmanship, and when they passed the *Washington Monument* he said nothing, forcing Khrushchev to ask what the structure was. Eisenhower replied, "It's news to me. It wasn't here yesterday."

The story may be apocryphal, but it does indicate something important about Washington: It is a city filled with imperial architecture—grand, expansive, deliberate—of a kind that simply doesn't happen overnight or by chance. And yet it is a city that did, indeed, happen almost by chance; a city that until World War II seemed to resist almost in its bones being what it has become today: the international showplace of the United States.

A walk along the *Mall* will remove any doubts you have about the quality of Washington's cityscape. The *Mall* is the grand promenade of the capital, connecting the *Capitol* to the *Lincoln Memorial* with 2 miles of open green and reflecting pools, lined by several of the superb *Smithsonian* museums. Familiar to everyone from picture postcards, the massive, columned buildings take on real dimensions and fulfill the promise of grandeur (particularly at night, when they are bathed in floodlights). But this city of wide tree-lined avenues offers enough open space for varied architectural styles to appear highly consistent. Newer government buildings of modern design and neat rows of townhouses fit in with Greek Revival and Federal architecture (the latter, featuring solid geometry and refined decorations and proportions, was the dominant style in the early 19th century, when much of Washington was built). And Washington will retain its impressive mien into the future. A city ordinance limits the height of buildings to 13 stories, so the *Capitol* remains the city's tallest building. Though others approach it, none surpasses the splendor of this domed edifice.

The fact that Washington is so impressive is especially remarkable when you consider its stormy birth. The selection of the site of the new nation's capital was preceded by years of wrangling between north and south. It wasn't until 1790 that both sides agreed upon a marshy site on the Potomac shore. Neither too far north nor too far south, it was far enough inland to protect against surprise attack, yet accessible to ocean vessels and at the head of a tidewater. Maryland agreed to give 69.25 square miles of land and Virginia 30.75 square miles to form the square to be known as the District of Columbia. The city was named for George Washington, who as first president was authorized to oversee its development.

Washington appointed Major Pierre L'Enfant, a French engineer, to lay out the city. L'Enfant arrived on the scene in 1791 and on viewing Jenkins Hill, the present *Capitol Hill,* he pronounced it "a pedestal waiting for a monument." He also set about designing avenues 160 feet wide that were to radiate from circles crowned with sculpture. The city's two focal points were to be the *Capitol* and the president's house, with Pennsylvania Avenue the principal ceremonial street between.

L'Enfant became involved in a controversy over the sale of lots that were to have raised money to finance construction of government buildings, and was fired before the year was out. George Washington died in 1799 before the development of the federal city was assured. But President John Adams's resolve was firm, and in 1800, Congress was moved to the howling wilderness of Washington. Abigail Adams was displeased by the *White House,* and nobody was pleased with the city. The streets were unpaved and mud-rutted, the sewers nonexistent, and the swampy surroundings infested with mosquitoes.

During the War of 1812 the city suffered a devastating setback when British troops burned the *White House* and gutted the *Capitol.* A torrential thunderstorm saved the city from total destruction, but much was burned beyond repair.

In 1901 the McMillan Commission was instituted to resurrect L'Enfant's original plans. Railroad tracks were removed from the *Mall,* plans were made for the construction of the *Lincoln Memorial* and *Arlington Bridge,* and 640 acres of swampland were converted into Potomac parklands. Unfortunately, things did not turn out as well for L'Enfant himself. He died a pauper in 1825; his remains were later transferred to a grave in *Arlington National Cemetery* overlooking the city that still bears the stamp of his magnificent design.

First-time visitors to Washington may well wonder if there's a life in Washington beyond the monuments, buildings, fountains, and statues. Behind the handsome façades lie many Washingtons, but it would take the combined skills of a historian, political analyst, city planner, expert on international, race, and social relations, and master satirist to explain each one. The writer Ben Bagdikian observed: "In many respects, Washington, DC, is a perfectly normal American city. Its rivers are polluted. The air is periodically toxic from exhaust fumes. It has traffic jams, PTA meetings, and other common hazards of urban life. . . . Beyond its official buildings the natives rise each morning, crowd into buses and car pools, go to work, return at night, to the naked eye no different from the inhabitants of Oklahoma City or Pawtucket, Rhode Island."

All true, but Washington has something no other city has—the federal government. The District is something of a one-industry town, but the industry is government, and that makes all the difference. Nearly half of the 600,000 people living in Washington and its immediate surroundings work for some branch of government (the population of the entire metropolitan area is over 3.5 million). As civil servants, they earn relatively high incomes, a factor that provides a solid economic base for the city. In addition to the permanent government employees, diplomats from more than 150 countries serve in Washington—considered to be the world's top post. The embassies lend a cultural sophistication to the capital and further diversify the population.

As a result of these influences, Washington is a major cosmopolitan center. Restaurants offer nearly as wide a representation of nationalities as do the embassies, and in some cases, even wider—you can eat in a Cuban restaurant, but try to find the embassy of Cuba (if you do, it's news to us; it wasn't there yesterday). In the *Smithsonian Institution*'s museums you can see anything and everything. On the cultural scene, the *Kennedy Center* draws star artists and provides a home for music, theater, and dance companies. And what is better proof of being an established cultural center than having branches of *Bloomingdale's* and *Neiman Marcus?*

Still, there are some long shadows across the Washington horizon. The city has a sufficiently high crime rate to have earned the nickname "Murder City," though the business and tourist areas, as well as most of the western end of the city, are relatively safe. It is highly inadvisable, however, to walk around alone after dark. The District's resident population, which is largely black, suffers from a distressingly high rate of unemployment, and the drug problem is epidemic. Drug-related crime has risen enormously in the last few years, and the 1990 arrest and conviction of then-Mayor Marion Barry on drug charges are testimony to how deep and pervasive the problem is. The combination of distrust in local elected officials and high crime figures precipitated a "white flight" to the suburbs, but recently there is some evidence of families returning to the city to renovate homes in once-seedy neighborhoods that are becoming more stable, integrated communities. Many of the city's worst slums, particularly in the southwest section, have been torn down and replaced by apartment houses, theaters, restaurants, townhouses, and a redeveloped waterfront area.

The forecast for the city remains murky. With home rule a reality (since 1973), Washington abandoned its status as "the last colony." Though residents now can vote for president, a mayor, a city council, and a representative to Congress, civic corruption has impeded reform and renewal. Still, the city a visitor sees has never been more vital and vibrant.

And so it goes with Pierre L'Enfant's city. The Washington he envisioned is what you see today. Every visitor to the *Capitol* should stand on its west terrace and appreciate one of the finest cityscapes in the world. And as you gaze, you might contemplate the words of Henry Adams. Over a century ago, he wrote, "One of these days this will be a very great city if nothing happens to it." Many things have happened to Washington, DC, but it is a great city nonetheless.

Washington At-a-Glance

SEEING THE CITY

The 555-foot *Washington Monument* commands a panorama of the capital in all its glory. To the north stands the *White House,* and below stretches the green *Mall,* with the *Lincoln Memorial* in the west and the *Capitol* perfectly aligned with it to the east. Beyond to the south and west flows the Potomac River, and across the river lies Virginia. (See *Special Places* for details.)

SPECIAL PLACES

In Washington, all roads lead to the *Capitol.* The building marks the center of the District. North–south streets are numbered in relation to it, east–west streets are lettered, and the four quadrants into which Washington is divided (NW, NE, SW, and SE, designated after addresses) meet here. *Note:* A surprising number of remarkable attractions in this city have no admission charge, as they are funded by federal monies.

An easy way to get around the principal sightseeing area, which includes *Arlington National Cemetery* (across the Potomac in Arlington, Virginia), is by *Tourmobile;* for details on this shuttle bus and other tours see "Tours" in *Getting Around.*

CAPITOL HILL AREA

THE CAPITOL The Senate and House of Representatives are housed in the *Capitol,* which is visible from almost every part of the city. The 258-foot cast-iron dome, topped by Thomas Crawford's statue of *Freedom,* was erected during the Civil War; beneath it, the massive *Rotunda* is a veritable art gallery of American history featuring Constantino Brumidi's fresco *The Apotheosis of Washington* in the eye of the dome, John Trumbull's Revolutionary War paintings on the walls, and statues of Washington, Lincoln, Jefferson, and others. The rest of the building also contains much artwork. You must join one of the excellent 40-minute guided tours that leave from the *Rotunda* every quarter hour in order to gain access to the visitors' galleries of Congress (congressional sessions start at noon). You also can ride the monorail subway that joins the House and Senate wings with the congressional office buildings and try the famous bean soup in the Senate dining room (also see *Quintessential Washington* in DIVERSIONS). Closed *Christmas, New Year's Day,* and *Thanksgiving.* The last tour is at 3:45 PM; from the first week of May through *Labor Day,* the *Rotunda* is open until 8 PM. No admission charge. First St. between Constitution and Independence Aves. (phone: 224-3121). *Metro: Capitol South* or *Union Station.*

SUPREME COURT BUILDING This neoclassical white marble structure, surrounded by Corinthian columns and with the inscription on its pediment "Equal

Justice Under Law," was designed by Cass Gilbert and completed in 1935. The impressive courtroom is flanked by Ionic columns. Court is in session intermittently from the first Monday in October through June; sessions are open to the public on a first-come, first-served basis. There are 20-minute courtroom presentations on the history and function of the *Court* every hour on the half hour from 9:30 AM to 3:30 PM except when court is in session. Closed weekends. No admission charge. First St. between Maryland Ave. and E. Capitol St. NE (phone: 479-3395). *Metro: Capitol South* or *Union Station.*

LIBRARY OF CONGRESS Three buildings—the *Jefferson,* the *Adams,* and the *Madison*—house the world's largest and richest library. Originally designed as a research aid to Congress, the *Library* serves the public as well with 84 million items in 470 languages, including manuscripts, maps, photographs, motion pictures, and music. The exhibition hall displays include Jefferson's first draft of the *Declaration of Independence* and Lincoln's first two drafts of the *Gettysburg Address.* Among the *Library*'s other holdings are one of three extant copies of the Gutenberg Bible, Pierre L'Enfant's original design for Washington, and the earliest surviving copyrighted film—the 14-second *Sneeze* by Thomas Edison. Forty-five-minute guided tours are offered on weekdays from 10 AM to 4 PM, Saturdays from 10 AM to 3 PM, and Sundays at 1, 2, and 3 PM. Open daily, with evening hours on Mondays, Wednesdays, and Thursdays. No admission charge. First St. between E. Capitol St. and Independence Ave. SE (phone: 707-5458). *Metro: Capitol South* or *Union Station.*

FOLGER SHAKESPEARE LIBRARY The nine bas-reliefs on the façade depict scenes from Shakespeare's plays; inside is the world's finest collection of rare books, manuscripts, and research materials relating to the foremost English-language playwright. The library, an oak-paneled, barrel-vaulted Elizabethan palace, also has a model of the *Globe Theatre* and a full-scale replica of an Elizabethan theater complete with a trapdoor called "the heavens," used for special effects. Visitors can see how productions were mounted in Shakespeare's day and how they are done today. The bookstore features the fine Folger series on the Elizabethan period as well as editions of Shakespeare's plays. Tours are at 11 AM; closed Sundays. No admission charge. 201 E. Capitol St. SE (phone: 546-4600). *Metro: Capitol South* or *Union Station.*

BOTANIC GARDENS If you feel as if you are overdosing on history, the *Botanic Gardens* provide a pleasant antidote of azaleas, orchids, and tropical plants. Closed *Christmas Day.* No admission charge. First St. and Maryland Ave. SW, at the foot of Capitol Hill (phone: 225-8333). *Metro: Federal Center Southwest.*

NATIONAL POSTAL MUSEUM The *Smithsonian*'s newest museum opened in the summer of 1993 and occupies a dramatic atrium area of the *City Post Office*

Building, which served as Washington's main post office from 1914 to 1986. It features the world's largest collection of stamps and philatelic materials, which was formerly housed in the *National Museum of American History* (see below). A variety of exhibits traces the colorful history of the ways the mail has been collected, sorted, and delivered over the years. Also included is an extensive, historical stamp collection. Be sure to take a stroll through the old post office's main lobby, with its marble floors and columns restored to their original luster. Also here are an educational *Discovery Center* and the *Library Research Center* (open by appointment from 10 AM to 4 PM on weekdays), specializing in philatelic and postal history. Closed *Christmas.* No admission charge. First St. and Massachusetts Ave. NE (phone: 357-1300). *Metro: Union Station.*

UNION STATION This early 20th-century Beaux Arts landmark was modeled after the *Baths of Diocletian* and the triumphal *Arch of Constantine* in Rome; its marble floors, granite walls, bronze grilles, and classic statuary dazzle visitors. In front of *Amtrak*'s rail terminal is a complex of chic boutiques and dining areas. (*Sfuzzi Washington* is one of our favorites; see *Eating Out.*) The main concourse, once the largest room under a single roof, has been divided into a series of levels and mezzanines for stores and eateries. The lower level houses movie theaters and a score of fast-food outlets. 50 Massachusetts Ave. NE (phone: 371-9441). *Metro: Union Station.*

THE WHITE HOUSE AREA

WHITE HOUSE Probably the most historic house in America; even though George Washington never slept here, every president since has. Designed originally by James Hoban, the *White House* still looks like an Irish country mansion from the outside; inside there are elegant parlors decorated with portraits of the presidents and first ladies, and antique furnishings of many periods. The five state rooms on the first floor are open to the public, and though you actually won't see the business of government going on, you'll be very close to it.

Visitors line up at the East Gate on East Executive Avenue. (Tickets, required during summer months and the week that begins with *Easter Sunday,* are available from the kiosk on the adjacent *Ellipse;* at peak times, for example around *Easter,* the lineup for tickets begins early in the morning.) Congressional tours of seven rooms, instead of the usual five, are available by writing to your congressman in advance. Be sure to specify alternate dates. Tours are conducted Tuesdays through Saturdays from 10 AM to noon. No admission charge. 1600 Pennsylvania Ave. NW (phone: 456-7041). *Metro: McPherson Square.*

LAFAYETTE SQUARE If you do not enter the *White House,* you can get a fine view of it from this square, which was originally proposed by city planner L'Enfant as the mansion's front yard. Statues commemorate Andrew Jackson and the foreign heroes of the American Revolution—Lafayette, de Rochambeau, von Steuben, and Kościuszko. Flanking the square are two early 19th-century buildings designed by Benjamin Latrobe, Washington's first public architect. *St. John's Church* (16th and H Sts. NW; phone: 347-8766), constructed along classically simple lines, is better known as the *Church of Presidents* because every president since Madison has attended services here. It's open to the public daily (also see *Historic Churches* in DIVERSIONS). The *Decatur House* (748 Jackson Pl. NW; phone: 842-0920), built for Commodore Stephen Decatur and occupied after his death by a succession of diplomats, is a Federal-style townhouse featuring handsome woodwork, a spiral staircase, and furniture of the 1820s. It's closed Mondays; admission charge. Near the southwest corner of the square is *Blair House* (1651-1653 Pennsylvania Ave. NW), the president's official guesthouse since 1942; it is not open to the public. *Metro: McPherson Square or Farragut West.*

ELLIPSE This grassy 32-acre expanse is the location of the zero milestone from which all distances in Washington are measured. It's the site of everything from demonstrations and ball games to the national *Christmas* tree. 1600 Constitution Ave. NW. *Metro: Farragut West.*

CORCORAN GALLERY OF ART One of the finest collections of 18th-, 19th-, and 20th-century American art anywhere is displayed in this museum's gracious, skylit halls. (It's privately funded, and despite its location is not a *Smithsonian* museum.) Among the distinguished works are paintings by Sargent, Bierstadt, and Copley. You'll also find European paintings and sculpture (some by Corot, some by the animal sculptor Antoine Barye), as well as Renaissance drawings, and a variety of changing exhibitions of contemporary art and photography. Closed Tuesdays; open until 9 PM on Thursdays. No admission charge. One block from the *White House* at 17th and E Sts. NW (phone: 638-3211). *Metro: Farragut West.*

RENWICK GALLERY The nation's first art museum, this beautiful French Second Empire building was designed by *Smithsonian Castle* architect James Renwick in 1859 to house W. W. Corcoran's art collection. Now run by the *Smithsonian Institution,* it is worth a visit for its changing exhibitions of contemporary American crafts and design. The gallery's other noteworthy sights are the entrance foyer, with its impressive staircase, and the 1870 Grand Salon, with overstuffed Louis XV sofas and potted palms. Open daily. No admission charge. Pennsylvania Ave. at 17th St. NW (phone: 357-2531). *Metro: Farragut North or West.*

DAUGHTERS OF THE AMERICAN REVOLUTION MUSEUM Though any member of the DAR must prove that she is descended from those who served the cause of American independence with "unfailing loyalty," the museum is open to everyone. Exhibitions feature more than 30 period rooms, including the parlor of a 19th-century Mississippi River steamboat, and the *Oklahoma Room,* with a prairie farm kitchen's utensils. *Continental Hall,* the building that houses the museum, is also one of the world's largest genealogical archives (there's a small charge to do research here). The museum is open and tours are given on a walk-in basis; closed all day Saturday, and Sunday morning. No admission charge. 1776 D St. NW (phone: 628-1776). *Metro: Farragut West.*

OCTAGON HOUSE This stately red brick townhouse, a notable example of Federal architecture, is where President James Madison and his wife Dolley lived for six months after the British burned down the *White House* (and the *Capitol*) in 1814. The British may have spared this structure because the French ambassador had been living here since the outbreak of the War of 1812, and the French tricolor was flying over the house. Today it is maintained as a museum; the American antique furnishings from the Federal period give visitors an idea of the high style of the early 19th century. Tours are available. Closed Mondays. Donations suggested. 1799 New York Ave. NW (phone: 638-3105). *Metro: Farragut West.*

ORGANIZATION OF AMERICAN STATES Architects Paul Cret and Albert Kelsey blended the styles of North and South America in this building of imposing formality and inviting elegance. The *OAS* links the US with the countries of Latin America and the Caribbean, and through its symposiums, lectures, and general precepts tries to promote better political and trade relations. For example, the *OAS* was involved in planning the celebration of the 500th anniversary of Columbus's voyage to the New World. Note the statue of Queen Isabella I as you enter. Also inside are the *Hall of Heroes and Flags;* the *Hall of the Americas;* several Louis Tiffany chandeliers; and the *Aztec Gardens,* a year-round tropical spot that is overgrown with exotic plants sent here from the member nations of the *OAS.* Closed weekends. No admission charge. The *Art Museum of the Americas* is just behind the *Aztec Garden.* Closed Sundays. No admission charge. In the *Pan American Union Building,* 17th St. and Constitution Ave. NW (phone: 458-3000 for *OAS;* 458-6016 for the art museum). *Metro: Farragut West.*

THE MALL AREA

This 2-mile stretch of green from the *Lincoln Memorial* to the *Capitol* forms something of the grand avenue envisioned by Pierre L'Enfant in his original plans for the city.

WORK IN PROGRESS

Due to extensive repairs to the *Lincoln* and *Jefferson Memorials,* visitors might see more scaffolding than monuments for the next year or so. The statues themselves, however, will not be obstructed. Although both will remain open to the public, walking entirely around the colonnades will be prohibited until repairs are completed, sometime next year.

LINCOLN MEMORIAL From the outside, this columned white marble building looks like a Greek temple; inside, the spacious chamber with its colossal seated statue of Lincoln, sculpted by Daniel French, is just as inspiring. Carved on the walls are the words of the *Gettysburg Address* and *Lincoln's Second Inaugural Address*. *National Park Service* guides present brief talks at regular intervals. Open 24 hours a day, with park rangers on duty until midnight. No admission charge. *Memorial Circle* between Constitution and Independence Aves. (phone: 426-6841 or 426-6895). *Metro: Foggy Bottom.*

WASHINGTON MONUMENT Dominating the *Mall* is the 555-foot marble and granite obelisk designed by Robert Mills (completed in 1888) to commemorate George Washington. The top, reached by elevator, commands an excellent panoramic view of the city. On *National Park Service* tours on weekends, you can walk down the 897 steps, where you see many stones donated by such groups as the "Citizens of the US residing in Foo Chow Foo, China." Open daily, 8 AM to midnight, from the first Sunday in April through *Labor Day;* 9 AM to 5 PM the rest of the year. No admission charge. 15th St. between Independence and Constitution Aves. (phone: 426-6841). *Metro: Smithsonian.*

VIETNAM VETERANS MEMORIAL Maya Ying Lin, while a *Yale* architecture student, designed this simple memorial which evokes complicated feelings about the American soldiers who died or are missing as a result of the Vietnam War. The two arms of the long, V-shaped, polished black granite walls point toward the *Washington Monument* and the *Lincoln Memorial.* On the 492-foot-long wall are inscribed the names of more than 58,000 men and women killed in the war or still missing. A sculpture by Frederick Hart, depicting three soldiers, stands a short distance from the memorial. Also nearby is a memorial honoring the estimated 10,000 women who served in the Vietnam War. The memorial, a bronze sculpture by Gienna Goodacre, depicts two women in uniform attending a wounded male soldier. Many make pilgrimages here to find the names of lost friends and family members, some of them quietly etching an inscribed name onto a piece of paper to take home with them. Constitution Ave. NW and Henry Bacon Dr. (phone: 634-1568). *Metro: Foggy Bottom.*

JEFFERSON MEMORIAL Dominating the south bank of the Tidal Basin, this domed temple-like structure (designed by John Russell Pope) is a tribute to our third president and the drafter of the *Declaration of Independence.* The bronze statue of Jefferson was executed by Rudolph Evans, and inscribed on the walls are quotations from Jefferson's writings. This is the place to be for the most dramatic view of the cherry blossoms in early spring. Open daily. No admission charge. South Basin Dr. SW (phone: 426-6822). *Metro: Smithsonian.*

UNITED STATES HOLOCAUST MEMORIAL MUSEUM Opened in April of 1993, this is a museum dedicated to educating visitors about one of the twentieth century's darkest periods: the persecution and systematic execution by the

Nazis of Jews, Gypsies, homosexuals, and other "undesirables" during World War II. Located between the *Washington Monument* and the *Jefferson Memorial,* the red brick and sandstone building was designed by James I. Freed. Upon entering, you are given an ID card bearing the picture and name of an actual victim; you then wend your way through exhibits about book burning, *Kristallnacht,* and the "Final Solution," eventually discovering the fate of "your" victim. There is also a library, archives, and the *Learning Center,* an interactive exhibit that allows visitors access to maps, documents, videos, and music via touch screens. A limited number of (free) same-day tickets are available when the museum opens at 10 AM, but demand has been high and people line up early. Advance tickets (a much better idea), with a fixed date and time of entry, can be ordered through *TicketMaster* (phone: 432-7328); there is a small service charge per ticket when ordering. Closed *Christmas.* No admission charge. 100 Raoul Wallenberg Pl. SW, between 14th and 15th Sts. (phone: 488-0400). *Metro: Smithsonian.*

BUREAU OF ENGRAVING AND PRINTING At the world's largest securities manufacturing establishment, you can watch the making of currency on 25-minute self-guided tours. Open weekdays from 9 AM to 2 PM only. Closed weekends, federal holidays, and from *Christmas* through *New Year's Day.* No admission charge. 14th and C Sts. SW (phone: 874-3019). *Metro: Smithsonian.*

J. EDGAR HOOVER BUILDING If you want to find out a little more about an organization that already knows everything about you, take a tour of the *Federal Bureau of Investigation (FBI).* In addition to a film on some past investigative activities, you'll get to see the laboratory and a firearms demonstration. One-hour tours start every 20 minutes on weekdays from 8:45 AM to 4:15 PM. Line up early. No admission charge. Pennsylvania Ave. between Ninth and 10th Sts. NW (phone: 324-3447). *Metro: Metro Center* or *Archives/Navy Memorial.*

NATIONAL ARCHIVES The repository for all major American records. The 76 Corinthian columns supporting this handsome building designed by John Russell Pope are nothing compared to the contents. Inside, in special helium-filled glass and bronze cases, reside the very pillars of our democracy—the *Declaration of Independence,* the *Constitution,* and the *Bill of Rights.* Open daily; there are evening hours from April through *Labor Day.* No admission charge. Constitution Ave. between Seventh and Ninth Sts. NW (phone: 501-5205). *Metro: Archives/Navy Memorial.*

US NAVY MEMORIAL PLAZA The plaza has a statue of a lone US sailor overlooking the US portion of a granite world map. The visitors' center includes a gift shop, IMAX theater, and museum. Military bands perform during spring and summer evenings; pick up a brochure at any hotel or call for schedule. Pennsylvania Ave. between Seventh and Ninth Sts. NW (phone: 737-2300; 800-821-8892). *Metro: Archives/Navy Memorial.*

NATIONAL GALLERY OF ART In a John Russell Pope building whose 500,000 square feet make it one of the world's largest marble structures, this museum, built to introduce Americans to the cream of European art, is what one local critic called "the sort of place paintings would aspire to if masterpieces went to heaven." Columns of Tuscan marble, floors of green marble from Vermont and gray marble from Tennessee, and walls of Indiana limestone and Italian travertine produce an unadulturatedly sumptuous effect. Leonardo da Vinci's *Ginevra de' Benci* (America's only da Vinci), Jan Vermeer's *Woman Holding a Balance,* a Rembrandt *Self-Portrait,* Jean-Honoré Fragonard's *A Young Girl Reading,* Pierre-Auguste Renoir's *Girl with a Watering Can,* and Claude Monet's *Rouen Cathedral, West Façade* are among literally thousands of breathtaking canvases and sculptures housed in the original building and the striking *East Building,* designed as a grouping of interlocking triangles by I. M. Pei. It all can be a bit bewildering, so, as an introduction, you might want to join one of the regular tours, rent a taped tour, or pick up the excellent *Brief Guide.* A monthly calendar of events includes free films, lectures, and concerts. Closed *Christmas* and *New Year's Day.* No admission charge. Fourth St. and Constitution Ave. NW (phone: 737-4215). *Metro: Judiciary Square, Federal Center Southwest,* or *Archives/Navy Memorial.*

SMITHSONIAN INSTITUTION Completed in 1855, the red Gothic castle on the *Mall,* built to house the institution's collections, is now the site of the *Smithsonian*'s *Information Center* and the offices of the staff that oversees the *Smithsonian*'s scattered museums and galleries. There are nine *Smithsonian* properties on the *Mall,* five (including the *National Zoo—* see below) in other parts of DC, two in New York City (the *Cooper-Hewitt National Museum of Design* and the *National Museum of the American Indian*), and a half-dozen scientific research facilities around the country. The total collection contains over 137 million items and gains almost one million more every year; only an infinitesimal percentage is displayed at any given time, so there's always something new to see. The *Smithsonian*'s $73-million, three-floor complex just south of the *Castle* on Independence Avenue SW at 10th Street is a bit controversial because it is underground. It houses two museums—the *Arthur M. Sackler Gallery,* featuring Asian art, and the *National Museum of African Art,* which was moved from its former *Capitol Hill* location (see below for details on both). The third floor houses the *International Center* for exhibitions, and atop it all is the *Enid A. Haupt Garden,* a $3-million Victorian delight built around a century-old linden tree. The *Castle* is at 1000 Jefferson Dr. SW (phone: 357-2700).

The following are the *Smithsonian Museums* on the *Mall;* they are listed in clockwise order, starting from the *Smithsonian Castle.* All are closed only on *Christmas Day;* hours are slightly longer in summer. There's no admission charge for any of the *Smithsonian* museums.

National Museum of African Art The most extensive collection of African art in this country, and the only one dedicated exclusively to the arts of sub-Saharan Africa. Exhibitions include figures, masks, and sculptures in ivory, wood, bronze, and clay from 20 African nations; also color panels and audio-visual presentations on the people and environments of Africa. One gallery has an intriguing display concerning the influence of Africa's cultural her-itage on modern European and American art. There's also a delightful gift shop. 950 Independence Ave. SW, next to the *Sackler Gallery of Art* (phone: 357-4600). *Metro: Smithsonian.*

Arthur M. Sackler Gallery Donated by Dr. Arthur M. Sackler, a New York medical researcher, the extensive collection of over 1,000 pieces of Eastern art includes Chinese bronzes from the Shang (1523–1028 BC) through Han (206 BC–AD 220) dynasties, Chinese jade that dates from 3000 BC, and Near Eastern works in silver, gold, bronze, and lesser ores. There are also Persian and Indian paintings, Chinese Ming Dynasty furniture, and more. 1050 Independence Ave. SW (phone: 357-4880). *Metro: Smithsonian.*

Freer Gallery An eclectic collection of Asian art, plus late-19th- and early-20th-century American art. Wealthy Detroit businessman Charles Lang Freer donated the works from his personal collection. *The Peacock Room,* painted by Freer's friend, James McNeill Whistler, is a must-see. Jefferson Dr. at 12th St. SW (phone: 357-4880). *Metro: Smithsonian.*

National Museum of American History The wealth of Americana that fills this uniquely austere *Mall* museum includes George Washington's false teeth, the original Star-Spangled Banner that inspired the Francis Scott Key poem (that inspired the national anthem), the desk on which Thomas Jefferson wrote the *Declaration of Independence,* Eli Whitney's cotton gin, Alexander Graham Bell's telephone, and other prized possessions—such as the gowns worn by First Ladies from Martha Washington to Hillary Clinton, modeled by mannequins standing in authentic reproductions of rooms in the *White House.* The museum's ground floor traces the role of machines in our nation's history, from railroad locomotives and a 1913 Model T to atom smashers and computers. The second floor focuses on our nation's people, our home life, our community life, and our relation-ship to the world beyond. The third floor is packed with exhibits ranging from musical instruments to instruments of war. One of the more inter-esting exhibits is an entire pre–Civil War post office taken from Headsville, West Virginia, that is still in operation and accepts letters for mail, frank-ing them with a unique *Smithsonian* seal. The various galleries, from the *1776 Gallery* to the *Pain Gallery* (in the *Medical Gallery*), offer a variety of demonstrations—visitors can learn about the workings of the ham radio, methods of type founding and printing, and much more. The *Smithsonian Bookstore* (phone: 357-1784) has the area's best selection of American history books. Constitution Ave. between 12th and 14th Sts. NW (phone: 357-2700). *Metro: Smithsonian* or *Federal Triangle.*

National Museum of Natural History This massive museum on the *Mall* is bloated with 118 million items (only a fraction of which are on display) that tell the story of human beings and their environment. The exhibits cover the entire spectrum of the life sciences, from anthropology to marine zoology. Among the more popular exhibits are the *Dinosaur Hall,* exhibits on the evolution of humans, fossils, a collection of beasts bagged by Teddy Roosevelt on his African adventures, the *Insect Zoo,* and displays on birds, plants, rocks, and gems. The gem collection contains the legendary Hope Diamond, smuggled out of India in the 17th century and reputed to bring tragedy to its owners; at 45.5 carats, this blue diamond is the largest in the world. The largest elephant on record, a giant Fenkovi African bush elephant more than 13 feet tall, greets visitors in the museum's octagonal rotunda, where banners point the way to the worlds of fossils, birds, mammals, bones, and the geology of the Earth. Another favorite occupant is "Uncle Beazly," the life-size model of a triceratops dinosaur. The *Sea Life Hall* contains live aquatic specimens and a living coral reef, and the *Discovery Room* is a godsend to parents, with its touchable exhibits of elephant tusks and arrowheads, plus a costume room (in which children can try on costumes from around the world). The museum's gift shops and *Associates Court* cafeteria are excellent. Constitution Ave. at 10th St. NW (phone: 357-2700). *Metro: Smithsonian* or *Federal Triangle.*

National Air & Space Museum This member of the *Smithsonian* complex, housing a fascinating assortment of aerodynamic treasures, draws more visitors annually than any other museum in the world; consequently, a visit here often means braving crowds. But in exchange for a little jostling and waiting, you will learn about the history of flight from people's earliest yearnings and attempts to fly, to World War II rockets, to the modern space probes that now explore the outer reaches of our solar system and beyond. In addition to the mechanics of flying, the 23 galleries in this lofty building explore the politics, physics, and art linked to man's dreams of flight. The entry hall's *Milestones of Flight Gallery* holds Charles Lindbergh's *Spirit of St. Louis,* the Wright brothers' *Kitty Hawk Flyer,* and the *Gossamer Albatross,* the first human-powered plane to cross the English Channel, but this is just the beginning. In all, there are 240 aircraft and 50 missiles in the collection. The museum's *Albert Einstein Planetarium* is truly a cosmic experience and the *Langley Theater,* which projects films onto a towering five-story-high screen, is the next best thing to having your own wings. Different films are featured periodically but the historic mainstay of the theater is *To Fly,* a hell-for-leather romp through the skies in everything from a hot-air balloon to a fighter jet. Other exhibits allow visitors to design aircraft, observe the history of aerial photography, and inspect a model of Skylab.

There's an admission charge for movies. Sixth St. and Independence Ave. SW (phone: 357-2700). *Metro: L'Enfant Plaza.*

Hirshhorn Museum and Sculpture Garden This is the most modern of the city's museums of modern art. The *Hirshhorn* houses the ever-astonishing collection amassed by Joseph H. Hirshhorn (1899–1981), who grew up in such poverty that he never even owned a toy. The collection focuses on American art and includes works by Estes, Golub, Gorky, Henri, Hopper, de Kooning, Noland, and Stella; modern European masters such as Bacon, Balthus, Kiefer, and Magritte also are represented. The extraordinary vitality of the sculpture collection reflects the genius of Calder, Degas, Matisse, Moore, Rodin, Serra, and David Smith—many of whose works are displayed in the sculpture garden—plus the innovations of more recent artists. For this variety alone the museum is fascinating; the building itself—circular and fortress-like—is intriguing as well. Seventh St. and Independence Ave. SW (phone: 357-1300). *Metro: L'Enfant Plaza.*

Arts and Industries Building Just east of the *Castle,* this is the second-oldest *Smithsonian* building on the *Mall.* The *Centennial Exhibition,* displayed in Philadelphia in 1876, has been re-created with marvelous displays of fashions, furnishings, and machinery. Jefferson Dr. and Independence Ave. at Ninth St. SW (phone: 357-1300). *Metro: Smithsonian.*

FOR THE YOUNG AND YOUNG-AT-HEART

The beautiful early 20th-century carousel set in the shadow of the *Smithsonian Castle* operates in the warm weather between 10 AM and 5:30 PM. *Metro: Smithsonian.*

DOWNTOWN

NATIONAL PORTRAIT GALLERY AND NATIONAL MUSEUM OF AMERICAN ART In the *National Portrait Gallery,* an excellent example of Greek Revival architecture, many Americans who have gone down in the history of this country have gone up on the walls (in portrait form, that is). Among those hanging are all the American presidents, Pocahontas, Horace Greeley, and Harriet Beecher Stowe. The *National Museum of American Art* features American painting, sculpture, and graphic arts, including Catlin's paintings of Indians and a choice group of works by the American Impressionists. Both museums (also administered by the *Smithsonian Institution*) are open daily. No admission charge. Eighth St. at F and G Sts. NW. (phone: 357-2700). *Metro: Gallery Place.*

FORD'S THEATRE The site of Abraham Lincoln's assassination by John Wilkes Booth is a national monument, restored and decorated as it appeared on the fatal night of April 14, 1865. In the basement is a museum of Lincoln memorabilia, including displays showing his life as a lawyer, statesman, husband, father, and president; the clothes he was wearing when he was shot;

the flag that covered his casket; the derringer used by the assassin; and Booth's personal diary. Theater performances are held throughout the year. Open daily. Admission charge for shows only. 511 10th St. NW (phone: 426-6924; 347-4833 for theater tickets). *Metro: Metro Center* (11th St. exit).

PETERSON HOUSE Directly across the street from *Ford's Theatre* is the house in which Lincoln died the morning after the shooting. The small, sparsely furnished home appears much the way it did in 1865. Open daily. No admission charge. 516 10th St. NW (phone: 426-6830). *Metro: Metro Center* (11th St. exit).

NATIONAL LAW ENFORCEMENT OFFICERS' MEMORIAL Dedicated in late 1991, this monument honors federal, state, and local law enforcement officers who have died in the line of duty, dating as far back as 1794. The enclosed plaza has walled pathways that encircle a terraced pool, and are guarded on each side by majestic bronze lions. E St. between Fourth and Fifth Sts. NW (phone: 703-827-0518). *Metro: Judiciary Square.*

ADAMS MORGAN

This funky, international neighborhood is now rivaling Georgetown as the area for after-hours fun and frolicking in the nation's capital. Long the bohemian section of town, it has been home to many Salvadoran, Ethiopian, and African immigrants. Surrounding the intersection of Columbia Road and 18th Street NW are foreign-language book and record stores, clothing boutiques with products from Asia and Africa, Ethiopian and Vietnamese restaurants, reggae bars, and hot nightspots. *Adams Morgan Day,* an annual cultural street fair held in early September, is alive with music from all over the world; local restaurants provide a host of international foods to satisfy any palate. *Metro: Dupont Circle.*

GEORGETOWN

Once the Union's major tobacco port, the only tobacco left in Georgetown is in the smoke shops. Still holding fast to its own identity, this neighborhood is particularly nice in the spring when it's pleasant to walk along the Chesapeake and Ohio Canal. The whole area's great for strolling (though too much tourism has produced the occasional tacky stretch). In summer, it's possible to catch a slow barge up the canal. Tickets can be purchased at the *Foundry Mall* (1055 Thomas Jefferson St. NW; phone: 472-4376). Beside the canal (between Jefferson and 31st Sts.), the streets off Wisconsin Avenue house the city's social and political elite in beautifully restored townhouses with prim gardens and lovely magnolia trees. Many of the buildings are on the *National Register of Historic Places* and are well worth seeing. The main drags—Wisconsin Avenue and M Street—are where most of the action is. In addition to boasting a shopping mall and some of the hottest nightlife in town (including sports and blues bars), the area is rich with boutiques, movie theaters, and restaurants offering a vast variety of food—from Vietnamese to Indian to French.

At the northern edge of Georgetown (along R St. east of Wisconsin Ave.), large 18th-century country estates mingle with smaller, more modern row houses. The *Dumbarton Oaks Garden* has beautiful formal grounds, and the *Dumbarton Oaks Museum* has a fine collection of early Christian and Byzantine art. The museum is open Tuesdays through Sundays from 2 to 5 PM; no admission charge. The gardens are open daily from 2 to 5 PM; admission charge from April through October (phone: 342-3200 or 338-8278). The entrance to the museum is at 1703 32nd Street NW; the entrance to the gardens is at 31st and R Streets NW.

At 37th and O Streets is the campus of *Georgetown University.* Established in 1789, it is the oldest Jesuit university in the United States and is renowned for its schools of foreign service and languages, as well as for one of the best law schools in the country.

ELSEWHERE IN DC

ROCK CREEK PARK New York has its *Central Park,* Chicago its *Grant Park,* and Philadelphia its *Fairmount Park.* Washington's premier city park, where one can escape the traffic, the noise, the concrete, and (mostly) the crowds, is found in a 1,700-acre swath of green in the northwest section of town. From its narrow south tip just outside Georgetown, *Rock Creek Park* (named for the meandering stream that bisects it) widens gradually until it's big enough to contain the *National Zoo* (see below) and, a few miles farther north, a modest 18-hole golf course (see *Golf*). There are bike and jogging trails, picnic tables, even riding stables, but mostly untended greenery, which covers the park's steep hills. A two-lane road meanders down its spine; the northern section of the park is closed to automobiles on Sundays to allow cyclists, Rollerbladers, and strollers free reign. In the northwest quadrant of the city (phone: 426-6829). *Metro: Fort Totten* or *Van Ness* (though it's a bus ride or long walk from either station).

NATIONAL ZOO The *Smithsonian Institution* is best known for its museums on the *Mall,* but its largest facility is located in the midst of verdant *Rock Creek Park* (see above) in the northwest quadrant of the city. Created in 1889 for "the advancement of science and the instruction and recreation of the people," this 163-acre zoological park clings to the side of a gently rolling hill. The *Amazonia* exhibit recreates a tropical river and rain forest, while the *Reptile Discovery Center* allows visitors to meet reptiles and amphibians up close and personal. The *Great Flight Cage* features exotic birds. Sadly, the zoo's female panda Ling-Ling died in late 1992, leaving her male companion Hsing-Hsing the only panda in the zoo; there are no offspring (although the pair's numerous attempts at mating are documented in a photo display!). There are, however, many infant animals born each year to such species as giraffes, orangutans, and elephants. The *Panda Café* serves refreshments, and souvenir shops are filled with, among other things, panda paraphernalia. Closed *Christmas.* No admission charge. 3301 Connecticut Ave. NW (phone: 673-4800). *Metro: Woodley Park/Zoo* or *Cleveland Park* (the easier walk is from *Cleveland Park;* it's a stiff uphill climb from *Woodley Park/Zoo*).

EXTRA SPECIAL

Just 16 miles south of Washington on George Washington Memorial Parkway is *Mount Vernon,* George Washington's estate from 1754 to 1799 and his final resting place. This lovely 18th-century plantation shows a less familiar aspect of the military-political figure—George Washington as the rich Southern planter. The mansion, overlooking the Potomac, and the outbuildings that housed the shops that made *Mount Vernon* a self-sufficient economic unit have been authentically restored and refurnished. Some 500 of the original 8,000 acres remain; all are well maintained, and the parterre gardens and formal lawns provide a magnificent setting. There's also a museum with Washington memorabilia; the tomb of George and Martha lies at the foot of the hill. During the spring or the summer, start out early to avoid big crowds. Bicycle paths lead from the DC side of Memorial Bridge to *Mount Vernon*—a lovely ride along the Potomac. Open daily. Admission charge (phone: 703-780-2000).

Also overlooking the Potomac is *Arlington National Cemetery,* a solemn reminder of the more turbulent parts of our country's history. Here lie the bodies of many who served their country, both in the military forces and in other ways, among them Admiral Richard Byrd, General George C. Marshall, Robert F. Kennedy, Justice Oliver Wendell Holmes, and John F. Kennedy, whose grave is marked by an *Eternal Flame.* Former first lady Jacqueline Kennedy Onassis, who died last spring, is interred beside her husband. The *Tomb of the Unknown Soldier,* a 50-ton block of white marble, commemorates the dead of World Wars I and II and the Korean, Vietnam, and Persian Gulf wars and is always guarded by a solitary soldier. Changing of the guard takes place every hour on the hour (every half hour during summer months). The beautifully landscaped grounds of the cemetery once were part of Robert E. Lee's plantation but were confiscated by the Union after Lee joined the Confederacy. Lee's home, *Arlington House,* has been restored and is open to the public. Cars are not allowed in the cemetery, but you can park at the visitors' center and go on foot or pay and ride the *Tourmobile* (phone: 554-7950). Both *Arlington House* and the cemetery are open daily. Directly west of Memorial Bridge in Arlington, Virginia. *Metro: Arlington Cemetery.*

Sources and Resources

TOURIST INFORMATION

The *Washington, DC, Convention and Visitors Association* (*WCVA;* 1212 New York Ave. NW, Suite 600, Washington, DC 20005; phone: 789-7000; fax: 789-7037) coordinates all Washington tourism information and runs the visitors' center (at 1455 Pennsylvania Ave. NW; phone: 789-7038). The center (closed Sundays) provides free maps and information on where to stay, eat, and shop, and on events.

LOCAL COVERAGE The *Washington Post* and the *Washington Times* are the city's morning daily newspapers; *Washingtonian* magazine is published monthly. All are available at newsstands. *Museum and Arts Washington* lists current museum exhibits. The *City Paper,* a free weekly tabloid published on Thursdays, is an excellent source of cultural and club listings; it's available in shops, restaurants, and *Metro* stations. *Best Restaurants and Others* by Phyllis Richman (101 Productions; $8.95) lists fine dining places in Washington, DC, and environs.

TELEVISION STATIONS WRC Channel 4–NBC; WTTG Channel 5–Fox; WJLA Channel 7–ABC; WUSA Channel 9–CBS; Cable Channel 42 or 11–CNN; and WETA Channel 26–PBS.

RADIO STATIONS AM: WTEM 570 (sports); WMAL 630 (news/talk/sports); WWRC 980 (talk); and WTOP 1500 (all news). FM: WPFW 89.3 (jazz/community radio); WETA 90.9 (classical/National Public Radio); WKYS 93.9 (urban contemporary); WMZQ 98.7 (country); WGAY 99.5 (easy listening); WGMS 103.5 (classical); and WCXR 105.9 (classic rock).

TELEPHONE The area code for the District is 202; for Maryland, 301; and for Virginia, 703. The telephone numbers in this chapter are in the 202 area code unless otherwise indicated.

SALES TAX The city sales tax is 6%; there is an 11% tax on hotel rooms.

GETTING AROUND

BUS The *Metro Bus* system serves the entire District and the surrounding area. Transfers within the District are free; the rates increase when you go into Maryland and Virginia. For complete route information call the *Washington Metropolitan Area Transit Authority* office (phone: 637-7000). *Greyhound/Trailways* runs to and from its main bus station (First St. and L St. NE; phone: 301-565-2662).

CAR RENTAL For information on renting a car, see GETTING READY TO GO.

SUBWAY The fastest way to get around Washington is by *Metrorail,* the subway system. The lines provide a quick and quiet ride, for $1 to $3.15 depending on the route and time of day. (Fare schedules are posted in each station.) You need a farecard to enter and exit platform areas; they are on sale inside the stations. Transfers to the bus system are free. Note: Be sure to pick up a transfer at your boarding station (not the exiting station). Children ages five and under ride free. *Metro* hours are weekdays from 6 AM to midnight; Saturdays and Sundays from 8 AM to midnight. Inquire about discount passes; for example, a two-day *Family/Tourist Pass,* which costs $5, is good for unlimited travel on the *Metro* buses and subway for up to four persons. For complete route and travel information and a map of the system, contact the *Washington Metropolitan Area Transit Authority* office (600 Fifth St. NW; phone: 637-7000).

TAXI Cabs in the District charge by zone. Sharing cabs is common, but ask the driver whether there is a route conflict if you join another passenger. Cabs may be hailed in the street, picked up outside stations and hotels, or ordered on the phone, but there is an extra charge of $1.50 for phone dispatch. By law, basic rates must be posted in all taxis. The major cab companies are *Yellow* (phone: 544-1212) and *Diamond* (phone: 387-6200).

TOURS The *Tourmobile* operates in the downtown sightseeing area between the *Lincoln Memorial* and *Capitol* area (the *Mall*), and also goes to *Arlington National Cemetery.* These 88-passenger shuttle trams make 18 stops, and passengers may get on or off as they wish (*Tourmobiles* pass each stop every 30 minutes). Commentary about the sights also is provided. Tickets can be purchased from the driver or from a booth near the tour sites. For complete information contact the *Tourmobile* office (1000 Ohio Dr. SW; phone: 554-7950).

Old Town Trolley Tours offers two-hour group charter tours or individual tours of the District (phone: 682-0079). *Gray Line* offers guided, narrated bus tours of the District and outlying areas (phone: 289-1995 or 301-386-8300); another bus touring company is *All About Town* (phone: 966-3800). Museum tours as well as special group tours emphasizing historic Washington are run by *National Fine Arts Associates* (4801 Massachusetts Ave. NW; phone: 966-3800). *Spirit Cruises* runs tours such as the "Spirit of Washington" and the "Spirit of Mt. Vernon" (March to mid-October only to *Mount Vernon*) aboard sightseeing boats on the Potomac, from March to December (Pier 4, Sixth and Water Sts. SW; phone: 554-8000 or 554-1542). The *Potomac Riverboat Company* also offers tours from the waterways of the capital area (phone: 703-684-0580). For further information on companies offering tours in and around Washington, see GETTING READY TO GO.

TRAIN More than 50 *Amtrak* trains daily pull into historic *Union Station* on *Capitol Hill,* including the *Metroliner,* linking the capital to New York and other Northeast Corridor cities. For reservations and information, call 800-872-7245.

LOCAL SERVICES

AUDIOVISUAL EQUIPMENT *Avcom* (1006 Sixth St. NW; phone: 408-0444) and *Total Audio-Visual Systems* (303 H St. NW; phone: 737-3900).

BABY-SITTING *Kids First* (15th and K Sts.; phone: 289-5437).

BUSINESS SERVICES *Ecco Temporary Services* (1001 Connecticut Ave. NW; phone: 293-2285). *The Capital Informer* (3240 Prospect St. NW; phone: 965-7420) helps plan conventions and meetings.

DRY CLEANER/TAILOR *Bergmann's* offers pickup and delivery at several locations (2318 Rhode Island Ave. NE; phone: 529-2440; 714 Sixth St. NW; phone: 737-6925; or call 703-247-7600).

LIMOUSINES *Congressional Limousine* (phone: 966-6000) offers 24-hour service. *International Limousine Service* (phone: 388-6800) has multilingual drivers; sedans are also available.

MECHANIC *Call Carl* (5030 Connecticut Ave.; phone: 364-6368) makes repairs from 7:30 AM to 5 PM; gas is available 24 hours a day.

MEDICAL EMERGENCY For information on area hospitals and pharmacies, see GETTING READY TO GO.

MESSENGER SERVICES *U.S. Couriers* (phone: 393-1111).

PHOTOCOPIES *City Duplicating Center* (1615 L St. NW; phone: 296-0700); *Beaver Press* (1333 H St. NW; phone: 347-6400; and 18 Ogelthorpe St. NW; phone: 882-6690) offers pickup and delivery service.

POST OFFICES For information on local branch offices, see GETTING READY TO GO.

PROFESSIONAL PHOTOGRAPHER *Garrison Studio* (52 O St. NW; phone: 265-5163).

SECRETARIES/STENOGRAPHERS *Courtesy Associates* (655 15th St. NW, Suite 300; phone: 347-5900).

TELECONFERENCE FACILITIES *Four Seasons* (2800 Pennsylvania Ave. NW; phone: 342-0444; 800-332-3442) and *Loews L'Enfant Plaza* (480 L'Enfant Plaza SW; phone: 484-1000; 800-243-1166).

TRANSLATORS *Berlitz* (1050 Connecticut Ave. NW; phone: 331-1160) for written translations only; *International Translation Center* (1660 L St. NW, Room 613; phone: 296-1344).

WESTERN UNION/TELEX *Western Union* (phone: 624-0100 or 800-325-6000) has offices throughout the city. For information on money transfers, see GETTING READY TO GO.

SPECIAL EVENTS

A town that knows how to throw presidential inauguration parties is a town that knows how to celebrate. There's plenty to keep the District going between inaugurations, too. The first sighting of white single blossoms and a flood of pink double blossoms means it's *Cherry Blossom* time in Washington. In early April, a big festival celebrates the coming of the blossoms and the spring with concerts, parades, balls, and the lighting of the Japanese Lantern at the Tidal Basin.

Around the same time (give or take a few blossoms) is the *Easter Monday Egg Rolling,* when scads of children descend on the *White House* lawn, usually to be greeted by the First Family; adults are admitted only if accompanied by a child.

House, garden, and embassy tours are given in April and May, allowing entrance to some of Washington's most elegant interiors. For information on the tours, see the "Weekend" section in Friday's *Washington Post.*

During the summer, the *Festival of American Folklife,* sponsored by the *Smithsonian Institution,* sets up its tents on the *Mall* near the *Museum of American History,* and groups from all regions of the country do their stuff; jug band concerts, blues performances, Indian dances, and handicraft demonstrations are just a few of the possibilities. In midsummer the *Twilight Tattoo* features military pageantry. And the *Fourth of July* celebrations in the capital are among the best in the country, with a parade, concerts, fireworks, and other entertainment.

In early September, *Adams Morgan Day* is celebrated in the Adams Morgan neighborhood. The festival, which reflects Spanish, Ethiopian, and African influences, features music, crafts, and food. The city is especially festive at *Christmas.* Special music programs are presented at the *Kennedy Center* and at many other spots around town.

MUSEUMS
In addition to those described in *Special Places,* other notable Washington, DC, museums include the following:

HILLWOOD Exquisite 18th- and 19th-century French and Russian icons, portraits, and Fabergé creations are housed in the elegant former home of cereal heiress Marjorie Merriweather Post. Other buildings on the 25-acre site include a dacha, or Russian country house, with a small collection of Russian art; the C. W. Post collection of paintings, sculpture, and furnishings; and a lodge housing Native American artifacts. Be sure to stroll around the *Rose Garden, French Garden,* and *Japanese Garden.* Closed Sundays and Mondays. Open to the public only via tours, which must be arranged by appointment; call well in advance for reservations. Admission charge. 4155 Linnean Ave. NW (phone: 686-5807). *Metro: Van Ness–UDC.*

HISTORICAL SOCIETY OF WASHINGTON, DC A museum devoted to Washington's history, housed in the spectacular Victorian mansion of brewer Christian Heurich. There is also a library and a bookstore. Tours are offered on the hour on Wednesdays through Saturdays starting from noon; the last tour leaves at 3 PM. The museum is closed Mondays. The library is open to the public Wednesdays, Fridays, and Saturdays from 10 AM to 4 PM. Admission charge. 1307 New Hampshire Ave. NW (phone: 785-2068). *Metro: Dupont Circle.*

NATIONAL BUILDING MUSEUM Housed in the old and wonderful *Pension Building,* this museum has permanent and changing exhibits relating to architecture, building, engineering, and design. Presidential inaugural balls are held in its *Great Hall.* Open daily. No admission charge. 401 F St. NW (phone: 272-2448). *Metro: Judiciary Square.*

NATIONAL GEOGRAPHIC SOCIETY EXPLORERS HALL Headquarters for the society; exhibits here document research and discoveries made by its explorers and documentarians. Open daily. No admission charge. 17th and M Sts. NW (phone: 857-7588). *Metro: Farragut North.*

NATIONAL LEARNING CENTER/CAPITAL CHILDREN'S MUSEUM A hands-on museum where children can dress up in period costumes, feed animals, and work on high-tech equipment. Open daily. Admission charge. 800 Third St. NE (phone: 543-8600). *Metro: Union Station.*

NATIONAL MUSEUM OF WOMEN IN THE ARTS In a former Masonic temple, this permanent collection of 500 pieces of pictorial, sculpted, and ceramic art spans 400 years of women's work. Open daily. Admission charge. 1250 New York Ave. at 13th St. NW (phone: 783-5000). *Metro: Metro Center* (13th St. exit).

PHILLIPS COLLECTION Opened in 1918, this is America's oldest museum of "modern art." Set in an elegant Victorian brownstone, the works of such masters as El Greco, Manet, and Chardin are shown together with their artistic progeny: Cézanne, Monet, Klee, O'Keeffe, Rothko, and many others. The pièce de résistance is Renoir's *Luncheon of the Boating Party.* The mahogany-paneled *Music Room* features a long-standing Sunday evening concert series of chamber music from September through May at 5 PM; admission charge). Closed *New Year's Day, July 4, Thanksgiving,* and *Christmas.* Admission charge weekends. 1612 21st St. and Q St. NW (phone: 387-0961). *Metro: Dupont Circle.*

TEXTILE MUSEUM A diverse collection of fabrics from around the world, in a former mansion with a charming garden. Featuring woven goods of both artistic and archaeological significance, it is one of only two museums in the world devoted entirely to woven rugs and fabrics. Even if your interest in the field runs no deeper than finding something to cover that stain on the den rug, this may be the place (although goods for sale in the shop are high-priced). Open daily. Admission charge. 2320 S St. NW (phone: 667-0441). *Metro: Dupont Circle.*

WASHINGTON DOLL'S HOUSE AND TOY MUSEUM Featured here is the private collection of dollhouse historian Floragill Jacobs. On display are antique dollhouses and toys, including a section of presidents' games that includes the "Game of Politics or Race for the Presidency," a board game created in 1887, and the "Game of Presidents," a card game dating from the early 20th century. Closed Mondays. Admission charge. 5236 44th St. NW, one block west of Wisconsin Ave., between Jennifer and Harrison Sts. (phone: 244-0024). *Metro: Friendship Heights.*

WOODROW WILSON HOUSE Home to Woodrow Wilson (from 1921 to 1924) and Mrs. Wilson (from 1921 to 1961), this is now a memorial to our 28th president and his wife. Gifts of state, presidential memorabilia, and other items from the 1920s are displayed. Considering Wilson's tireless efforts to establish the *League of Nations* and to expand America's role in international affairs, it is altogether fitting that he relocated to the Embassy Row district. On display are his library, the dining room, bedrooms, a solarium overlooking a garden, and many personal effects such as the typewriter he used to compose speeches. Only guided tours—which take approximately 45 minutes—are available; the house is closed Mondays. Admission charge. 2340 S St. NW (phone: 387-4062). *Metro: Dupont Circle North.*

MAJOR COLLEGES AND UNIVERSITIES

Washington has several universities of high national standing, including *American University* (Massachusetts and Nebraska Aves. NW; phone: 885-1000); *Gallaudet University* for the deaf (Seventh St. and Florida Ave. NE; phone: 651-5000); *Georgetown University* (37th and O Sts. NW; phone: 687-5055); *George Washington University* (2121 I St. NW; phone: 994-1000); and *Howard University* (2400 Sixth St. NW; phone: 806-6100).

SHOPPING

When you've had your fill of monuments, the nation's capital has enough shopping venues to satisfy even "shop-till-you-drop" appetites. Following the sprucing up of Pennsylvania Avenue some years ago, Washington is now home to a number of excellent shopping malls. For unique gifts, however, the city's impressive museums are the best bet. Most museums, shrines, and churches have their own shops, some offering reproductions of priceless treasures at very affordable prices. For details on antiques hunting in Washington, see *Capital Antiques* in DIVERSIONS. Here's a capital shoppers' guide:

SHOPPING MALLS

Connecticut Connection This three-story shopping and dining complex is conveniently located atop the *Farragut North Metro* station. Connecticut Ave. and L St. NW (no main phone number).

Eastern Market An open-air extravaganza on weekends with fresh produce, flowers, and crafts. North Carolina Ave. and Seventh St. SE.

Georgetown Park The centerpiece of Georgetown shopping, this handsome brick complex, with its magnificent Victorian interior, houses more than 100 elegant shops—including *Ann Taylor, FAO Schwarz,* and *Williams-Sonoma*—and restaurants. 3222 M St. NW at Wisconsin Ave. (phone: 298-5577).

International Square In this 12-story atrium with a cascading fountain are 30 retail shops, restaurants, and fast-food eateries. 1850 K St. NW (phone: 223-1850).

Mazza Gallerie On the north end of Wisconsin Avenue, this enclosed mall features high-fashion shops and specialty stores such as *Neiman Marcus.* 5300 Wisconsin Ave. NW (phone: 966-6144).

Pavilion at the Old Post Office The city's oldest Federal building, complete with a bell tower and skylight, has shops, cafés, and restaurants on its lower floors. 12th St. and Pennsylvania Ave. NW (phone: 289-4224).

Shops at National Place A prime shoppers' paradise, it includes such national chains as *Victoria's Secret, Sharper Image,* and *Express.* F St. between 13th and 14th Sts. NW (phone: 783-9090).

2000 Pennsylvania Avenue On the edge of the *George Washington University* campus, this mall, located within a brick townhouse complex, has a variety of specialty shops. Between 20th and 21st Sts. NW (phone: 452-0924).

Union Station The capital's Beaux Arts train station has been restored to its former glory and contains numerous shops as well as unique and entertaining eating spots. 50 Massachusetts Ave. NE (phone: 371-9441).

Washington Harbour This expansive office/retail/residential complex on the Potomac River features unique architectural designs, with fountain-filled courtyards and specialty shops and restaurants. 3000 K St. NW, next to the Whitehurst Freeway in Georgetown (phone: 944-4140).

Watergate A prestigious shopping arcade in the Watergate complex, including *Yves Saint Laurent, Gucci, Valentino,* and *Guy Laroche.* (It also has excellent restaurants and a hotel; see the *Watergate* listing in *Checking In.*) New Hampshire and Virginia Aves. NW (phone: 298-5500).

FOR BUDGET WATCHERS

Thirty minutes south of Washington is *Potomac Mills,* one of the world's largest outlet malls, and a big attraction for Washington shoppers on weekends. Among the almost 200 discount stores are outlets of such well-known retailers as *Eddie Bauer, Laura Ashley, Nordstrom's,* and *Benetton.* Open daily. On I-95S, exit 52, in Prince William, Virginia (phone: 703-643-1770; 800-VA-MILLS).

DOWNTOWN SHOPS

Border's Books and Music One of downtown's new superstores, this print and music emporium has a wide selection, plus a café. 18th and L Sts. NW (phone: 466-4999, books; 466-6999, music).

Britches of Georgetown Casual menswear and womenswear. 1219 Connecticut Ave. NW (phone: 347-8994).

Earl Allen Office clothing for women. *International Sq.,* 1825 I St. NW (phone: 466-3437).

Hecht's One of Washington's top department stores. 12th and G Sts. NW (phone: 628-6661).

Kramer Book Stores A wide selection of classics and new titles. Two locations: *Kramerbooks and Afterwords,* with a café in the rear of the store, open until 1 AM Sundays through Thursdays; all night Fridays and Saturdays (1517 Connecticut Ave. NW; phone: 387-1400); and *Sidney Kramer Books* (1825 I St. NW; phone: 293-2685).

Post Office Exchange Designer and souvenir Washington T-shirts. *Pavilion at the Old Post Office,* 12th St. and Pennsylvania Ave. NW (phone: 842-0504).

Tannery West Leather and suede clothing and bags. *Union Station,* 50 Massachusetts Ave. NE (phone: 371-1705).

Windsor Shirt Company Men's shirts. *International Square,* 1850 K St. NW (phone: 887-0011).

Woodward and Lothrop A popular, traditional department store. 11th and F Sts. NW (phone: 347-5300).

GEORGETOWN

Appalachian Spring Handmade crafts, quilts, and jewelry from all over the US. 1415 Wisconsin Ave. NW (phone: 337-5780).

Britches of Georgetown Casual clothing for men and women. 1247 Wisconsin Ave. NW (phone: 338-3330).

Hats in the Belfry Funny, unusual, elegant, and antique toppers for all occasions. 1237 Wisconsin Ave. NW (phone: 342-2006).

Little Caledonia Unusual furnishings, fabrics, and stationery. 1419 Wisconsin Ave. NW (phone: 333-4700).

The Newsroom In the heart of the embassy district, this newsstand has a wide selection of international newspapers and magazines. 1753 Connecticut Ave. NW (phone: 332-1489).

Orpheus Records Specializes in vintage and rare recordings. 3249 M St. NW (phone: 337-7970).

Phoenix Mexican jewelry, crafts, and clothing. 1514 Wisconsin Ave. NW (phone: 338-4404).

Santa Fe Style Crafts and art from the American Southwest. 1525 Wisconsin Ave. NW (phone: 333-3747).

Threepenny Bit Irish items—including hand-knit sweaters, shorts, shirts, ties, and shoes. 3122 M St. NW (phone: 338-1338).

MUSEUM SHOPS

Some fine souvenirs of a visit to the nation's capital await in its museum shops: Lincoln memorabilia, arty T-shirts, posters, and reproductions of historical furnishings and jewelry are just some possibilities.

Arts and Industries Building Stocks items shown in the *Smithsonian* mail-order gift catalogue. Between Jefferson Dr. and Independence Ave. at Ninth St. SW (phone: 357-1367).

Bethune Museum Gift Shop Books on such famous black women as Harriet Tubman and Josephine Baker. 1318 Vermont Ave. NW (phone: 332-1233).

Corcoran Gallery of Art Art reproductions. 17th St. and New York Ave. St. NW (phone: 638-3211).

Dumbarton Oaks The private collection of Byzantine and pre-Columbian jewelry is reproduced for sale. 1703 32nd St. NW (phone: 342-3209).

Ford's Theatre The book and gift store here stocks materials pertaining to President Lincoln, his assassination, and the Civil War. 511 10th St. NW (phone: 426-0179).

Friends of the Kennedy Center Jewelry, tote bags, T-shirts, scarves, cards, cookbooks, and more. New Hampshire Ave. and Rock Creek Pkwy. NW (phone: 416-8343).

Hirshhorn Museum Contemporary jewelry and art reproductions. Independence Ave. and Seventh St. SW (phone: 357-1429).

Mt. Vernon Estate Replicas of George Washington memorabilia, books, and prints. George Washington Memorial Pkwy. (phone: 703-780-2000).

National Air and Space Museum NASA flight jackets, US rocket model kits, and freeze-dried astronauts' dinners. Sixth St. and Independence Ave. SW (phone: 357-1387).

National Geographic Society Its shop offers some of the best bargains around in atlases and maps. 17th and M Sts. NW (phone: 857-7588).

National Museum of African Art Arts and crafts, jewelry, books, graphics, posters, and postcards. 950 Independence Ave. SW (phone: 786-2147).

National Museum of American Art Books, prints, postcards, and jewelry. Eighth St. at F and G Sts. NW (phone: 357-1545).

National Museum of American History Everything from a reproduction of the Hope Diamond to First Lady dolls. Constitution Ave. between 12th and 14th Sts. NW (phone: 357-1527).

National Portrait Gallery Busts of past presidents. Eighth St. at F and G Sts. NW (phone: 357-1447).

National Shrine of the Immaculate Conception Religious items. Fourth and Michigan Sts. NE (phone: 526-4433).

National Trust for Historic Preservation Books, scarves, replicas of antique furniture. Decatur House, Lafayette Sq. NW (phone: 842-1856).

Renwick Gallery Pieces by American crafts artists, including ceramics, woodcarvings, clocks, scarves, and quilting. Pennsylvania Ave. at 17th St. NW (phone: 357-1445).

Washington Doll's House and Toy Museum Replicas of dolls and president's games. 5236 44th St. NW (phone: 244-0024).

Washington National Cathedral An extensive gift shop featuring religious items. Massachusetts and Wisconsin Sts. NW (phone: 537-6267).

SPORTS AND FITNESS

BASKETBALL The NBA's *Bullets* hold court from October through April at the *USAir Arena* (1 Harry S. Truman Dr., Landover, Maryland; phone: 301-350-3400). It can be reached via signposted access roads off the Beltway; either take Beltway exit 18 and go east on MD Route 214/Central Avenue for about 100 yards, or take exit 17 and go south about half a mile on MD Route 202. Tickets can be ordered by calling NBA-DUNK.

BICYCLING Rent from *Metropolis Bike & Scooter* (709 Eighth St. SE; phone: 543-8900); *Big Wheel Bikes* (1034 33rd St. NW, Georgetown; phone: 337-0254); or *Thompson's Boat Center* (Virginia Ave. at Rock Creek Pkwy. NW; phone: 333-4861). The latter also has mountain bikes, beach bikes, and tandems available. See *Bicycling* in DIVERSIONS for details on several of the best places to ride.

FITNESS CENTER Most major hotels have health and fitness centers (see *Checking In*).

FOOTBALL The NFL *Redskins* play at *Robert F. Kennedy Stadium* (E. Capitol and 22nd Sts. SE; phone: 547-9077) from September through December. Tickets are hard to come by during the season; it's much easier to get into pre-season games, held in late July and August. Try *TicketMaster* (phone: 432-7328) or the stadium box office.

GOLF The most convenient public golf courses in the city are at *East Potomac Park* (phone: 554-7660) and *Rock Creek Park* (phone: 882-7332). For the best courses nearby, see *Good Golf Outside the City* in DIVERSIONS.

HOCKEY The *Capitals,* Washington's pro hockey team, play at the *USAir Arena* (see *Basketball*) from October to April. Tickets are available at *TicketCenter* outlets or by calling the arena.

JOGGING Join plenty of others in making a round trip from the *Lincoln Memorial* to the *Capitol* (4 miles); also run in *Rock Creek Park* and in Georgetown, along the Chesapeake and Ohio Canal.

SKATING From November through March you can ice skate on the rink on the *Mall.* Seventh St. and Constitution Ave. NW (phone: 371-5340).

SWIMMING Year-round facilities are available at the *East Capitol Natatorium* (635 North Carolina Ave. SE; phone: 724-4495). Many of the hotels also have pools (see *Checking In*).

TENNIS There are more than 1,000 courts in the Washington area, most of which are public and many of which have fallen into disrepair. Some of the better courts in the area require a fee, and some insist on reservations. It is best to call in advance to check the regulations. Below, we list some of the better public tennis venues in and around Washington.

CHOICE COURTS

Chinquapin Center This sports complex has four lighted, outdoor tennis courts, operated on a first-come, first-served basis with a log book for times when it gets especially crowded. These are the only public courts in Alexandria that the area's park service recommends. 3210 King St., Alexandria (phone: 703-931-1127).

Hains Point This complex of 24 public tennis courts includes five heated and air conditioned indoor courts. Of the 19 outdoor courts, 10 are clay. Located on Hains Point and reasonably close to *Capitol Hill,* the courts have been known to attract members of Congress and have counted among their players Chief Justice William Rehnquist and former HUD Secretary Jack Kemp. Courts should be reserved at least one week in advance. The fee is steep ($15 to $24 per hour, depending on the day and time). 1090 Ohio Dr. (phone: 554-5962).

Washington Tennis Center This collection of 17 soft-surface and five hard-surface courts is open from April through November. They are perhaps the District's best courts since they are in a particularly lovely area of *Rock Creek Park* north of the *National Zoo.* Reservations are necessary. 16th and Kennedy Sts. NW (phone: 722-5949).

Wheaton Regional Park & Cabin John Park These are the best of the 235 public courts in Montgomery County, Maryland (for information on other courts, call 301-495-2525). Along with a number of outdoor courts in *Wheaton Regional Park* (10 miles from DC at 11715 Orebaugh Rd., Wheaton, MD; phone: 301-649-4049), there are six indoor courts that can be reserved. *Cabin John Park* features six indoor courts. Though these are a little busier, court time is ordinarily available. 7801 Democracy Blvd., Bethesda, MD (phone: 301-365-2440).

THEATER

Washington is America's third city of theater, according to *Variety,* the bible of showbiz. With New York as the undisputed leader of the nation's theater scene and Boston a respectable but distant second, Washington, with its strong cast of over 20 professional stage theaters and a dozen professional dinner and community theaters in the area, is a major cultural force. Clearly, as its presidential namesake intended, it was the behemoth *Kennedy Center* that created the beginning of a theatrical renaissance in this once sleepy town. Today, boasting one of the country's premier stages and one of its finest Shakespearean theater companies, Washington has won a place on the theatrical map of America. For half-price, same-day performance tickets try *Ticketplace (Lisner Auditorium,* 21st and H Sts. NW; phone: TICKETS). If all else fails, a hotel concierge might have some pull. The following is a list of Washington's most outstanding stages.

CENTER STAGE

Arena Stage One of the oldest and most consistently admired American theater companies and the first outside New York to receive a Tony for theatrical excellence, the *Arena Stage* is noted for developing American drama and for introducing foreign (particularly Eastern European) plays to the US. The theater's three stages seat 827, 514, and 180; the last is used for small musical revues and experimental works. Sixth St. and Maine Ave. SW (phone: 554-9066; 488-3300, box office; 484-0247, TTY number for hearing-impaired patrons).

Ford's Theatre The infamous theater in which Lincoln was shot has been faithfully restored to the way it looked that fateful April night in 1865. The flag-draped presidential box remains empty, a memorial to the slain president. The performances hosted by the theater these days are professional productions of contemporary plays and musicals. After Lincoln's assassination the theater was closed for 100 years out of respect. Its basement houses a select collection of Lincoln memorabilia (see *Special Places*). 511 10th St. NW (phone: 347-4833).

Kennedy Center Now a DC cultural landmark, the *Kennedy Center for the Performing Arts* attracts world-renowned dance, theater, and musical companies to its five theaters and concert halls. Among the performances staged here over the years have been *The Phantom of the Opera,* a revival of *Bye Bye Birdie, Grand Hotel, Tru, Buddy: The Buddy Holly Story, The Will Rogers Follies,* the latest of August Wilson's plays, and the like. This massive classical building also is a tourist attraction in its own right. Before attending a performance, come early to walk through the red-carpeted *Grand Foyer;* lit by 18 chandeliers, it's a prime pre- and post-performance schmoozing area for VIPs and politicos. Currently in an open-ended run at the center's *Theater Lab Cabaret* is the hit play *Shear Madness,* a participatory thriller in which the audience is invited to guess whodunit. Original productions and Broadway-bound shows also are presented in the *Eisenhower Theater,* a comfortable and intimate house paneled with East Indian laurel. Also on the premises are the *Concert Hall, Opera House, Terrace Theater,* and *American Film Institute Theater* (phone: 785-4600). An oft-overlooked feature of the *Kennedy Center* is the rooftop terrace, which offers a spectacular panorama of the Potomac and of Washington. Check with specific theaters for events, showtimes, and ticket prices. Guided tours are given daily from 10 AM to 1 PM. One block south of the intersection of New Hampshire and Virginia Aves. NW (phone: 467-4600; 800-444-1324 for all theaters; or write to the *Kennedy Center,* Washington, DC 20566). *Metro: Foggy Bottom.*

National Theatre Established in 1835, this is Washington's oldest operating community theater. It has provided entertainment for every American president since Eisenhower (who was not known for being a culture vulture). The theater, which now hosts performances of pre- and post-Broadway shows, is managed by the *Shubert Organization.* Visitors should be forewarned that this is the stomping grounds of a legendary phantom—the ghost of an actor named John McCollough is said to roam the theater. McCollough, as the story goes, was killed in a fight with another actor, who then stuffed McCollough's body between the theater's old and new foundation walls—an area now known as the "cemetery." The ghost of the actor is said to have been spotted a number of times—it disappears when addressed. Several years ago, electricians found part of a musket, which is believed to have been the murder weapon. Life (or death?) is still more compelling than art. 1321 Pennsylvania Ave. NW (phone: 628-6161; 800-233-3123, *Telecharge*). *Metro: Metro Center* (13th St. exit).

Shakespeare Theater Washington's popular Shakespearean productions are held at this sleek theater, with a seating capacity of 449. Though Shakespearean works dominate the repertoire, the company is also known for its thoughtful productions of other classics, plus the occasional new play. 450 Seventh St. NW (phone: 547-3230; 393-2700, box office). *Metro: National Archives/Navy Memorial.* Note: In the summer (usually August), the troupe performs a free outdoor play at the *Carter Barron Amphitheater,* in *Rock Creek Park* near Kennedy Street NW; call the above number for information.

Washington also has what one theater critic calls the "off-off *Kennedy Center* movement"—a network of small avant-garde houses on or near the stretch of 14th Street NW above Thomas Circle: *Studio Theater* (1333 P St. NW; phone: 332-3300); *Woolly Mammoth Theater Company* (1401 Church St. NW; phone: 393-3939); and *Source Theater* (1835 14th St. NW; phone: 462-1073). During the summer the *Olney Theater* (2001 Rte. 108, Olney, Maryland; phone: 301-924-3400), about a half-hour drive from the District, offers summer stock with well-known casts. In winter, the *Barns at Wolf Trap,* a 350-seat theater at *Wolf Trap Farm Park for the Performing Arts* (1624 Trap Rd., off Rte. 7 near Vienna, Virginia; phone: 703-938-2404), holds performances indoors. To get there, take the *Dulles Airport* toll road Rte. 267, or the *Metro* to West Falls Church, Virginia, where there's a connecting shuttle bus. For a unique dinner-theater experience, see *Mystery on the Menu.* Held only on Saturday evenings, it's a participatory play that takes the form of a Georgetown wedding reception for a senator and his bride. During the reception, a murder occurs and all the audience members/"guests" get a chance to solve the crime. A three-course meal with a glass of champagne is included in the ticket price. Locations vary and reservations are necessary; call for details (phone: 333-6875).

MUSIC

The *National Symphony Orchestra* performs at the *Kennedy Center Concert Hall* (phone: 467-4600) from September through June; in June the concert hall also hosts a *Mostly Mozart Festival.* In addition, concerts are presented at the city's *former* premier venue, *Constitution Hall* (18th and C Sts. NW; phone: 638-2661), which is renowned for its acoustics. The *Washington Opera* (phone: 416-7800) presents seven operas a year, between November and March, at the *Kennedy Center Opera House.* The *Juilliard String Quartet* and other notable ensembles usually perform chamber music concerts on Stradivarius instruments in the *Library of Congress's Coolidge Auditorium* Thursday and Friday evenings in the spring and fall. However, at press time concerts were temporarily being held at the *National Academy of Sciences* (2100 C St. NW), while the *Coolidge* undergoes renovations, scheduled for completion later this year; for tickets, call 707-5502. During the summer, *Wolf Trap Farm Park for the Performing Arts* near Vienna, Virginia (see *Theater,* above), presents musicals, ballet, pop concerts, and symphonic music in a lovely outdoor setting—bring a picnic basket. A shuttle bus runs to the park from downtown (phone: 703-255-1868). There are often free concerts by the service bands on the plaza at the West Front of the *Capitol* or in front of the *Jefferson Memorial.* Consult newspapers for where and when. *Army and Navy Band* concerts are presented at different locations in the winter (phone: 696-3643). The *British Embassy Players* delight audiences with old-fashioned music hall performances; the *British Embassy Rotunda* (3100 Massachusetts Ave. NW) is magically transformed into a cabaret, with some embassy staff and other area Britons providing the entertainment. There are four productions beginning in the fall and ending with three *Music Hall* weekends in June. Tickets are limited and must be reserved well in advance (phone: 703-271-0172).

NIGHTCLUBS AND NIGHTLIFE

For some, Washington is an early-to-bed town, but there's plenty of pub crawling, jazz, bluegrass, soul, rock, and folk music going on after dark—you just have to know where to look for it. Best bets are Georgetown, Adams Morgan, Dupont Circle, and the *Capitol Hill* areas. For up-to-the-minute listings of DC's ever-shifting club scene, consult the weekly *City Paper* (see *Local Coverage*). Some sure favorites: *Blues Alley* (1073 Wisconsin Ave. NW; phone: 337-4141), for mainstream jazz and Dixieland; *Tortilla Coast* (201 Massachusetts Ave. NE; phone: 546-6768), decorated with hot tropical murals and featuring killer margaritas; the *Dubliner Restaurant and Pub* (520 N. Capitol St. NW; phone: 737-3773), the place to hear old Irish and Celtic tunes and jigs; *Market Inn* (200 E St. SW; phone: 554-2100), a popular steak and seafood house near *Capitol Hill* where live jazz is featured nightly; and *Cities* (2424 18th St. NW; phone: 328-7194), a watering hole–cum-restaurant-cum-nightclub in what once was a three-story auto dealership. *Cities,* which changes its city theme every six months, is located in the heart of Washington's newest nightlife scene—Adams Morgan, a funky mélange of bars, dance clubs, ethnic restaurants, and shops radiating from the intersection of Columbia Road and 18th Street NW. In recent years Adams Morgan has come to rival Georgetown as "the" place to see and be seen after dark in the capital.

On Saturday nights, the *Bayou* in Georgetown (3135 K St. NW; phone: 783-7212) presents *Clintoons,* a production of *Gross National Product,* a satirical and sometimes ridiculous political revue targeting Washington politicians in the spotlight. Reservations are necessary. Political satirist Mark Russell also performs occasionally in local nightspots (check local newspapers for details). Watch local listings, too, for performances by the *Capitol Steps,* a satirical singing group. The *Comedy Café* (1520 K St. NW; phone: 638-5653) features nationally known comedians in an informal, downtown club. The dining room staff at Georgetown's *La Niçoise* (1721 Wisconsin Ave. NW; phone: 965-9300) not only serves French fare while on roller skates, but the talented crew also presents an amusing after-dinner cabaret. *Déjà Vu* (2119 M St. NW; phone: 452-1966) is a lively dance club with music from the 1960s to today. *West End Café* at the *One Washington Circle* hotel (One Washington Circle; phone: 293-5390) is a popular piano bar where classical and jazz music are featured. Two ever-popular chains have Washington branches: the rock 'n' roll–centered *Hard Rock Café* (999 E St. NW; phone: 737-7625), and the movie world's *Planet Hollywood* (11th St. and Pennsylvania Ave. NW; phone: 783-7827), both brasserie-style bar restaurants.

BAR NONE

Because Washingtonians are serious about their sports teams, especially the *Redskins,* sports bars are scattered around the area and are prime spots for game nights (if you don't have seats at *RFK Stadium*). Try *Champions* (1206 Wisconsin Ave. NW; phone: 965-4005), a Georgetown favorite; *Bottom Line* (1716 I St. NW; phone: 298-8488), a rugby bar popular with local players and their cheering squads; *Poor Robert's* (3419 Connecticut Ave. NW; phone: 363-1839), which offers satellite TV for special sporting events; and *Joe Theismann's* (1800 Diagonal Rd., Alexandria, Virginia; phone: 703-739-0777), a sports bar owned by the former, fabulous *Redskins* quarterback.

The capital is also a major saloon town, and some of the best stomping grounds are on the "Hill." *Bullfeathers* (410 First St. SE; phone: 543-5005), where the Congressional crowd hangs out, has a bar that's always hopping. The *Hawk 'n' Dove* (329 Pennsylvania Ave. SE; phone: 543-3300), a dark, rustic bar, is perfect for after work (or after play), and crowded with both Capitol Hillers and law students. *Clyde's* in Georgetown (3236 M St., NW; phone: 333-9180) is your typical wood and brass fern bar, with cozy pub decor, and *Hamburger Hamlet,* also in Georgetown (3125 M St. NW; phone: 965-6970), offers a casual, warm atmosphere, great summer drinks, and crayons for drawing on the paper tablecloths.

Best in Town

CHECKING IN

Washington enjoys a wealth of good-quality hotel establishments because of a building boom in the late 1980s. Still, accommodations at the best stopping places can dwindle fast, so reservations should be made in advance. Visitors in town for only a few days should stay downtown to make the best use of their limited time; weekends offer the best package deals. Inexpensive taxis, the *Metro* system, and buses facilitate getting around without private cars, which can be difficult and expensive to park (although some hotels offer reasonable valet parking). If you're traveling by car, it may make more sense to stay at one of the major motel chains located at the principal entry points to the district—Silver Spring and Bethesda in Maryland, and Arlington, Rosslyn, and Alexandria in Virginia. Expect to pay $175 or more (sometimes much more) per night for a double room at a hotel described as expensive, $100 to $175 at a place in the moderate category, and $70 to $100 at a hotel listed as inexpensive. For information about bed and breakfast accommodations, contact *The Bed and Breakfast League/Sweet Dreams & Toast* (PO Box 9490, Washington, DC 20016; phone: 363-7767). *Washington, DC, Accommodations* (phone: 800-554-2220) provides assistance with hotel reservations at no charge. *Capitol Reservations* (phone: 800-847-4832) offers a free reservation service and discount rates at Washington area hotels.

Most of Washington's major hotels have complete facilities for the business traveler. Those hotels listed below as having "business services" usually offer such conveniences as meeting rooms, photocopiers, computers, translation services, and express checkout, among others. Call the hotel for additional information. Unless otherwise noted, hotel rooms have air conditioning, private baths, TV sets, and telephones. All telephone numbers are in the 202 area code unless otherwise indicated.

For an unforgettable experience in DC, we begin with our favorites, followed by our cost and quality choices of hotels, listed by price category.

GRAND HOTELS

Four Seasons If the difference between a good and a great hotel is in the details, this is one of the capital city's very best. The full spectrum of guest needs is given personalized attention. Each room is furnished with an ample number of chairs, a desk large enough to scatter papers over, juices, spirits, and chocolates in the armoire, plus a thick terry cloth robe behind the bathroom door. The hotel is flanked by the Chesapeake & Ohio Canal (a run along the canal is a Washington ritual) and by *Rock Creek Park,* Washington's premier parkland; in fact, most of the 197 rooms overlook the tranquil green space. The property is regal yet relaxed, attracting many entertainers and Hollywood types. Body-conscious guests can use the fitness club, with a skylit lap pool, a whirlpool bath, a sauna, and a steamroom. The *Garden Terrace* serves afternoon tea, replete with scones, double Devonshire cream, and homemade preserves. The terrace affords a view of the verdant park and canal area, and the hotel bar is a popular after-work cocktail spot. The main restaurant, *Seasons* (formerly *Aux Beaux Champs*), serves nouvelle and classic French cuisine; its champagne breakfast and excellent wine list also have quite a following (see *Eating Out*). *Le Petit Champs* is a private dining enclave with its own waiters and dinner "captains"; there's seating for up to 14 for lunch, dinner parties, or breakfast meetings. Business services and 24-hour room service are available. 2800 Pennsylvania Ave. NW (phone: 342-0444; 800-332-3442; fax: 342-1673).

Hay-Adams This architecturally stunning hostelry sits on some of DC's most prized real estate: Many of its 143 Edwardian- and Georgian-style rooms overlook *Lafayette Square* and the *White House;* others afford a point-blank view of *St. John's Church,* "the Church of the Presidents." Rooms are decorated with 18th-century period furniture and antiques. Designed in the Italian Renaissance style by a former palace architect of a Turkish sultan, the structure is built of white Indiana limestone, with a paneled lobby, Tudor dining rooms, and obsequious doormen dressed like Prussian generals. Charles Lindbergh, Amelia Earhart, Sinclair Lewis, prominent heads of state, and foreign dignitaries have stayed here. The *John Hay Room* offers classic French fare and an elegant afternoon tea with all the tasty trappings of this ancient British custom (from 3 to 5 PM daily). The subterranean *Eagle Bar and Grill* is an informal spot; the *Adams Room* is a pleasant place to mull over breakfast and the *Washington Post;* it also offers an excellent lunch and weekend brunch. Room service is available 24 hours a day, and there is a concierge desk and business services. 800 16th St. NW (phone: 638-6600; 800-424-5054; fax: 638-2716).

Jefferson Federal-style understatement is the hallmark of this downtown establishment within walking distance of the *White House.* Relatively intimate, with 69 rooms and 35 suites, its room service never dozes, nor does it refuse even the most extravagant requests—even during the wee hours. The multilingual concierge service is ideal for arranging dinner reservations or theater tickets; business services also are available. One of the hotel's real gems is the *Hunt Club,* a restaurant and bar on the ground floor; the kitchen features American and French food, including such dishes as Jefferson macaroni (named after our third president, who, according to the hotel, introduced pasta to the US after his travels through Europe) and vegetable strudel. There is also a display of 18th-century historical prints and portraits (many of the originals hang in the *White House*). For those with an expensive thirst, an $800 bottle of Louis XIV brandy is locked in a glass case to the right of the bar. You can order a single snifter for only $75! A cigar box containing fine complimentary smokes sits on a cherrywood table near the exit. 1200 16th St. NW (phone: 347-2200; 800-368-5966; fax: 331-7982).

Ritz-Carlton From the hand-carved mahogany headboards and embroidered English bedspreads to the quaint afternoon tea and the extra-dry martinis served amid the intimate alcoves of the *Fairfax Bar,* this property is everything one would expect from the Ritz name. In the middle of tree-lined *Embassy Row,* the Georgian-style red brick building has the feel of an elegant—yet "understated" (as the staff is quick to add)—European home; Federal-style antiques complement the colonial decor in the 230 rooms. The hotel maintains a data base of customer profiles so that if a guest returns, the staff knows his or her preference for soft or firm pillows, chocolates, reading material, and other personal items to make the traveler feel at home; business services, a concierge, and 24-hour room service also are available. The *Jockey Club* restaurant is steeped in clubby congeniality, the food French-influenced (see *Eating Out*). 2100 Massachusetts Ave. NW (phone: 293-2100; 800-241-3333; fax: 466-9867).

Stouffer Mayflower This historic property, one of the capital's treasures, has earned laurels over the years for catering to the world's movers and shakers with elegance and style. The yellow brick-and-limestone Beaux Arts building boasts a block-long lobby adorned with Italian marble, glittering chandeliers, and intricately carved, 23-karat gold-leaf ceilings. Its location in the heart of downtown (not far from the *White House* and the *Mall*) is ideal for sightseers, and its nearly 700 rooms can accommodate legions of them. The *Grand Ballroom* recalls the splendor of a bygone era, and the *Nicholas* restaurant is a fitting place to feast on mid-Atlantic American fare (a jacket and tie are required for men). Guests also can enjoy a health center, round-the-clock room service, valet parking, and full concierge service. Business services are available. 1127 Connecticut Ave. NW (phone: 347-3000; 800-HOTELS-1; fax: 466-9082).

Willard Inter-Continental A temporary home for no fewer than 10 American presidents-elect, including Lincoln and Harding, this sprawling, imposing Beaux Arts building looks much as it did in the days when it was known as the "Residence of the Presidents." This is also where Julia Ward Howe—after meeting with a haggard and war-weary President Lincoln—wrote the "Battle Hymn of the Republic," and where Dr. Martin Luther King Jr. wrote his "I Have a Dream" speech. The carpeting, columns, and much of the furniture are reproductions based on photographs of the original decor; the 365 rooms are decorated in turn-of-the-century style. *Peacock Alley,* the opulent, block-long hall with marble columns that connects the hotel's two entrances, was, according to legend, the very spot in which the term "lobbyist" was coined. As the story goes, Ulysses Grant would, on occasion, escape the rigors of the *White House* and head for the *Willard.* A legion of influence peddlers would follow him there and linger about as he enjoyed his brandy in *Peacock Alley.* And if the hotel's distinctive architecture and impressive history are not enough, the service is nothing less than superb. A special staff assists guests with plane reservations, theater tickets, and transportation, and business services are available. In addition, there's an exercise room, a café, two lounges, and the *Willard Room,* which serves contemporary American fare and regional favorites amid Edwardian decor (see *Eating Out*). A special treat is afternoon tea served in the *Nest* lounge. The *Occidental Grill,* one of the city's finest dining spots and a popular meeting place for primary powers, is adjacent to the hotel but not under the same ownership (see *Eating Out*). Round-the-clock room service, a concierge, and business services complete the list of amenities. 1401 Pennsylvania Ave. NW (phone: 628-9100; 800-327-0200; fax: 637-7326).

EXPENSIVE

ANA This outstanding link in the Westin chain is as elegant inside as it is outside. There is a lovely interior garden, and 415 luxuriously appointed rooms, including 36 Executive Club rooms and 26 suites; three Executive Premier King suites have cable TV, three phones, voice mail, and terry cloth robes. The *Colonnade* is a fine restaurant for formal dining, and there's a more casual brasserie and a lobby lounge in a glass loggia just off the garden. A professionally staffed fitness center, complete with a pool, a Jacuzzi, saunas, squash courts, an aerobics room, weights, and state-of-the-art exercise equipment, plus a beauty salon and juice bar, is on the premises. Business services are available. Children under 18 stay free in their parents' rooms. 24th and M Sts. NW (phone: 429-2400; 800-228-3000; fax: 457-5010).

Canterbury Near the downtown business district and not far from the *White House,* this small place has 99 suites with a stocked bar in each, a restaurant, and a bar. Pluses include a complimentary continental breakfast, underground parking, nightly turn-down service, and a complimentary cocktail each evening in the *Union Jack Pub.* Business services are available. Inquire about weekend package rates. 1733 N St. NW (phone: 393-3000; 800-424-2950; fax: 785-9581).

Capital Hilton One of Washington's most luxurious hostelries is also one of the most conveniently located, just a few minutes from the *White House.* It has 549 expansive rooms, each with a marble foyer, two telephones, a fully stocked mini-bar, and terry cloth robes. The Deluxe Towers' rooms on the top four floors also have VCRs and a separate concierge and check-in area. Restaurants include *Trader Vic's,* which serves Chinese and Polynesian fare, the sophisticated *Twigs Grill,* and the lobby bar. There's also a state-of-the-art fitness center. Business services and 24-hour room service are available. 1001 16th at K St. NW (phone: 393-1000; 800-445-8667; fax: 639-5784).

Carlton Host to many presidents and dignitaries, this hotel has an elegant Italian Renaissance lobby, 197 comfortable rooms, and a bar that's good enough to win approval from feisty New York *Newsday* columnist Jimmy Breslin. The *Allegro* dining room is excellent and has a terrific Sunday brunch (see *Eating Out*); there's also a cocktail lounge. Business services are available. 923 16th St. NW (phone: 638-2626; 800-325-3535; fax: 638-4231).

Grand A distinctive copper dome wedged between walls of brick and granite marks this West End hostelry. In architecture and ambience, it is reminiscent of a small European hotel: A white marble staircase cascades through the lobby, the inner courtyard is meticulously landscaped, and all 263 rooms feature Italian marble baths and three phones; there are working fireplaces in some suites. The elegant *Mayfair* serves *cuisine courante,* a step beyond nouvelle, with a menu that changes daily; the *Promenade Lounge* features breakfast, lunch, dinner, and afternoon tea in a more informal atmosphere. Besides a multilingual concierge and currency conversion service, there is 24-hour room service, valet and dry cleaning, and valet parking. Business services are available. 2350 M St. NW (phone: 429-0100; 800-848-0016; fax: 429-9759).

Grand Hyatt Washington Located in the heart of downtown DC, across from the *Washington Convention Center,* this property has 907 rooms, including 60 suites, and a Regency Club floor with a private lounge and concierge service. The suites, all with living areas, wet bars, and lots of greenery, also feature saunas and marble baths. All rooms have turn-down service, free cable television with HBO and ESPN, and full-service honor bars. Dining facilities include the New York–style *Zephyr Deli;* the *Grande Café,* an informal eatery for breakfast, lunch, and dinner; the more formal *Hamilton's; Palladio's,* a three-level lobby bar; and *Grand Slam,* a sports bar with two large-screen TV sets. Business services are available. There's also a health club with an exercise room, a sauna, a Jacuzzi, a lap pool, and aerobics classes. 1000 H St. NW (phone: 582-1234; fax: 637-4781).

J. W. Marriott A significant step above other members of the Marriott chain, this property is connected to a mall complex of 160 stores and the *National Theatre.* There are 772 rooms, an indoor pool, and a health spa; the Marquis floors (14 and 15) are especially nice. Concierge Level (14th floor only) extras include breakfast, complimentary hors d'oeuvres, and a private lounge. There also is a *Grand Ballroom* for up to 2,000 people, and the *Capital Ballroom,* which can accommodate up to 800. Room service is available around the clock, and business services are available. 1331 Pennsylvania Ave. NW (phone: 393-2000; 800-228-9290; fax: 626-6991).

Madison With 374 luxurious rooms, this property features gracious Federal decor and excellent service by a well-trained staff. Extras include interpreters, refrigerators, and bathroom phones; there is also a health club. The *Montpelier Room* is quite a good restaurant; it serves a buffet on weekdays and brunch on Sundays. The *Retreat* restaurant is open for afternoon tea on weekdays and for dinner daily; the lobby bar has nightly entertainment. Business services are available. 15th and M Sts. NW (phone: 862-1600; 800-424-8577; fax: 785-1255).

Sofitel Washington Formerly the *Pullman Highland,* this link in the French hotel chain boasts 145 spacious, elegantly decorated rooms with such extras as fax and computer hookups, mini-bars, safes, and coffee makers. There is a restaurant, and business services are available. There's also a multilingual concierge, access to a health club, tennis, and golf, and 24-hour room service. Located in the heart of the embassy district. 1914 Connecticut Ave. NW (phone: 797-2000; 800-424-2464; fax: 462-0944).

Vista Washington François Mitterrand and Elizabeth Taylor are among those who have stayed at this 399-room hostelry, only six blocks from the *White House*. Its six very expensive one-bedroom suites, designed by Givenchy, feature full-length mirrors, large private balconies, and bathrooms with Jacuzzis; they are completely separate from the rest of the hotel, sharing no walls with any other rooms. Favorite recipes of past presidents are on the menu at the *American Harvest* restaurant; cardiovascular fitness gear is available at the health club along with treadmills and a sauna. Business services are available, as is 24-hour room service. 1400 M St. NW (phone: 429-1700; 800-847-8232; fax: 785-0786).

Watergate Though this modern hotel-apartment-office complex doesn't look too historic, appearances can be deceiving (as can small pieces of tape). This property boasts 235 large contemporarily furnished rooms, an indoor swimming pool and health club, the excellent nouvelle French *Jeun-Louis* restaurant (see *Eating Out*), and the less pricey, bistro-like *Palladin* (both dining spots are named after chef Jean-Louis Palladin). There is also a cocktail lounge, and *The Watergate Shopping Mall* (with even more dining possibilities), all at a location adjacent to the *Kennedy Center*. There's a concierge desk and 24-hour room service, and business services are available. 2650 Virginia Ave. NW (phone: 965-2300; 800-424-2736; fax: 337-7915).

Wyndham Bristol There are 239 rooms (37 of which are suites) in this English-style hostelry; guests also have access to a health club for a small fee. The *Bristol Grill* offers fine food. Business services and 24-hour room service are available. 2430 Pennsylvania Ave. NW (phone: 955-6400; 800-822-4200; fax: 955-5765).

MODERATE

Morrison-Clark Inn This popular bed and breakfast–style inn served as the hostel for the *Soldiers, Sailors, Marines, and Airmen Club* from 1923 to 1984. A 1988 addition to the two historic buildings comprises 41 of the 54 tastefully decorated rooms, some furnished with Victorian antiques. The hotel has an excellent restaurant; breakfast is included in the rate. There's also a concierge desk, and business services are available. Located one block from the *Convention Center* and four blocks from *Metro Center* (*Metrorail* stop) at Massachusetts Ave. and 11th St. NW (phone: 898-1200; 800-332-7898; fax: 289-8576).

Tabard Inn On a charming semi-residential street near the heart of the business district, this establishment offers guests an ambience rare in an American city. The 40 rooms are furnished with antiques and some of them share baths (23 have private baths); there are no in-room TV sets. A restaurant serves breakfast, lunch, and dinner, and brunch on weekends (see *Eating Out*); there's also a library. Business and concierge services are available. 1739 N St. NW (phone: 785-1277; fax: 785-6173).

Washington One of the city's older properties, this comfortable hotel offers an incomparable view from its rooftop restaurant (which makes it a particularly good place to be during an inaugural parade). The 370 rooms feature such luxury amenities as telephones in the bathrooms; downtown shopping is nearby. Room service is available until 11 PM. 15th St. and Pennsylvania Ave. NW (phone: 638-5900; fax: 638-4275).

INEXPENSIVE

Harrington A 310-room, older establishment in the center of Washington's commercial area, it has seen better days but provides clean accommodations and is within walking distance of the Mall. Popular with high school and family groups. 11th and E Sts. NW (phone: 628-8140).

Windsor Inn Small and unpretentious, near the trendy Adams Morgan district. A magnet for relocating embassy employees as well as government workers who prefer a modest, homey atmosphere. There are 46 rooms; the staff is personable and attentive. Continental breakfast comes with a newspaper; and for a European touch, afternoon sherry is served. 1842 16th St. NW (phone: 667-0300 or 800-423-9111).

Windsor Park It's modest, but this 40-room property is within walking distance of the *Woodley Park/Zoo Metro* station and near the French diplomats' residence and the *Chinese Embassy*. Continental breakfast is included in the rate. 2116 Kalorama Rd. NW (phone: 483-7700; 800-247-3064; fax: 332-4547).

EATING OUT

Considering the international aspects of Washington—2,000 diplomats and a large number of residents who have lived abroad and brought back a taste for foreign fare—it's not too surprising that the District can provide an international gastronomic tour de force. But though it's always helpful to have an ermine-lined wallet or, better yet, a generous expense account, those who have only a yen for good food needn't go hungry. Expect to pay $100 or more for a dinner for two at places described as very expensive; between $75 and $100 at places listed as expensive; $40 to $75 at restaurants in the moderate category; and less than $40 at dining spots described as inexpensive. Prices do not include drinks, wine, or tips. Reservations are a must at the top-flight restaurants. Unless otherwise noted, restaurants are open for lunch and dinner, and telephone numbers are in the 202 area code.

For an unforgettable dining experience, we begin with our culinary favorites, followed by our cost and quality choices, listed by price category.

CAPITAL DINING

L'Auberge Chez François This Alsatian country inn, 30 minutes west of the District in northern Virginia's hunt country, is a perennial favorite. Everything from the attentive service to the cozy yet refined setting of a country house and the sublime preparation of the Alsatian specialties makes dinner here an enchanting experience. There are several working fireplaces, antique grandfather clocks, a mounted elk's head, lots of other knickknacks from the Alsace region in France, and a staff dressed in Alsatian garb. The fare blends the hearty proportions of Germanic cooking with such French touches as superb sauces, fine cheeses, and artistic presentation. The reasonably priced menu includes a number of Alsatian specialties, among them the famed *choucroute garnie,* a collection of sausages and duck served atop heavily seasoned sauerkraut; an Alsatian version of cassoulet with sausages and lentils; stuffed rabbit; and chicken stewed in Alsatian Riesling. The assortment of pâtés is renowned, and for dessert, we recommend the lime tart. The prices listed for the main course include a selection from the list of first courses, a house salad, a family-style serving of vegetables, and a dessert. Open daily for dinner only. The reservation book is always filled, so plan far in advance (a well-kept secret among the regulars is that no reservations are necessary for dining in the garden during the warm months). Major credit cards accepted. 332 Springvale Rd., Great Falls, VA (phone: 703-759-3800).

Galileo *Washingtonian* magazine ranked this as not only the capital's best Italian dining spot, but possibly the best restaurant in town. (It is one of only two restaurants to which the food scribes at the *Washingtonian* are willing to affix their coveted four stars.) And no wonder. Chef Roberto Donna uses his northern Italian ingenuity in creating poultry, meat, and game dishes—along with the city's finest breads, which accompany each meal. Try the risotto or the homemade *agnolotti,* a pasta filled with spinach and ricotta. The rack of veal with mushroom and rosemary sauce is also popular. Preferred seating is in the *Wine Room,* a cozy alcove where the impressive selection of wine is stored. (In fact, the wine list has earned a coveted Award of Excellence from *The Wine Spectator.*) Portraits and reproductions of the writings of the Italian astronomer for whom the restaurant is named adorn the walls. Unfortunately, reaching the heights of popularity results in extremely steep prices. Closed for lunch on weekends. Reservations advised. Major credit cards accepted. 1110 21st St. NW (phone: 293-7191).

Maison Blanche This elegant French dining room is so close to the *White House* that even a snail could crawl over on its lunch hour. The only place you'll find a snail here, however, is on a plate: Chef Christian Gautrois is well known for his exquisite escargots (as well as other French classics such as bouillabaisse). Other favorites are his nouvelle version of Norwegian salmon in a vegetable sauce and shrimp with angel hair pasta. The wine list boasts over 350 labels. Elegant decor—walnut, brown-velvet armchairs, a crystal chandelier from Belgium, and a remarkable carpet sporting a bouquet of 36 colors—and excellent cuisine make this a favorite among lobbyists and *White House* staffers. It's also a haunt of newsfolk, including columnist Art Buchwald, who dines here regularly. The prix fixe menu (available nightly from 6 to 9:30 PM) is a bargain. The *Kennedy Center* is a short drive or an eight-block walk away. Closed Sundays. Reservations advised. Major credit cards accepted. 1725 F St. NW (phone: 842-0070).

Mr. K's The strength of this bustling "Restaurant Ridge" (K Street) establishment lies in the hushed competence of its staff—who arrive at tableside in threes—and the excellent food that hails from four areas of China (northern food from Peking, spicy Hunan and Szechuan dishes from central China, the milder Shanghai fare from eastern China, and the classic Cantonese dishes from the country's south). Favorites include beef mimosa, Peking duck, and any one of several lobster dishes. There are four private dining rooms with impressive jade statues of dragons and a phoenix. The tables in the spacious main dining room are arranged with privacy in mind—a nod to the high-powered lawyers and lobbyists who frequent here. Surprisingly for a Chinese restaurant, a real treat awaits coffee aficionados at the end of the meal: A high-tech coffee urn is wheeled out, a burner lit underneath, and after the water in the pipes boils, causing quaking, burbling, and gurgling, a delicious brew issues forth (they serve tea, too). Open daily. Reservations advised. Major credit cards accepted. 2121 K St. NW (phone: 331-8868).

Occidental Grill Though this historic Washington eatery has shed its stuffy, formal atmosphere, fortunately, its first-rate fare hasn't changed. Longtime chef Jeff Buben's specialties include a super swordfish sandwich, escalope of salmon *au poivre* with black bean purée, crab cakes, and a selection of grilled meat, fish, and sausage. The wine list is impressive and the dessert list comprehensive.

Given its proximity to the houses of American government, don't be surprised if you wind up rubbing elbows with a member of Congress, a *White House* aide, or a Supreme Court Justice or two. The walls of this clubby brass and leather dining room are covered with more than 3,000 signed photographs of statesmen dating back to the early 1900s. The mahogany bar on the lower level is a wonderful venue for a cocktail; always dense with legislators, it's popular among lobbyists, too. Open daily. Reservations advised. Major credit cards accepted. 1475 Pennsylvania Ave. NW (phone: 783-1475).

Prime Rib Arguably Washington's premier steakhouse; anybody who can't stare down a two-inch-thick cut of the signature entrée shouldn't be here. Nevertheless, the menu does offer, in addition to prime ribs, an impressive rack of lamb, crab Imperial, and some fish specialties. The ambience—featuring soothing piano music from a baby grand against a motif of black and white and polished brass—evokes the mood of a 1940s New York supper club, but without the mammoth Manhattan prices. In fact, meals here are remarkably reasonable. Perhaps the city's best lunch value is an on-the-bone cut of prime ribs served with two vegetables (and the aforementioned music) for $13. Dinner is more expensive, but still well priced, considering that you're getting a large portion of some of the finest steak in the area. Closed Saturday lunch and Sundays. Reservations advised. Major credit cards accepted. 2020 K St. NW (phone: 466-8811).

VERY EXPENSIVE

Jean-Louis Named for its chef, this is a small (only 14 tables) and elegant restaurant with gracious service and fine nouvelle cuisine. Jean-Louis Palladin changes his menu frequently to accommodate the seasons and his whims. His presentations are as legendary as his cooking, with meals that often look too beautiful to eat; terrines, truffles, and warm seafood salads are among the highlights. There are also fixed-price dinners available, and the pre-theater seating (5:30 to 6:30 PM) offers tremendous value. Closed Sundays. Reservations necessary. Major credit cards accepted. In the *Watergate Hotel,* 2650 Virginia Ave. NW (phone: 298-4488).

Le Lion d'Or This establishment is reputed to have the finest French food in town, although some say that the service is unpredictable. If you want formal dining, however, this is the restaurant for you; selections from the long and exquisite menu by chef Jean-Pierre Goyenvalle include lobster stew, fillet of lamb, roasted pigeon, and red snapper. Don't leave without tasting one of the spectacular desserts. Closed Saturday lunch and Sundays. Reservations necessary at least two weeks in advance. Major credit cards accepted. 1150 Connecticut Ave. NW, near 18th and M Sts. (phone: 296-7972).

Seasons This handsome dining room in the *Four Seasons* hotel (formerly *Aux Beaux Champs*) is distinguished by stylish service and a highly creative menu that changes daily, specializing in *cuisine courante*—a mixture of French and California food. Specialties include breast of quail stuffed with woodland mushrooms in a zinfandel sauce with wild rice and scallion cake, and stuffed lamb with pistachio crust and risotto fritters in a minted madeira glaze. Open daily. Reservations advised. Major credit cards accepted. 2800 Pennsylvania Ave. NW (phone: 342-0810).

EXPENSIVE

Bice This northern Italian eatery, owned by the proprietors of the New York establishment of the same name, specializes in risotto, fresh pasta, fish dishes, and duck entrées. Only Italian and California wines are served, but the champagne is French. Closed Saturday lunch. Reservations advised. Major credit cards accepted. 601 Pennsylvania Ave. NW, between Sixth and Seventh Sts.; enter on Indiana Ave. (phone: 638-2423).

Jockey Club This *Ritz-Carlton* restaurant is a favorite meeting and eating spot for local movers and shakers. The decor looks like New York's old *"21."* Beyond the soft-shell crabs, the menu is French-influenced; chef Fabrice Canelle was formerly with *Maxim's* in Paris. Open daily. Reservations necessary. Major credit cards accepted. 2100 Massachusetts Ave. NW (phone: 659-8000).

Red Sage This dining spot is accented with hand-blown chandeliers, silver and gold decor, and food that is as exquisite as the surroundings. Chef Mark Miller creates dishes with a Southwestern flavor; among the selections is a stew of lobster, scallops, mussels, and clams. Also try plum *ancho* (glazed quail with jalapeño slaw and spoonbread). Open daily. Reservations necessary. Major credit cards accepted. 605 14th St. NW at F St. (phone: 638-4444).

I Ricchi One of the city's hottest eateries, here chef Francesco Ricchi concocts fabulous Florentine fare such as broad noodles tossed with hare sauce, leg of rabbit with rosemary, and quail stuffed with homemade sausage. This trattoria has a warm homey feeling. Closed Saturday lunch and Sundays. Reservations necessary. Major credit cards accepted. 1220 19th St. NW (phone: 835-0459).

Willard Room Bruno Bonnet, formerly of *Le Lion d'Or,* creates delicious, regional American–style dishes all made from local produce. Try the rack of lamb, Dover sole, or Chesapeake Bay fish. Open for all three meals Mondays through Saturdays, brunch and dinner on Sundays. Reservations advised. Major credit cards accepted. In the *Willard Inter-Continental Hotel,* 1401 Pennsylvania Ave. NW (phone: 637-7440).

Allegro This lovely dining room of the *Carlton* hotel is known for its fabulous business buffet lunch featuring jumbo shrimp, salmon, pâté, and carved roast of the day, and is perfect for those under time constraints. Afternoon tea is accompanied by a harpist and Sunday brunch by a pianist. Breakfast might include assorted breads, healthy options such as Bircher muesli and honey yogurt, and international offerings such as miso soup and grilled salmon à la Japanese. Dinner highlights include saffron ravioli with shiitake-morel sauce and asparagus tips, and curry oyster tempura with sake herb sabayon. Open daily for all three meals. Reservations advised, especially for the business lunch and brunch. Major credit cards accepted. 16th and K Sts. NW (phone: 879-6900).

La Colline Charming and reasonably priced, it serves adventurous French food and daily specials as well as wonderful desserts. Try the bouillabaisse and *choucroute alsacienne* (sauerkraut, sausages, pork). Open daily for all three meals. Reservations advised. Major credit cards accepted. 400 N. Capitol St. NW (phone: 737-0400).

Ernie's Original Crab House Across the Potomac in Alexandria, this is an old favorite of crab lovers. Open daily. Reservations advised on weekends. Major credit cards accepted. Two locations: 1623 Fern St. (phone: 703-836-1623) and 7929 Richmond Hwy. (phone: 703-780-0100).

Germaine's The varied Pan-Asian menu includes Japanese, Korean, Vietnamese, and Indonesian fare. Specialties are pine cone fish, scallop salad, *satay,* and squirrelfish. Closed for lunch on weekends. Reservations advised. Major credit cards accepted. 2400 Wisconsin Ave. NW (phone: 965-1185).

I Matti *Galileo* owner Roberto Donna's popular eatery in the Adams Morgan section of town offers both northern Italian dishes and Italian nouvelle cuisine. Aromatic stews, pizza with a paper-thin crust, and meltingly wonderful ricotta cheesecake are the highlights. Open daily. Reservations necessary. Major credit cards accepted. 2436 18th St. NW (phone: 462-8844).

Au Pied de Cochon An informal place for a good meal at a decent price 24 hours a day. If *pieds de cochon* (pigs' feet) aren't your style, try asparagus vinaigrette, coq au vin, and other bistro specialties. Open daily. No reservations. Major credit cards accepted. 1335 Wisconsin Ave. NW (phone: 333-5440).

Sfuzzi Washington Northern Italian food with an American touch is served in this *Union Station* dining establishment, founded by the owners of New York City's *Sfuzzi* restaurant. The grilled salmon is recommended, as are the pizza and pasta. Try the chicken *romano tagliatelle* (grilled chicken with gorgonzola cheese and noodles). There's an outdoor café in the summer and a happy hour on weekdays. Open daily. Reservations advised. Major credit cards accepted. 50 Massachusetts Ave. NE (phone: 842-4141).

Tabard Inn The nouvelle-influenced menu at this charmingly quirky inn is strong on fresh seafood such as grilled tuna and swordfish. The vegetables are shipped fresh daily from a nearby farm in Virginia. Sunday brunch is a popular affair, and there's a fire in the hearth in winter. Open daily. Reservations advised. MasterCard and Visa accepted. 1739 N St. NW (phone: 833-2668).

INEXPENSIVE

America The menu at this eatery (whose sister restaurant is in New York City) offers choices from all regions of the United States, from grits to Cajun shrimp to grilled tuna salad. Open daily. Reservations advised. Major credit cards accepted. In *Union Station,* 50 Massachusetts Ave. NE (phone: 682-9559).

China Inn In Washington's Chinatown, this eatery serves primarily Cantonese fare, although there are some Szechuan dishes on the menu. Try the lemon chicken, butterfly shrimp, or sea bass with scallions, ginger and spices. Open daily. Reservations unnecessary. Major credit cards accepted. 631 H St. NW (phone: 842-0909).

Hard Rock Café A relative newcomer to Washington, this outpost of the famous rock-music hangout serves hearty sandwiches, burgers, and salads. Open daily. Reservations advised for large groups. Major credit cards accepted. Corner of 10th and E Sts. NW (phone: 737-7625).

Madurai Vegetarian Indian food is the specialty of this Georgetown establishment. Try the eggplant curry or the vegetable *biryani* (mixed vegetables cooked with rice). Open daily. Reservations advised. Major credit cards accepted. 3318 M St. NW (phone: 333-0997).

Peyote Café This Southwestern bar and grill is located below *Roxanne's* (see below) in the heart of Adams Morgan. Try the chuck wagon beef and pinto bean chili, the mashed potatoes (with skins), and the Texas yardbird (barbecued chicken with melted Monterey Jack cheese). Open daily. Reservations advised. Major credit cards accepted. 2319 18th St. NW (phone: 462-8330).

Roma A solid Italian family-style place, best in warm weather when the large outdoor garden is open and musicians and singers add to the relaxed ambience. All the old favorites, from pizza to pasta, are here. Open daily. Reservations advised. Major credit cards accepted. 3419 Connecticut Ave. NW (phone: 363-6611).

Roxanne's Chef Phil DeMott worked with New Orleans's Paul Prudhomme for five years before coming to this Cajun-style eatery in Adams Morgan. Try the barbecued shrimp, the blackened tuna, or the grilled lamb with white bean salad. Open daily. Reservations advised. Major credit cards accepted. 2319 18th St. NW (phone: 462-8330).

Sarinah Satay House A favorite among locals, this place specializes in Indonesian fare. Recommended are the grilled chicken in coconut sauce, the *satay,* and the *gado gado* (salad with peanut sauce). Closed Mondays. Reservations advised. Major credit cards accepted. 1338 Wisconsin Ave. NW (phone: 337-2955).

Star of Siam This is the best Thai restaurant in the district. Try one of the 10 different kinds of curries, the crispy noodles, or the fish cakes. Open daily. Reservations necessary for parties of four or more. Major credit cards accepted. 1136 19th St NW, between L and M Sts. (phone: 785-2838/9). There are two other locations: in Rosslyn, Virginia, across the Key Bridge from Georgetown (1735 N. Lynn St.; phone: 703-524-1208), and in Adams Morgan (2446 18th St. NW; phone: 986-4133).

Vietnam Georgetown Small and intimate, this simple place serves the best Vietnamese food in town. Specialties include deep-fried crispy spring rolls, shrimp with sugarcane, and beef in grape leaves. Open daily. Reservations unnecessary. MasterCard and Visa accepted. 2934 M St. NW (phone: 337-4536).

FOR THE SWEET OF TOOTH

Washington has a homegrown ice cream empire founded by renegade attorney Bob Weiss. *Bob's Famous Ice Cream* has stores on Capitol Hill (236 Massachusetts Ave. NE; phone: 546-3860), near the *Cleveland Park Metro* station (3510 Connecticut Ave. NW; phone: 244-4465), and in Bethesda, Maryland (4706 Bethesda Ave.; phone: 301-657-2963). *Bob's* ice cream also is sold at the *Ice Cream Shop* (2416 Wisconsin Ave. NW; phone: 965-4499).

Diversions

Exceptional Pleasures and Treasures

Quintessential Washington

Many Americans at one time or another have stood—ice cream dripping down their shirtfronts on a hot and humid August day—in awe of Washington's white marble grandeur. As schoolchildren, we saw pictures in textbooks of our republic's eminent federal buildings and monuments—the *White House,* the *Capitol Building,* the *Supreme Court,* the *Washington Monument*—so in a way, the images are familiar. Yet there's nothing quite like seeing them in person. For whether home is Bangor or Bakersfield, a close encounter with the nation's capital brings the textbook dazzlingly to life. Only here can you sense the vision of Washington, Jefferson, architect Pierre Charles L'Enfant, and company, who founded this city in the hope that it would become the workshop and showcase of American government.

The monuments, memorials, and marble façades are the magnets that draw upwards of 19 million visitors a year, but there is much more to this major metropolitan area—from jazz clubs and ethnic restaurants to trendy shops and the *Redskins.* Don't be reluctant to behave like a tourist: Ask questions, enjoy your ice cream cone, and buy a *Redskins* or *Georgetown University* T-shirt. Many of those who live and work here—senators, congressmen, and the like—are also tourists of sorts. It's just that they will stay a little longer (two or six years, at least) before returning home.

NATIONAL ARCHIVES Most of us take freedom for granted. We salute the flag and stand for the singing of the "Star-Spangled Banner," but few if any Americans stop to think about the founding principles of "the land of the free and the home of the brave." A visit to the *Archives,* home to the sacred documents on which our nation was built—the *Declaration of Independence,* the *Constitution,* and the *Bill of Rights*—is likely to inspire such thoughts. There is little glitz to this exhibit, which essentially consists of faded parchment paper in a glass case. But for those who come to pay solemn tribute to these paper pillars of democracy—unlike those who just wander in to kill time before the movie begins over at the *Air and Space Museum*—it is refreshing to look beyond the *Fourth of July* fireworks to see what the hubbub is all about.

The shimmering white marble and classical design of the *National Archives Building* lend an air of permanence to what is in essence our nation's file cabinet. Walking up the steps on the *Mall* side (Constitution Ave.), through the legion of Corinthian columns and the six-and-a-half-ton bronze doors, you pass into the building's grand Rotunda. On a pedestal atop a set of steps inside are the documents, flanked on either side by sweeping murals depicting Jefferson presenting a draft of the Declaration of Independence to John Hancock, the President of the *Continental Congress* (left); and James Madison submitting the Constitution to George Washington and the *Constitutional Convention* (right).

First explore the exhibit in the hall that encircles the Rotunda, a slice of Americana serving up such changing themes as Yankee ingenuity or the history of political cartoons. After clearing the metal detector and bag search, proceed up the steps for a look at the *Charters of Freedom*—which you can read through several layers of tinted, laminated glass and special filters that protect them from the ravages of light. An electronic-sensored vault underneath the case is ready to seal up the documents for safekeeping if it senses trouble. Indeed, the security arrangement that protects against anything short of Armageddon reinforces the notion of our impenetrable commitment to preserving our freedom and its symbols.

In addition to the billions of documents housed here, there are a few rather bizarre holdings, such as a brown paper bag containing a hamburger with one bite missing. It is the evidence in a 1940 case involving a sailor on the USS *Dubuque* and a young woman who came aboard with a hamburger—and a yen for men in uniform. After the sailor and the woman found privacy in a gun locker, she took a bite of the burger. She also had been sniffing chloroform to get high, and promptly died in the sailor's arms. The sailor was acquitted of involuntary manslaughter and rape charges, but the hamburger remains in custody (note that it is not on general display). Constitution Ave. between Seventh and Ninth Sts. NW (phone: 202-502-5205).

CRAB FEAST Just as refusing a lobster in Maine is, to some, grounds for deportation, so is passing up a crab in the Washington area. No other dining experience, at least in this country and in this century, compares with a traditional, unpretentious Chesapeake crab feast. Setting the tone for the proceedings is a brown paper tablecloth, which is soon joined by the weapons—a wooden mallet and a stubby knife—followed by a tall pitcher of beer. Before long, a heaping mound of red, spiced steamed crabs is hoisted onto the table. Let the games begin. Some restaurants have placemats with instructions. Other places sell T-shirts that illustrate ten easy ways to approach a crab—and live to tell about it. One way or another, a brief tutorial is in order for the uninitiated, since strategy is crucial for getting at the edible parts of the crab. (A good waiter or waitress can be of help in identifying the most succulent morsels.) The sound of mallets pounding and the odd crab leg landing in your lap only add to the experience. A true crab aficionado will get down and dirty, emerging from the whole feast covered in spices and shards of shell.

Though ordinary appetites are sated by only a half-dozen to a dozen crabs, a hearty appetite is recommended for a feast (all you can eat). The best time for a crab orgy is from mid-March to November, since crabs are rarely taken from the Chesapeake during the winter (when they're flown up from the Carolinas). The granddaddy of such feasts is served by *Ernie's Original Crab House,* across the Potomac in Alexandria (1623 Fern St.; phone: 703-836-1623; and 7929 Richmond Hwy.; phone: 703-780-0100). For a more upscale version, try the *Dancing Crab* (4611 Wisconsin Ave. NW; phone: 202-244-1882).

CHERRY BLOSSOM TIME For those whose spirits are lifted by bursting buds, the best time to visit Washington is early April, when the *Cherry Blossom Festival* celebrates the arrival of spring. The exact date the blossoms appear varies each year, depending on the weather, but it usually falls between March 20 and April 17—and the sight is the only event known to stir Washingtonians more than a *Redskins* victory or a juicy political scandal. When the trees, a gift from the Japanese government, are in full bloom, Washingtonians descend upon the Tidal Basin, an ordinarily tranquil body of water to the north of the *Jefferson Memorial.* Couples amble slowly amid the blossoms, artists dig in their easels, and boaters paddle about, observing the spectacle from the water. One of the most colossal traffic jams of the calendar year ensues as motorists, who never seem to learn, clog the streets circling the Tidal Basin.

The trees are of two varieties: Most are Akebeno trees, with delicate white blossoms, and scattered among them are Yoshino trees, with pale pink petals. Today's trees are actually a replacement bunch. The first batch were besieged by insects and fungus, and the *Department of Agriculture* had them destroyed. The Japanese graciously avoided an international incident by sending another batch with a better bill of health three years later. (In the 1960s, the US came to the rescue of Japan's pollution-ravaged native cherry trees by sending cuttings from these trees back to their homeland.) The delicate beauty of the blossoms is best viewed up close amid the majesty of the nearby *Lincoln* and *Jefferson Memorials* (see *Walk 1: The Mall and Monuments* in DIRECTIONS).

Whether or not the blossoms have arrived, the *Cherry Blossom Festival* is always held during the first week in April. The ceremonial lighting of the Japanese lantern, a stone lantern located among the trees, begins a week of festivities that includes a parade, pageants, concerts, and a marathon.

TEA AT THE WILLARD At Washington's historic *Willard* hotel—known for many years as the "Residence of the Presidents" because of the distinguished company it kept (see "Grand Hotels" in *Checking In,* THE CITY)—the English custom of afternoon tea is strictly observed. Washington's elite gathers in the L-shape *Nest* lounge to sip Earl Grey tea and daintily munch on the full complement of finger sandwiches, scones, Devonshire cream, and pastries. Strategically set on the mezzanine of this restored Beaux Arts building, the lounge has a decidedly feminine look, with light, marble-topped tables draped in white linen, small vases holding irises, delicate china, and soft blue drapes and carpeting. The decor reflects a bygone era when women were banished up the spiral staircase to sip tea and chat amongst themselves while their husbands swilled spirits in the bar below. Today, taking tea at the *Willard* is popular among movers and shakers who want a break from moving and shaking, business folks escaping the rigors of the office, and the regular contingent of society ladies who sip champagne along with their tea; it's also a popular spot for baby and bridal showers. Tea is served daily from 3 to 5 PM. Everyone is welcome—even men.

SENATE BEAN SOUP Though none can explain its origin with authority, a beige and rather bland bean soup has been the official dish and a trusty staple of the *US Senate Dining Room* since the turn of the century. Historians have boiled the blame (or credit) down to either Minnesota Senator Knute Nelson, whose affinity for a brimming bowl of bean soup was well documented, or Idaho Senator Fred Thomas Dubois, who, using his clout as chairman of the *Senate Restaurant Committee,* cooked up a law ensuring that bean soup would enjoy special status on the *Senate Dining Room* menu. Whatever the reason, this most capital soup is made and served here daily by special order of Congress.

Unfortunately, one must get elected or be a personal guest of a US Senator to enter the sanctity of the true *Senate Dining Room.* For the tourist committed to experiencing this taste of pure Americana while on "the Hill," bean soup receives star billing at the *Capitol Refectory* (also called the *Senate Dining Room*) on the Senate side. The *Refectory* serves up a respectable bowl of bean soup on white linen tablecloths in a hurried but pleasant atmosphere. Pen-and-ink drawings of the *Capitol Building* adorn the walls, and a legislator or two may well stride past while you dine. It's open weekdays from 8 AM until the Senate session ends, which is sometimes not until after midnight; when the Senate is not in session, it closes at 3:30 PM. A good bowl of soup is also served at the admittedly characterless cafeteria in the *Dirksen Senate Office Building* (1st St. and Constitution Ave. NE, the middle of three Senate office buildings, located in the basement; phone: 202-224-7196). But perhaps Washington's best bean soup can be found down in the lowlands of Foggy Bottom. After finding the bean soup in the *Senate Dining Room* (the exclusive one) too watery for his taste, restaurateur Dominique D'Ermo, owner of *Dominique's* (1900 Pennsylvania Ave. NW; phone: 202-452-1126), concocted a "better recipe" and now, with much fanfare, serves the steamy staple in his highly touted restaurant. *Dominique's* canned version, though not as good as the real thing, makes for a tasty souvenir.

A MOUNT VERNON AFTERNOON Lovingly preserved, George Washington's *Mount Vernon* home, a short drive south of Washington, is a far more meaningful monument to the man who was our first president than is the impersonal obelisk that bears his name. A leisurely afternoon spent at *Mount Vernon* provides both a relaxing reprieve from the bustling city and a respectful glimpse into the life and times of this US patriot.

Start by visiting the mansion, preferably in the morning (the estate attracts some 10,000 visitors a day during the summer, and the line gets unwieldy in the afternoon). By Virginia Tidewater standards today, this colonial country house, like our first president's financial status at the time, is modest. Still, there is much to appreciate at *Mount Vernon.* Inside this mid-Georgian style building are some of the landscapes and riverscapes that recall Washington's interest in the commercial navigation of Virginia's waterways. There is an elegantly embellished Palladian window in the *Banquet Hall.* Elsewhere are found the *Key to the Bastille,* given to Washington by his chum Lafayette; a harpsichord he imported from England for his adopted daughter; a trunk he carried with him throughout the Revolutionary War; and the bed in which he died.

The real draw of *Mount Vernon* is the tranquillity of its sylvan setting and its history-steeped displays. Visit the spinning room, stable, open-hearth kitchen house, period garden, remaining slave quarters, and burial vaults for George and Martha, and walk the shaded paths that connect them all. Washington wrote of *Mount Vernon* that "no estate in America is as pleasantly situated as this home." Gaze out upon the wide sweep of the Potomac from the Windsor chairs arranged on the mansion's portico, down the verdant *Bowling Green* that Washington himself laid out in 1785, and across the river to the Maryland hills, on an area preserved to look much as it did in Washington's day, and it will be clear to you that the proprietor's claim was no idle boast.

A KENNEDY CENTER OPENING Dust off your tux, shake out your mink, and prepare for a gala night out. Opening night at *Kennedy Center* is Washington at its glitziest. It's an opportunity for people to see and be seen, but more important, it's a staid, history-rich, red-tape-ridden city's salute to some of the finest theater this side of Broadway. Recent programs have featured such hits as David Mamet's *Oleanna, Guys and Dolls, Tommy Tune Tonite!,* and Kander and Ebb's *The World Goes 'Round.*

The opening-night experience begins with dinner at one of several choice restaurants near the *Center,* where fixed-price pre-theater dinner deals abound. Book a table at *Maison Blanche,* near the *White House,* which specializes in French classics (phone: 202-842-0070); *Dominique's,* a favorite of Elizabeth Taylor (phone: 202-452-1126); or *Jean-Louis,* the *Watergate* complex's premier eatery and one of the most expensive in the nation (phone: 202-298-4488). The *Kennedy Center* features its own excellent eatery, the *Roof Terrace,* which concentrates on regional food such as Maryland crab cakes (phone: 202-416-8855).

Then it's time to mingle with the pundits, policymakers, and power brokers who exchange witty anecdotes, swap government gossip, and slap backs, all under the crystal chandeliers (a gift from Sweden) of the plush, red-carpeted *Grand Foyer*. Critics strut about, senators mingle with lobbyists, cabinet secretaries chat with *White House* aides, and veteran socialites exchange the latest scuttlebutt quietly among themselves. Often, the playwright is in attendance, scanning the crowd for a friendly reviewer. An early arrival is imperative in order to drink in the social spectacle, along with a glass of champagne from the refreshment concession.

Before the curtain rises, take a walk around the *Kennedy Center*'s roof terrace, which offers a view of the Potomac in one direction and the glimmering capital city opposite. A leisurely terrace stroll takes about 15 minutes. On your way back into the theater, note the seven-foot bronze bust of John F. Kennedy in the *Grand Foyer;* it was Kennedy's plan for the performing arts center that stirred Washington out of its deep cultural sleep.

THE GEORGETOWN EXPERIENCE The spirited community west of Rock Creek that locals stubbornly call Georgetown (though its official name, according to the DC municipal government, is West Washington) is the city's source of adrenalin. Through its main arteries, M Street and Wisconsin Avenue, flows the energy that makes this historic former tobacco port the city's most popular nightlife destination. Some of the folks who gravitate to Georgetown after sundown are hustling off to *Blues Alley,* a reformed hole-in-the-wall down a forgotten alley where cool jazz and Cajun food are the standard fare (is it a coincidence that Duke Ellington grew up nearby?). Others are meeting friends—or an ambassador—at one of Georgetown's ethnic restaurants (see below), or just ruminating over a late-night coffee and dessert at *Au Pied de Cochon*. Other folks who deluge Georgetown's narrow streets on weekend nights, attracted by the area's vitality, have no particular destination in mind.

Restaurants abound here. Among the best are *Bamiyan,* serving Afghan food; *El Caribe,* offering Spanish food, zippy sangria, and a festive atmosphere; and *Vietnam Georgetown* (see *Eating Out* in THE CITY for more details), the restaurant that started the Southeast Asian food boom in Washington. Tony boutiques, inviting bookshops, and relaxed pubs orbit the corner of M Street and Wisconsin Avenue, Georgetown's nerve center. But Georgetown's real activity unfolds on the street. While waiting to cross an intersection, it is not unusual to find yourself flanked by black-garbed Existential types headed to a down-home café or a gaggle of suited matrons off for tea and a chat about today's politics. Georgetown is a hodgepodge of students, socialites, Senate staffers, and street eccentrics—like the man who positioned himself as a tour guide outside the historic *Old Stone House* and convinced some visitors that George Washington entertained prostitutes there. After a lively tour of the main drags, wander along the cobblestone residential backstreets, where Georgetown's true colonial charm lies. The towpath of the C & O Canal (go there only by day), which slices through Georgetown, is another pleasant dimension to this once-tacky tobacco town.

A Few of Our Favorite Things

This city of around-the-clock politicking and cherished national monuments and museums also has a proud roster of elegant hotels, restaurants, and theaters. Follow our lead; we promise you won't be disappointed.
Each place listed below is described in greater detail in THE CITY.

GRAND HOTELS

Washington's hotels in large part reflect the historic and ceremonial character of the nation's capital. The following are our accommodation favorites. Complete information about our choices can be found on pages 62 to 65 of THE CITY.

Four Seasons
Hay-Adams
Jefferson
Ritz-Carlton
Stouffer Mayflower
Willard Inter-Continental

CAPITAL DINING

This sophisticated, multicultural city offers cuisine styles as numerous as the flags that grace the long rows of embassies here, and boasts many world class chefs. The following are our picks of the city's top dining rooms. Complete information about our choices can be found on pages 69 to 71 of THE CITY.

L'Auberge Chez François
Galileo
Maison Blanche
Mr. K's
Occidental Grill
Prime Rib

CENTER STAGE

There are five stellar stages in Washington, each one either a historic or contemporary performing arts landmark. Complete information about our choices can be found on pages 57 to 58 of THE CITY.

Arena Stage
Ford's Theatre
Kennedy Center
National Theatre
Shakespeare Theater

Capital Antiques

To find the best concentration of antiques in the Washington area, one must first locate the area's most historic districts: Old homes beget old furnishings. Thus, with the exception of lengthier trips to the Pennsylvania Dutch country or to Leesburg and the other Virginia "burgs" to the south, Georgetown and Old Town Alexandria are the antiques buff's best hunting grounds. These old Potomac port cities, rich in well-preserved 18th-century architecture, predate the nation's capital. In exchange for the hogsheads of tobacco that left these ports for England, ships returned carrying furniture and other trappings of European culture to fill the houses of the area's wealthy tobacco merchants, who were part of the colonial aristocracy. And so, in addition to the more austere American collectibles one might find in this area, there is usually a respectable selection of European antiques. All of the following offer shipping services for furniture and larger items.

MILLER & ARNEY ANTIQUES The owner of this shop characterizes his inventory as a "general store of antiques." Housed in a turn-of-the-century, two-story Victorian building are American, English, and continental furniture and decorative objects from the 18th and 19th centuries. Owner Joe Miller, who is proudest of his English discoveries, travels to Great Britain to rummage and restock when the exchange rate is favorable. (Lately, he has had to concentrate on scouring for antiques in his own back yard.) Known by local antiques mavens as much for his purchases as for his sales, Miller always seems to carry a large selection of mahogany desks, "occasional tables," standing clocks, and lamps of all kinds for traditional homes. If notified in advance, the shop will provide chauffeur service to and from downtown DC (an especially welcome feature as there is no *Metro* stop nearby). Information: *Miller & Arney Antiques,* 1737 Wisconsin Ave. NW, Georgetown (phone: 202-338-2369).

SUSQUEHANNA ANTIQUES COMPANY The inventory of this spacious Georgetown shop, filling a two-story house just off Wisconsin Avenue, includes mainly American and English furniture, paintings, and clocks. Among the vast collection of early American bracket and shelf clocks is a Federal-period standing piece made in 1780 by a clockmaster whose family held on to it for all of its 200-year history. Owner David Friedman, a third-generation antiques dealer, is an aficionado of American art, and his collection reflects it. Included here are works by Charles Warren Eaton, Paul Cornoyer, and Herbert Morton Stoops. The shop also features myriad antique brass andirons and a collection of pre-1920 quilts, most from Maryland or Pennsylvania. The owner will let you have a peek at the stuff in his nearby warehouse (call for an appointment), which he uses as a workshop and place to store the overflow. Information: *Susquehanna Antiques Company,* 3216 O St. NW, Georgetown (phone: 202-333-1511).

THIEVES MARKET This antiques mall, the first of its kind in the country when it opened in 1953, is a place to really get a steal (thus the name—it's also the namesake of a famous Parisian market). For example, this market sold the oldest painting of Abraham Lincoln, pre-beard, for $3 in the 1970s, and a box filled with assorted papers was sold for $8—much to the delight of the patron who discovered that it contained a rough draft of General Robert E. Lee's farewell address. Stories abound of customers walking away with ordinary antique desks and, after some inspection, finding secret compartments containing diamonds, emeralds, and rubies. One canny shopper paid $1,200 for an American-made table that fetched over $28,000 several weeks later at an auction. Though the presentation of its inventory might not be as demure as that of the more exclusive dealers, many dealers and decorators shop here and turnover is quick (the market attracts several thousand people every week). Owner Kaplan Cohen, a third-generation art dealer, offers American, English, and continental china, silver, crystal, armoires, antique paintings, Venetian chandeliers, bronze and marble statuary, 18th-century mahogany desks, and other unusual items. Information: *Thieves Market,* 8101 Richmond Hwy., Alexandria, VA (phone: 703-360-4200).

WASHINGTON ANTIQUES CENTER The plain exterior of this red brick office building belies the venerable treasures inside. From an excellent collection of silver, including some 17th-century pieces, to furniture, rugs, books, porcelain, crystal, and fine arts, this gallery seemingly has it all. Among the 35 dealers whose antiques are tastefully displayed here are Roberta Tankel, Washington's premier dealer in porcelain; *G & M Antiques,* which carries an unholy alliance of affordable retro (from the 1950s) and Victorian furniture; and a bookseller who specializes in collectible first editions. One showcase sparkles with vintage costume jewelry. The management has created the sophisticated mood of a gallery, and is careful not to overwhelm the patron with bric-a-brac. Classical music serves as background, and the collections are carefully placed so as not to clutter the area, as they do at flea markets. Information: *Washington Antiques Center,* 209 Madison St., *Old Town* Alexandria, VA (phone: 703-739-2484).

RULES OF THE ROAD FOR AN ODYSSEY OF THE OLD

Buy for sheer pleasure, not for investment. Forget about the carrot of supposed retail values that dealers habitually dangle in front of amateur clients. If you love something, it will probably grace your home long after you've left the nation's capital.

Buy the finest example you can afford of any item, in as close to mint condition as possible. Chipped or broken "bargains" will haunt you later with their shabbiness. They also don't increase in value the way the mint stuff does.

Train your eye in museums and/or collections of items in the period that interests you. These are the best schools for the acquisitive senses, particularly as you begin to develop special passions. (Old Town Alexandria and Georgetown have a wealth of historic 18th- and 19th-century homes and buildings, many of which offer tours.)

Get advice from specialists when contemplating major acquisitions. Much antique and collectible furniture and many paintings have been restored several times. If you want to be absolutely certain that what you're buying is what you've been told it is, stick with the larger dealers. Some auction houses and even small museums have an evaluation office whose experts will make appraisals for a fee.

Don't be afraid to haggle—a little. Most dealers don't have fixed prices, so sharpen your negotiating skills and make an offer they can't refuse. A word of warning: While most larger dealers take credit cards, smaller shops do not.

When pricing an object, don't forget to figure the cost of shipping. The price of shipping home a large piece—furniture, sculpture, antique garden paraphernalia—can be considerable. Be sure to figure this into the cost of your purchase.

Historic Churches

Presidents pray in them, while others come to marvel at their vaulting interiors and historic relics. Pierre L'Enfant, the capital city's chief architect, targeted an area where a "national pantheon or church" would be built, like London's *Westminster Abbey* or *Notre-Dame* in Paris. Unfortunately, the Greek Revival temple at 12th Street and Pennsylvania Avenue that was finally completed in 1867 was quickly diverted into use as a Civil War hospital, and after the war it was further demoted into service as a US Post Office and then the *Pavilion at the Old Post Office,* an office and shopping complex (see *Shopping* in THE CITY). L'Enfant's concept of a national pantheon or church is today served by the *Washington National Cathedral* (below), which—although not built for such grand purposes—has come to serve as a treasured national shrine. The two other venerable churches listed here also have national stature.

NATIONAL SHRINE OF THE IMMACULATE CONCEPTION This architectural blend of contemporary, Byzantine, and Romanesque styles is the largest Roman Catholic church in the Western Hemisphere and the seventh-largest religious building in the world. Interestingly, it is the only Catholic house of worship in the US to have been built with funds contributed by every parish in the country. Its sheer expanse is awesome: It seats over 6,000 worshipers in its 57 chapels. Begun in 1920, the edifice is noted for its statuary, over 200 stained glass windows, and intricate mosaics depicting the history of Catholicism in America. A mosaic on the ceiling of the dome, *Christ in Majesty,* is reputedly the largest of its kind in the world. (One of the church's mosaics used up all the stone in one Italian quarry.) Though the church—appropriately located near *Catholic University*—was dedicated in 1959, decorative work and renovation of interior sections practically never stop. Summer organ recitals on Sunday evenings are widely attended. Information: *National Shrine of the Immaculate Conception,* Fourth St. and Michigan Ave. NE (phone: 202-526-8300).

ST. JOHN'S CHURCH Every American president since James Madison has worshiped in this charming yellow church across the street from the White House on *Lafayette Square.* It is nicknamed the "Church of the Presidents," and *Pew 54* is reserved for the president and his family. Several architects contributed to the construction of this building, but the one who deserves the most credit is Benjamin Henry Latrobe, a multi-talented fellow who not only designed the Greek Revival church, but served as its first organist and composed a hymn for its grand opening. The spectacular stained glass was designed by the curator of the stained glass windows at *Chartres Cathedral* in France; its installation was overseen by James Renwick, architect of the "castle," the *Smithsonian's* flagship building on the *Mall. St. John's* also offers free organ recitals every Wednesday, just after noon.

Next door is the *Parish House,* a lovely French Second Empire–style building that hasn't lost a bit of elegance in its scaled-down size, and that seems to harmonize like a church choir with the church. The *Parish House* is the former home of Lord Ashburton, a British minister who negotiated the boundary between the US and Canada with Daniel Webster, who lived not far from here. Open daily; services are held on Sundays at 8, 9, and 11 AM. Information: *St. John's Church,* 16th and H Sts. NW (phone: 202-347-8766).

WASHINGTON NATIONAL CATHEDRAL This colossal Gothic cathedral, which towers over northwest DC from its perch on Mount St. Albans, is formally named the *Cathedral Church of St. Peter and St. Paul.* The less pedantic just call it the *National Cathedral.* The idea for the church was born in 1893; an American (Henry Vaughn) and a Briton (George Bodley) collaborated on its original design, which was later completed by the tireless Philip Frohman. Ground was broken in 1907, but the church was not completed and consecrated until 1990. Originally and presently the seat of the Washington Episcopalian Diocese, the *Cathedral* nonetheless offers multi-denominational worship and serves in numerous ecumenical capacities.

This dramatic, twin-towered house of worship has been described as "the last of the great cathedrals." Its design and building materials are true to 14th-century Gothic form: No structural steel was used. It has all the classic components of Gothic architecture: flying buttresses, gargoyles, grotesques, ample stained glass, and spires that seem to tickle the heavens. And its interdenominational services and events are true to George Washington's dream of a national church. But the cathedral is not entirely a throwback to an earlier era. Embedded in the large, stained glass *Space Window* is a moon rock brought back to earth by astronauts Neil Armstrong, Michael Collins, and Edwin Aldrin from *Apollo 11*. And interred here are several contemporary heroes: President Woodrow Wilson, Admiral George Dewey, Cordell Hull (Secretary of State during World War II), and Helen Keller.

No visit to the *National Cathedral* is complete without a stroll through the 12th-century Norman arch and into the *Bishop's Garden,* a network of paths among rose bushes, medieval herbs, flowers, and well-groomed shrubbery. The benches in this English garden are a tranquil spot for resting the feet and restoring the soul. The circular *Herb Cottage* nearby sells jams and knickknacks. The *Pilgrim Observation Gallery* (which closes an hour before the cathedral does) affords a dramatic, panoramic view of Washington from one of the capital's highest points of elevation. Open daily until 4:30 PM. Information: *Washington National Cathedral,* Wisconsin Ave. at Woodley Rd. NW (phone: 202-537-6200).

Good Golf Outside the City

The late President Dwight D. Eisenhower is said to have left cleat marks in the *Oval Office* from his frequent putting practices between foreign policy briefings. President Bill Clinton is no stranger to the links, either. From the top brass on down, Washingtonians love golf. With the exception of the *Redskins* during football season, golf is perhaps the most popular subject of water-cooler conversation here. For those who strive to fit into Washington life, teeing up is as important as having voted in the last presidential election. Perhaps this is the genius behind the area's many golf-equipment discount shops (just check the yellow pages). And in spite of hot-and-humid-as-hell summers and an occasional snowstorm, golf is played almost every month of the year at the area's many courses. There's municipal golf to be played inside the District of Columbia's city limits (see *Golf* in THE CITY), but those who venture a little farther will be rewarded with a high-caliber round. Here are a few of the better public courses within a reasonable drive of DC.

ENTERPRISE This picturesque collection of holes just 10 minutes north of DC is known among locals as the *"Augusta National* of area public courses." Though golfers must keep their eye on the ball, the azaleas, Oriental dogwood blossoms, and other colorful plantings are delightful distractions. These 18 holes occupy 160 acres of the former farm and estate of Captain Newton H. White, the first commanding officer of the USS *Enterprise,* a

World War II aircraft carrier. The captain's stately mansion has been carefully preserved and sits next to the course's modern clubhouse, which has a snack bar for light breakfast or sandwiches, and plenty of cold beer. Though there are two ponds, only one presents a true obstacle (unless your backswing goes awry). The par 72, 6,200-yard course is still fairly challenging; bunkers tightly flank most of the sprawling greens. A putting green is available, as is club rental (even for southpaws like Mr. Clinton), and both pull and power golf carts. Tee-off time is on a first-come, first-served basis, and there are long backups on weekends. One spirited soul arrives around 2:30 to 3:30 AM on Saturdays; as a result, he has been the first to tee off every Saturday in recent memory. Information: *Enterprise Golf Course,* 2802 Enterprise Rd. (off Rte. 214 east), Mitchellville, MD (phone: 301-249-2040).

HERNDON CENTENNIAL Noted by area professionals for its thorough maintenance, this 18-hole, par 71 course features rolling, tree-lined fairways. Grassy mounds molded along the fairway often cause shots to veer sideways (which can mean either serendipity or doom, depending on which side of the mound the shot returns to earth). These mounds are reminiscent of the grand old game's Scottish origins—thankfully, without the added heather hazard. With ample bunkers intruding on most tee shots and every green, the course presents more than 50 opportunities to test one's mettle in the sand. Fortunately, the course's relative paucity of water (with the exception of three or four holes) and its forgiving length (5,865 yards from the men's tees) are enough to repair the ego if you're having a sandy day and getting some bad bounces. *Herndon* has a putting green and driving range, golf-club rental, and pull or power golf cart rental. Clubhouse amenities include a golf shop, a snack bar, and a well-stocked 19th hole. Best to reserve tee times a week in advance. The city of Herndon is about 15 miles southwest of Washington. From *Dulles Airport* Toll Road, take exit 2 to Route 657 north; Ferndale Avenue is on the left. Information: *Herndon Centennial Golf Course,* 909 Ferndale Ave., Herndon, VA (phone: 703-471-5769).

RESTON Visitors will enjoy (or at least be challenged by) this classically designed course, which is long (6,550 yards), lush, and rolling. Mature oak trees line many of the well-groomed fairways, and some attractive townhouses are just out of range (golfers hope) of this busy course's cross fire. Bring along a good sand wedge: The par 71 course contains a series of traps enclosing both the greens and those nettlesome fairway bunkers that can gobble up even the best-struck shot. For example, the 18th hole is pockmarked by no less than seven bunkers, five of them on the fairway. Also, the wind has been known to sweep away otherwise dazzling shots from their intended targets. (At least, this can be your reasoning while replaying the round in the clubhouse's snack bar over a cup of soup, a sandwich, or a brew.) Tee times are not needed during the winter months but are an absolute necessity during peak season. For weekday play, call the pro shop starting at 8

AM on Wednesdays; for Sunday play, at 8 AM on Thursdays. Clubs, and pull and power carts, can be rented. Located about 15 miles southwest of Washington. Information: *Reston Golf Course,* 11875 Sunrise Valley Rd. (off exit 3, *Dulles Airport* Toll Rd. and Reston Pkwy.), Reston, VA (phone: 703-620-9333).

SWAN POINT Though it's more than an hour's drive into the Maryland countryside south of Washington, this 6,403-yard course (par 72) is well worth the trip. Due in part to the marshy natural surroundings with lots of old pine trees, ominous mounds, and plenty of sand, its classic Carolina feel is also a credit to its recent redesign and reconstruction by Atlanta-based golf course architect Bob Crupp, an adviser for the *Augusta National,* home of the *Masters* tournament. Most of all, the narrow fairways demand placement that may seem as difficult as threading a camel through the proverbial eye of a needle—though thankfully there aren't many fairway bunkers. The fairways are Bermuda grass (almost unheard of in this area) and the greens are bent grass that make it feel as if you're putting on smooth ice. Some holes meander through marshland, and water could come into play on 13 of them (bring lots of extra balls). A driving range and putting green are also available. Golf carts are mandatory until 3 PM. There's also a fancy clubhouse with restaurant and 19th hole for delighted—or dejected—duffers. Tee times for weekday play should be arranged a week in advance; call on Thursdays beginning at 8 AM for weekend play. Information: *Swan Point,* Swan Point Rd. (off Rte. 301 to MD 257), Issue, MD (phone: 301-259-4411).

Bicycling

Biking in any major metropolitan area is akin to waging war with a peashooter; in Washington, it's more like firing off at the *Redskins'* offensive line with no more padding than a pair of dress slacks and a starched sports shirt. The menaces are many. Absentminded tourists in cars, preoccupied with monuments and parking spaces, weave about like the dragon in a Chinese parade. Bespectacled bureaucrats wander randomly into traffic. And because of the high turnover of its citizenry, few Washingtonians have really mastered the slants, one-ways, traffic circles, and perpetual road construction that comprise driving in DC. Downtown biking is best left to the couriers. Fortunately, however, a number of bike trails in the Washington area afford the cyclist an opportunity to get an invigorating workout while drinking in the serenity of several choice suburbs. If you've come with your wheels, happy trails. If not, three-speed, 10-speed, mountain, and kids' bikes can be rented from several establishments (see *Bicycling* in THE CITY). The following are several of the best bike paths in the area. As in any large city where crime is a problem, cyclists should take extra safety precautions.

ARLINGTON CEMETERY TO ROCK CREEK PARKWAY This 5-mile stretch of paved bike path runs from *Arlington National Cemetery* across the Arlington Memorial Bridge to the *Lincoln Memorial.* From here, head uptown on the lovely Rock Creek Parkway, a thickly wooded spindle of greenery that meanders along Rock Creek, toward the *National Zoo.* Teddy Roosevelt used to go on brisk hikes up this corridor of wilderness between Georgetown/Northwest and Adams Morgan. A good place to access the trail is from *Thompson's Boat Center,* at the northwest end of Virginia Avenue where Rock Creek feeds into the Potomac. From here the path can be taken toward *Arlington National Cemetery,* where it links up with the *Mount Vernon Bike Path* running south (see below). Another option from the *Lincoln Memorial* is to continue south to either Ohio Drive or West Basin Drive, which borders the Tidal Basin, and then follow the path around this serene body of water. This is especially recommended in April when the cherry blossoms are in bloom.

C & O CANAL TOWPATH This wide, packed-dirt trail borders the historic waterway that was supposed to revolutionize commerce in the early 19th century. Commerce was, indeed, revolutionized—but by the railroad instead. Thus, instead of being trod by mules towing barges, the towpath along the canal has become more famous for being trod by bikers and joggers. The entire length of the canal, from Georgetown to Cumberland, Maryland, can be biked (184 miles each way; some serious bikers make it a three- or four-day excursion). Though the towpath's incline is almost imperceptible, it rises slightly uphill as you leave Georgetown. There are camping facilities, historical points of interest, and a canal museum along the way. The Great Falls of the Potomac, a dramatic series of jagged falls that roar into a narrow gorge, is one of the most spectacular sights in the eastern US. There are plenty of walking trails that are ideal for mountain bikes. The *National Park Service* (phone: 202-426-6841) has put up mileposts along the towpath for the 14 miles from Georgetown to Great Falls.

MOUNT VERNON BIKE PATH This is Washington's premier bike trail. From the *Lincoln Memorial,* use the left side of the bridge across the Potomac and bear left once in Virginia. The well-maintained, paved path runs approximately 25 miles along the Potomac, all the way to George Washington's stately home in Mount Vernon, where there are ample bike racks near the snack bar, across from the parking lot. Along the way, enjoy the views of the city skyline, *National Airport,* vistas of the Maryland hills, the *Masonic Temple,* and a number of marinas along the Potomac shores. Fortunately, the path is wide, since cyclists must ride alongside runners and Rollerbladers. The path breaks up for a short stretch in *Old Town* Alexandria, where cyclists must forge through the streets, but the route is well marked and resumes at the other end of *Old Town.*

Boating

Traversed by rivers, tributaries, canals, and reservoirs, Washington offers a fleet of boating options on its various waterways—from plush dinner cruises on the Potomac River to paddleboats on the Tidal Basin. Perhaps the most intriguing water transport idea was proposed by architect Pierre L'Enfant, whose original plan of Washington envisioned a canal running from a point near the White House to the *Capitol Building:* When he paid a visit to Congress, the president would simply get there via barge. (The idea never got beyond L'Enfant's drawing board.) Even though the canal was paved over and is now Constitution Avenue, visitors can get a feel for what mule-drawn barge travel was really like on the C & O Canal (see below). In addition, the world's fastest and most expensive speedboats come to Washington in early June for the *President's Cup Regatta,* held off Hains Point; the extravaganza includes canoe and rowing races as well. The following are popular area boating experiences.

C & O CANAL BARGE The one-and-a-half-hour floating trips on the mule-drawn *Georgetown* or *Canal Clipper* barges are a close encounter with early-19th-century canal life. Built to resemble the cargo barges of yore, the boats used by the *National Park Service* are 85 feet long and 13 feet wide. The two mules that provide the journey's horsepower (that's two hp!) reach a top speed of 2 miles per hour (the canal's speed limit is 4 miles per hour, since higher speeds with a full load create a wake that would flood the towpath). Tour guides in 19th-century garb explain the fascinating history of the canal. Barges run from mid-April to mid-October. The *Georgetown* (phone: 202-472-4376) leaves from *The Foundry* at 1055 Thomas Jefferson Street NW. The *Canal Clipper* (phone: 301-299-2026) embarks at *Great Falls Park.*

POTOMAC DINNER CRUISE In the tradition of Paris's *bateaux-mouches,* a Potomac dinner cruise is a novel boating experience, affording a stunning view of America's luminous capital at night. One of the better such dinner cruises is aboard the *Dandy* (Zero Prince St.; phone: 703-683-6076), which leaves nightly from its dock in historic *Old Town* Alexandria and quietly makes its way up the Potomac. As dusk turns into night and dinner (a five-course meal with choice of prime ribs, cornish game hen, or poached salmon) is served, the *Dandy* passes the *Jefferson* and *Lincoln Memorials,* the *Washington Monument,* and the *Kennedy Center,* before turning about at Georgetown's *Washington Harbour.* And there's dancing—of the cheek-to-cheek variety so as not to rock the boat. The *Dandy* also sets sail for less expensive lunch cruises. Dinner prices range from $48 to $56 per person (depending on the day of the week) and do not include bar drinks, tax, or service. Lunch ranges from $26 to $30 per person. Sunday brunch includes a complimentary glass of champagne.

TACKING THE POTOMAC Though the Potomac is not generally known for its world class sailing—sandbars seem to pop up all the time, and floating timber is apt to get in the way—the *Washington Sailing Marina* (George Washington Memorial Pkwy., 1½ miles south of *National Airport;* phone: 703-548-9027) is the exception. The hazards are well marked in this intermediate, 3-mile zone between the Woodrow Wilson Bridge (to the south) and Hains Point (to the north). Sailing here offers unique views of the capital. The marina rents Sunfish for novices, 15-foot sloops, and 17-foot Islanders, as well as windsurfing boards. Adjacent to the marina is the *Potomac Landing* (phone: 703-548-0001), which serves up a bountiful catch of seafood. For really top-shelf sailing, an ideal day trip is a visit to historic Annapolis, Maryland (the home of the *United States Naval Academy*), and the Chesapeake Bay (a 45-minute drive from Washington). The *Annapolis Sailing School* (phone: 410-267-7205, a toll call from Washington) rents out 24-foot sailboats. During the warmer months, boat rentals are available throughout the capital area.

TIDAL BASIN This quiet reservoir is one of Washington's treasured water venues. Originally built to transfer water from the tidal Potomac to the Washington Channel, it is now the domain of Washington's beloved cherry trees, lovestruck couples who walk along its banks, and an armada of boats busily paddling hither and yon. In fact, there may be no more relaxing a spot in the District of Columbia than on these waters; though you can see it, the city seems light-years away. From this spot the marble steps of the *Jefferson Memorial* rise out of the water over the bow of the boat, and the *Washington Monument,* the *Mall* area, and the *White House* are visible beyond the stern. The morning hours when the fog hovers over the water, giving the reservoir a mystical feel, are the best time for boating. Rowboats, canoes, and paddleboats are all for hire for a nominal fee at the north end of the Tidal Basin at Maine Ave. and 15th St. SW (phone: 202-484-0206).

A Shutterbug's Washington

The ideal shutterbug in Washington is part tourist, part photojournalist, and part paparazzo. From the trickling fountain in Dupont Circle, the cobblestone streets of Georgetown and *Old Town* Alexandria, and the lovely English *Bishop's Garden* next to the *National Cathedral,* to the bright red mounds of steamed crustaceans at a crab feast (see *Quintessential Washington,* above), photo ops abound in the area. Beyond the photogenic white marble temples of our democracy is a charming tidewater city. And since a city like Washington—with its statuary, monuments, and memorials—can't help but suggest the symbolic, be on the lookout for that photograph that speaks volumes. Even a beginner can achieve remarkable results with a surprisingly basic set of lenses and filters. Equipment is, in fact, only as valuable as the imagination that puts it into use.

LANDSCAPES AND CITYSCAPES Washington's monuments and government buildings are most often visiting photographers' favorite subjects. But the *Mall,* the Potomac, and quaint Georgetown provide numerous photo possibilities as well. In addition to the *Capitol,* the *White House,* and the *National Cathedral,* be sure to look for natural beauty: Cherry trees that line the Tidal Basin, the lovely gardens in Dumbarton Oaks, the stately homes and buildings in the Embassy District, and the crew and sailboats that skim along the Potomac River are just a few examples.

Although a standard 50mm to 55mm lens may work well in some landscape situations, most will benefit from a 20mm to 28mm wide-angle. The *Mall,* with the *Washington Monument* and *Lincoln Memorial* in the distance, for example, is the type of panorama that fits beautifully into a wide-angle format, allowing not only the overview, but the opportunity to include people or other points of interest in the foreground. A flower, for instance, may be used to set off a view of the *Vietnam Veterans Memorial;* or people can provide a sense of perspective in a shot of Dupont Circle. To isolate specific elements of any scene, use your telephoto lens. Perhaps there's a particular statue that would make a lovely shot, or it might be the interplay of light and shadow on a cobblestone Georgetown street. The successful use of a telephoto means developing your eye for detail.

PEOPLE As with taking pictures of people anywhere, there are going to be times in Washington when a camera is an intrusion. Consider your own reaction under similar circumstances, and you have an idea as to what would make others comfortable enough to be willing subjects. People are often sensitive to having a camera suddenly pointed at them, but a polite request, while getting you a share of refusals, will provide a chance to shoot some wonderful portraits that capture the spirit of the city as surely as the scenery does. For candids, an excellent lens is a zoom telephoto in the 70mm to 210mm range; it allows you to remain unobtrusive while the telephoto lens draws the subject closer. And for portraits, a telephoto can be used effectively as close as two or three feet.

For authenticity and variety, select a place likely to produce interesting subjects. Georgetown is an obvious spot for visitors, but if it's local color you're after, visit *Eastern Market* on *Capitol Hill,* go to a game at *RFK Stadium,* walk around ethnically rich Adams Morgan, or wander around the *Georgetown University* campus. Aim for shots that tell what's different about our nation's capital. In portraiture, there are several factors to keep in mind. Morning or afternoon light will add richness to skin tones, emphasizing tans. To avoid the harsh facial shadows cast by direct sunlight, shoot in the shade or in an area where the light is diffused.

SUNSETS When shooting sunsets, keep in mind that the brightness will distort meter readings. When composing a shot directly into the sun, frame the picture in the viewfinder so that only half of the sun is included. Read the meter, set, and shoot. Whenever there is this kind of unusual lighting, shoot a few frames in half-step increments, both over and under the meter reading. Bracketing, as this is called, can provide a range of images, the best of which may well be other than the one shot at the meter's recommended setting.

Use any lens for sunsets. A wide-angle is good when the sky is filled with color-streaked clouds, when the sun is partially hidden, or when you're close to an object that silhouettes dramatically against the sky. Telephotos also produce wonderful silhouettes, either with the sun as a backdrop or against the palette of a brilliant sunset sky. Bracket again here. For the best silhouettes, wait 10 to 15 minutes after sunset. Unless using a very fast film, a tripod is recommended.

Red and orange filters are often used to accentuate a sunset's picture potential. Orange will help turn even a gray sky into something approaching a photogenic finale to the day. If the sunset is already bold in hue, however, the orange will overwhelm the natural colors. A red filter will produce dramatic, highly unrealistic results.

NIGHT If you think that picture possibilities end at sunset, you're presuming that night photography is the exclusive domain of the professional. If you've got a tripod, all you'll need is a cable release to attach to your camera to assure a steady exposure (which is often timed in minutes rather than fractions of a second).

For situations such as a night tour of the monuments or moonlight boat cruises, a strobe does the trick, but beware: Flash units are often used improperly. You can't take a view of the Tidal Basin and *Jefferson Memorial* with a flash. It may reach out as far as 30 feet, but that's it. On the other hand, a flash used too close to a subject may result in overexposure, resulting in a "blown out" effect. With most cameras, strobes will work with a maximum shutter speed of 1/125 or 1/250 of a second. If you set the exposure properly and shoot within range, you should come up with pretty sharp results.

CLOSE-UPS Whether of people or of objects such as antique door knockers, close-ups can add another dimension to your photography. There are a number of shooting options, one of which is to use a 70mm or a 210mm lens at its closest focusable distance. Unless you're working in bright sunlight, a tripod will be worthwhile. If you are very near your subject and there is a good deal of reflective light, it may pay to underexpose a bit in relation to the meter reading.

If you do not have a telephoto lens, you can still shoot close-ups using a set of magnification filters. Filter packs of one-, two-, and three-time magnification are available, converting your lens into a close-up lens. Even better is a special macro lens designed for close-up photography.

A SHORT PHOTOGRAPHIC TOUR

Here are are some of Washington's truly great pictorial perspectives.

TIDAL BASIN In the early morning the steam rises off this tranquil body of water just west of the *Mall* area, creating a mysterious veil over the *Jefferson*

Memorial. Position yourself next to the boathouse on the east side next to the *Bureau of Engraving and Printing* and get as close to the surface of water as possible (try lying on the concrete rim of the basin). If several of the crusty fellows who fish the area near the bridge on the left are in the viewfinder, so much the better. If the cherry trees that line the Tidal Basin are in bloom (late March or early April), giving this pool a pinkish fringe, you've got a keeper.

CAPITOL'S WEST FRONT Washington insiders who tread these paths every day swear that this rarely captured view is the best angle from which to appreciate the city. From here—on what constitutes the back patio of the *White House*—the *Mall* is in perfect alignment due west; the panorama extends toward the *Reflecting Pool* and, beyond it, the steps of the *Lincoln Memorial.* At a 25° angle to the right is Pennsylvania Avenue, "America's Main Street," the tree-lined thoroughfare that cuts its way through marble monuments and departmental monstrosities in its march to the *White House.* Every driver who has cursed Washington's street layout should study this photo. Though it may not calm the nerves, the aesthetic wisdom of L'Enfant's plan for a grid overlaid with broad avenues relieved by the intermittent traffic pinwheel is more easily understood from here.

LAFAYETTE PARK Even if there are a zillion postcards depicting this scene, it still makes for a great photograph. From the northern edge of *Lafayette Square* face the *White House.* The dramatic equestrian statue of *Andrew Jackson,* the fountain on the front lawn, the president's residence as white as crisp, clean linen, the Stars and Stripes atop the portico, and the top half of the *Washington Monument* all come into view, creating a photo of remarkable balance. Early evening is the best time to capture this shot.

STREET SCENES If you've got a yen for historic street scenes, there are three places of note. Tree-lined O Street in Georgetown near *Georgetown University* is one of Washington's most endearing little thoroughfares—especially in the fall, when the brilliantly colored Federal and Victorian townhouses are adorned by the changing leaves. The trolley tracks embedded in the cobblestones are a vestige of a bygone era. Lower Prince Street in *Old Town* Alexandria is also a cobblestoned street, dating back to the late 18th century. A photo from atop *Captain's Row* (the corner of Prince and Lee Streets)—a block of Federal-style townhouses built by sea captains, with the Potomac and the Maryland hills in the background—is a must. Finally, *Washingtonian* magazine calls N Street, between Connecticut and Rhode Island Avenues (downtown Washington) the most charming street in the city. Photo buffs in search of a historic Washington unintruded upon by modern structures will certainly agree.

Directions

Introduction

Like Canberra in Australia and Brasilia in Brazil, Washington was conceived as a capital city. And like the man who built a baseball field in the movie *Field of Dreams,* Washington's planners knew that if they built a city worthy of being a capital, tourists would come. Designed in the late 18th century by a Frenchman who had the network of broad, walker-friendly boulevards of Paris in mind—and at a time when walking was still a primary mode of transportation—Washington was created for the pedestrian.

In fact, most of the conventional tourist attractions in Washington—the fistful of *Smithsonian* museums, the *Capitol,* the *White House,* and most of the monuments—can be seen virtually without having to cross the path of motorized traffic. And that's probably just as well. But automobiles aren't even the major hazard. In a city driven by bureaucratic paper pushing, it's the bicycle couriers en route to the Department of Something or Other that pedestrians must really fear.

Unlike the condensed cities to the north where people crawl over one another to live, commute, and work, Washington, in true southern fashion, tends to sprawl. In the District alone, an area of roughly 70 square miles, getting from one side of town to another by foot is a major cardiovascular feat. Adding in historic *Old Town* Alexandria, Virginia, to the south—without which a tour of the capital's environs would be incomplete—the Washington area that is the subject of these walking tours represents a good chunk of real estate. So wear comfortable shoes, but also remember that if fatigue sets in you can always use Washington's *Metro* system, one of the finest in the world. The legitimate taxis here are also relatively trustworthy (they charge based on a zoned-fare system). What's more, the alphabet streets (running east–west) combine with the numbered streets (running north–south) to give order to the city's layout.

The following walking tours have been designed to take the tourist past Washington's more familiar sites, along with stops at some fascinating but often overlooked places. The tours will coax the inquisitive up flights of stairs, into nooks and near crannies, through hotel lobbies, under monuments, up inside church spires, and within reach of many shops and cafés.

The rewards of walking through Washington are monumental. However, be aware as you sightsee that Washington has the dubious honor of being the nation's crime capital, too. Although these walks will not deliberately steer you into known combat zones (the only real concern should be around *Capitol Hill*), keep in mind the general rules of caution you would apply in any place with inner-city crime, even in generally "safe" areas: avoid unfamiliar or uncrowded streets after dark, walk purposefully, and watch your wallet.

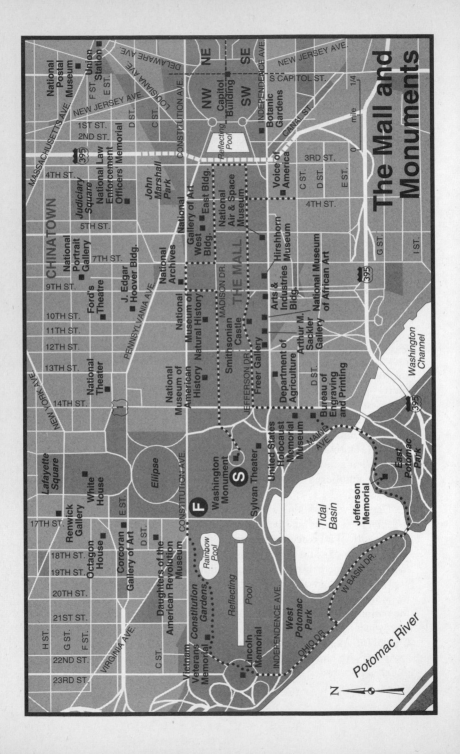

Walk 1: The Mall and Monuments

Washington's *Mall* area, the long rectangular strip of greenery that stretches from the *Capitol Building* through a canyon of museums to the *Washington Monument*, is both the nation's front lawn and its dusty storage attic.

In contrast to the sleepy ambience of many government buildings in the area and the sluggish pace of big government in general, the *Mall* is where most Washingtonians expend all the energy (and frustration) they have accumulated in the course of conducting the nation's business. Weather permitting, there is always something doing on the *Mall,* be it a combative game of congressional softball, jogging bureaucrats reversing the ravages of a sedentary lifestyle, vendors hawking souvenirs and snacks, contentious political demonstrators shouting slogans, distracted tourists precariously wandering into traffic, lovestruck picnickers ignoring the commotion around them, or, more than likely, all of the above.

The *Mall* is also the country's foremost repository of Americana and the cargo hold of our nation's collective bric-a-brac. On its fringe are nine sprawling museums devoted to everything from air travel and art to the evolution of the zebra. The country's pre-eminent museum complex, the *Smithsonian Institution,* accounts for the lion's share of the exhibits. Though more than 137 million objects are in its possession, there is only enough space in its sprawling buildings to display one percent of its holdings. However, the more than a million items on display are enough to keep an alert tourist awash in exhibits for several days. All of these museums are closed only on *Christmas Day;* there is no admission charge to any of them. (For more information on each of the museums, see *Special Places* in THE CITY.)

The *Mall* tour begins from the easiest site in Washington to spot: the *Washington Monument* (15th St. between Constitution and Independence Aves. NW; phone: 202-426-6841). The nearest *Metro* station is Smithsonian. The tour takes about four hours, allowing for a solemn moment at each of the monuments but only a stroll by the buildings of the *Smithsonian Institution.* At least a day, preferably longer, is recommended for inspecting the contents of these stately bastions to art and artifacts.

The mound on which the *Washington Monument* was built is an ideal place from which to observe and reflect on the history of the *Mall.* Although originally slated by city designer Pierre Charles L'Enfant as a grand avenue, à la Paris, lined with gardens and diplomats' mansions, that would run from the *Capitol Building* to the *Washington Monument,* the *Mall* was not always the hub of Washington activity. The Washington administration, dissatisfied with his design and exasperated by his unyielding arrogance, fired L'Enfant before he could execute his plan. For years, the *Mall* remained a no-man's-land, a simple common for pasturing cows. In the 19th century, a grid of railroad tracks were built, bringing in trains that shattered the area's tranquillity and sent up periodic plumes of noxious air.

Nearby lumber and coal yards and years of neglect sent the *Mall* area into further decline before its fortunes rose. By the early 20th century, the area where the *Reflecting Pool* is now located had become home to a sort of shantytown of wood and stucco shacks and temporary office buildings.

Nearby Southwest DC, which was originally scheduled to be the city's primary commercial district, became an impoverished working class housing district instead. It looked as if L'Enfant's grand plan had been a grand failure. Gradually, however, the French planner's original idea began to germinate, taking root in 1902 in Senator James McMillan's Senate District Committee. A veritable brain trust of landscaping, architecture, and sculpting genius was assembled to carry out the plan devised by the committee to save the *Mall.* Renowned landscape architect Frederick Law Olmsted, architects Daniel Burnham and Charles McKim, and sculptor Augustus Saint-Gaudens teamed up to give what has been dubbed the "nation's town green" a thoughtful, utilitarian, and sanctified feel.

The railroad was transported in 1908 from its location along the *Mall* to *Union Station,* a new terminal to the northeast. The conservatory of the *Botanic Garden* was removed from smack-dab in the middle of the *Mall* to its southeastern edge. The emotionally stirring *Lincoln Memorial* was built in the 1920s, staking out the *Mall*'s western boundary, and the *Jefferson Memorial,* a little farther afield, was dedicated in 1943. Once a blight, the *Mall* had been lovingly converted into an important attraction for tourists— in part because it had become a wonderful place from which to view many of Washington's most familiar and famous buildings and monuments.

Possibly its most recognizable structure—and certainly its most striking—is the *Washington Monument* (also see *Special Places* in THE CITY), a relatively simple obelisk with a clean design by Robert Mills. The monument is open daily; as with most federal properties, there is no admission charge. There will probably be a wait for the elevator that goes to the porthole atop the monument. While waiting, you may want to reflect on this famous spindle's history.

Perhaps it is the ultimate insight into the workings of Congress that the learned body approved a simple equestrian statue dedicated to George Washington in 1783, and that 105 years later the nation's taxpayers received a 555-foot, two-toned, sinking obelisk with an elevator of dubious design. Considering the other suggestions made by legislators—a crypt in the *Capitol* and a marble tomb were two of their more morbid ideas—Americans should be thankful for Congress's decision to build an obelisk. And indeed they are, if attendance is any indication: About 4,000 visitors a day ascend the monument during high season.

The cornerstone of the monument was laid in 1848, using the trowel Washington had used to lay the *Capitol* cornerstone 55 years earlier. After construction began, the *Washington Monument Society* continued to solicit funds from individuals and from each state in the union. Because Alabama was short on cash, it sent a stone instead. The idea caught on and stones arrived from around the world—until a stone from Pope Pius IX arrived. In the small hours of March 6, 1854, a band of intruders from the virulently anti-Catholic "Know-Nothing" party set upon the monument, stole the "pope's stone," and reportedly threw it into the Potomac. A local paper called it "a deed of barbarism." When the night watchman was asked why he hadn't used his shotgun to sound the alarm, his response was that he didn't know. (Perhaps he was a "Know-Nothing.")

Construction continued apace until the onset of the Civil War, when the nation's resources were diverted to the military. The stub of stone sat forgotten for 15 years, collecting rainwater, until building was finally resumed. Although the stone used was mined from the same Maryland quarry as before, it came from a different stratum, accounting for the discoloration between the bottom quarter and the rest of the monument.

When it opened in 1888, the *Washington Monument* was equipped with a steam-driven elevator, which was deemed too dangerous for women. The men who visited the monument, living life on the edge, rode the sluggish elevator, which took 20 minutes to reach the top. As for the women, they climbed the 897 steps—some collapsing and even dying—as the men toasted them with wine and beer from the top. The elevator is safe and quicker now, but more crowded and less convivial. On a clear day, the view from the top includes most of the District and parts of Virginia and Maryland. The stairs are off-limits except for "step tours" conducted by the *Park Service* on weekends (hours vary; phone: 426-6840). On these tours, you can go down all 897 stairs, viewing 188 memorial stones donated by various states, nations, societies, and individuals along the way.

After returning to terra firma, notice the *Sylvan Theater* on the southeast side of the monument's quadrant. This outdoor theater, with its massive lawn, hosts military bands, Shakespeare festivals, and musicals. There is a concert every day during the summer, including performances indigenous to Washington—for example, a Jesse Jackson speech backed up by three gospel singers, a five-piece electric band, and a voter-registration drive.

Walk the path leading northeast from the monument to Madison Drive. The *Ellipse* is to your left, and the familiar south side of the White House sits beyond. Begin walking on Madison Drive toward the *Capitol Building* in the distance. The first building ahead on the *Mall* proper, the *National Museum of American History* (Constitution Ave. between 12th and 14th Sts. NW; phone: 202-357-2700), is one of several *Smithsonian* properties clustered here.

The wealth of Americana at this site includes George Washington's false teeth, the original Star-Spangled Banner that inspired the poem that inspired the anthem, the desk on which Thomas Jefferson wrote the *Declaration of Independence,* a pocket compass used by Lewis and Clark, a collection of First Ladies' gowns, Eli Whitney's cotton gin, Muhammad Ali's boxing gloves, a collection of campaign paraphernalia, and an antebellum post office taken from Headsville, West Virginia, in which you can still mail a letter that will be postmarked with a unique *Smithsonian* seal. And there's more—much more—some of great historical significance and some with none whatsoever, such as Dorothy's ruby slippers and Radar O'Reilly's teddy bear. The museum's primary purpose is to document American civilization's achievements in science, technology, politics, and culture (the jury is still out on the inclusion of memorabilia from the hit TV series "Happy Days").

The next museum along the way is the *National Museum of Natural History* (Constitution Ave. between Ninth and 12th Sts. NW; phone: 202-357-2700), a veritable treasure trove of the life sciences. Housing 118 million objects inside its barrel-chested, early-20th-century façade, it sprouted two wings in the 1960s. If forced to categorize its contents, "artifacts from planet Earth" is the best we could do: Among the major attractions is "Uncle Beazly," a life-size model of a triceratops; the *Dinosaur Hall;* the *Insect Zoo,* featuring thousands of live insects, including the incredible hissing cockroach; the *Hall of Gems,* which is studded with 1,000 precious stones, making the contents of New York's *Tiffany's* seem like prizes in a Cracker Jack box; and the *History of Life* exhibit. To see even a fraction of the museum's contents is to get a good cultural workout.

At Ninth Street, the *National Archives* (phone: 202-501-5205) is on the left, set back on Constitution Avenue behind an area that is a garden in the summer and an ice rink in the winter (skates can be rented nearby). The *National Archives* is the nation's file cabinet, containing the *Declaration of Independence,* the *Constitution,* the *Bill of Rights* (all in the *Archives Exhibition Hall* on the Constitution Avenue side of the building), and a blizzard of paperwork documenting the nation's history, including President Gerald Ford's pardon of Richard Nixon and all the laws ever enacted by Congress. Many genealogy buffs find the *Archives* to be a crucial link in tracing their ancestry (the research rooms are reached from the Pennsylvania Avenue entrance and are open to the public). Also see *Quintessential Washington* in DIVERSIONS. The *Exhibition Hall* is open daily; there's no admission charge.

Return down Seventh Street to Madison Drive and turn left. The massive, marble *West Building* of the *National Gallery of Art* (phone: 737-4215) occupies a good chunk of of the real estate (five and a half acres) on the left. This gallery is among the finest in the world, with major works by all the Impressionist painters, one of the best collections of Italian art outside Europe, an extensive collection of American art, and works by Flemish, German, Dutch, Spanish, and British artists, plus many others. The *West Building* (the original *National Gallery of Art*) was constructed from funds provided by the Pittsburgh banker and philanthropist Andrew Mellon. Given control of the family's bank at age 26, Mellon wasted no time in converting his interest in art into one of the most impressive privately held collections in the world. The Mellon collection, still housed in the *West Building*, concentrated on the Old Masters of 16th-, 17th-, and 18th-century Europe (he sent $6 million to a cash-strapped Soviet Union for a collection of classics, including works by Raphael and Botticelli). After relocating to Washington to become Secretary of the Treasury in 1921, Mellon delighted European visitors by inviting them to dinner at his 15-room apartment to glimpse some of the works produced by their compatriots.

The dramatically angular *East Building* (phone: 202-737-4215) was designed by architect I. M. Pei, who was given the formidable challenge of building on a trapezoidal site between Madison Drive and a slashing Pennsylvania Avenue to the north, complicated by tennis courts and rose bushes planted by Lady Bird Johnson. His solution, a building shaped like two interlocking triangles made of stone from the same Tennessee quarry as the *West Building*, is as unorthodox as it is ingenious. Whether you love it or loathe it, its galleries are a who's who of 20th-century art and a delightful gambol amid greatness. Both branches of the *National Gallery of Art* are closed only on *Christmas* and *New Year's Day;* there's no admission charge to either.

Along the underground concourse between the two buildings is a rather generic cafeteria and the *Cascade Café,* where a waterfall trickles down a glass wall. Both are good places to relax over tea or coffee. The benches along the *Mall*'s gravel paths also offer a pleasant perch for short culture breaks, and there are plenty of food vendors along the *Mall* hawking everything from hearty hot dogs, giant pretzels, and candy bars to coffee, soft drinks, and snow cones.

After reaching Third Street, turn right to get to the museums on the south side of the *Mall.* Looking at the *Mall* from its east end, over your right shoulder you will see a stunning, linear display of the *Washington Monument* and the Lincoln Memorial beyond. Notice how the *Smithsonian Castle* building on the south side juts into the *Mall.* (This was built before L'Enfant's *Mall* plan had been resuscitated, when any area on the *Mall* was fair game for development.) Directly ahead beyond Jefferson Drive, between Third and Fourth Streets, is the last vacant lot on the *Mall.* There are tentative plans to build another *Smithsonian* museum here, this one devoted to Native Americans, within the decade. The museum presently has a branch in lower Manhattan in New York City.

Now, begin walking down Jefferson Drive on the south side of the *Mall* toward the *Washington Monument.* Turn left off the *Mall* on Fourth Street, cross Independence Avenue, and walk south one block to C Street. The building on the left is the home of *Voice of America* (phone: 202-619-4700), the government-operated radio station that broadcasts news throughout the world. At last count, *VOA* broadcasts could be heard in 44 languages, including Swahili, Armenian, and Urdu. Free guided tours, given on weekdays, explain the role of the *VOA* and its umbrella organization, the *US Information Agency (USIA)*. Return up Fourth Street to Jefferson Drive and turn left. The first building on the left, the *National Air and Space Museum* (phone: 202-357-2700), is Washington's most popular tourist attraction, hosting more than eight million visitors a year. The museum, which covers air travel from man's humblest efforts to the space probes sent to the outer reaches of the solar system, has many exhibits in 23 galleries that span several blocks of the *Mall.* The *Langley Theater* presents several memorable films about flight on its dizzying five-story-high screen. Even a mildly curious visitor could easily spend a day here. There's an admission charge to the films.

The next building to the west on Jefferson Drive is the *Hirshhorn Museum* (phone: 202-357-2700), a.k.a. "the doughnut on the Mall." This round building, now part of the *Smithsonian,* houses the copious art collection of a Latvian-born immigrant of the same name who made a fortune in the US running uranium mines. At a time when the art world revolved around Europe, Hirshhorn championed the cause of many contemporary American artists. His reward was a collection worth, by most accounts, $50 million when he went on to that great gallery in the sky. The entrance is on the Independence Avenue side. The collection includes works by Mark Rothko, Jackson Pollock, Georgia O'Keeffe, and Andy Warhol. Equally impressive are the more than 2,000 sculptures, including the definitive collection of Henry Moore sculpture, on display across Jefferson Drive in the sunken *Sculpture Garden.* Also in the garden are works by Honoré Daumier, Alberto Giacometti, Auguste Rodin, and Pablo Picasso.

After wandering among the statuary, forge ahead to the next museum, the *Arts and Industries Building* (phone: 357-2700). Along with the *Castle* next door, this Victorian structure, made of red sandstone with giant industrial trusses and balconies, represents the old-guard *Smithsonian* building style. Erected in 1881 to shelter the horse-drawn carriages, pistols, machinery, and furniture exhibited at the *Philadelphia Centennial Exhibition* of 1876, this was the second of the Institution's buildings. Across the street is a festive and carefully preserved carousel, always a hit with the kids.

The granddaddy of the *Mall* is the *Castle* (phone: 202-357-2700), the original *Smithsonian Institution.* This dramatic building is generally regarded as one of the best specimens of Gothic Revival architecture in the US. You may want to stop and admire the outside of the building, but there's not much need to go in—except to stop at its *Visitors' Center*—since today it houses the *Smithsonian Institution's* administrative offices and the *Woodrow Wilson International Center for Scholars.* Also inside is the *Crypt Room,* containing the tomb of the institution's eccentric founder, James Smithson.

Smithson, a well-heeled British scientist who lived in the late 18th and early 19th centuries, was ostracized by English society because he was the illegitimate son of a duke. Although he never visited the US, his will, drafted three years before his death in 1829, left his estate to his nephew—with one stipulation. If his nephew should die without children, Smithson's entire fortune—worth $515,169 at the time—was to go to the US "to found at Washington, under the name of the *Smithsonian Institution,* an establishment for the increase and diffusion of knowledge among men." Fortunately for the enrichment of knowledge among men, the nephew died young and childless. But the US Congress, which is known for its reluctance to change, took a full 11 years to decide whether it should accept the money.

Directly behind the *Castle* is the Quadrangle, an underground complex that houses the *Smithsonian's* two newest additions, the *Arthur M. Sackler Gallery* and the *National Museum of African Art* (phone: 202-357-2700 for both). The *Sackler's* three floors afford an opportunity for the *Smithsonian* to tastefully show off its impressive holdings of Eastern art: The museum has Chinese bronzes that date back to the Shang dynasty (1523–1028 BC) and Chinese jade that dates to 3000 BC. The museum library shelves over 35,000 volumes in Chinese and Japanese.

The *National Museum of African Art's* 6,000-object collection is one of the finest of its kind in the world—and the only one dedicated exclusively to the arts of sub-Saharan Africa. One gallery has an intriguing display that shows the influence of Africa's cultural heritage on modern European and American art.

The wrought-iron benches, beds of bright flowers, and greenery on ground level between the entrance buildings of the *Sackler* and *Museum of African Art* comprise the *Enid A. Haupt Garden,* named after the New Yorker who contributed the money for its construction. The *Fountain Garden,* next to the parterre of the *Haupt Garden* near the *African Art Museum,* is a godsend on sweltering August days in the District.

Finally, the *Freer Gallery of Art* (phone: 202-357-2700) on the west side of the *Castle* is an intimate museum with an impressive collection of Asian art. It also boasts perhaps the finest cluster of paintings by American artist James McNeill Whistler, who was a friend of the museum's founder, plus a good many paintings by Winslow Homer and John Singer Sargent. The gallery was built to resemble a Florentine palace. Because the building is small and works are constantly being juggled, visitors can call to schedule an appointment to see anything not on display. It is also part of the *Smithsonian.*

The remainder of the *Mall* to 14th Street is graced by the elegant white marble *Department of Agriculture Building,* one of the first structures to take root as a result of the McMillan Commission's resurrection of Pierre L'Enfant's plan. The *Mall* seemed an ideal location for this department, as it was thought that the ground in front of the building could be used as a garden for growing experimental crops. (It wasn't.) Etched in the cornices on this side of the building are symbols of some of the staples of this department's bureaucratic toil: grains and forests, flowers and fruit. The majestic, castle-like structure across 14th Street is the *Auditor's Building,* which, in 1879, was the first building dedicated to the task of printing the nation's legal tender. Turn left on 14th Street and walk past Independence Avenue. Notice the bridge that spans this thoroughfare. Known as the "Bridge of Sighs," it is dedicated to a former secretary of agriculture as well as to Seaman Knapp, a distinguished warrior in the fight against the scourge of cotton, the dreaded boll weevil. The bridge connects the old and new buildings of the *Agriculture Department.*

Now, cross 14th Street and walk down to C Street and the *Bureau of Engraving and Printing* (phone: 202-874-3188). This is where the nation's paper money, postage and food stamps, military certificates, and presidential invitations are printed. The 25-minute, self-guided tour is a favorite of out-of-towners and gives the tourist a good view of crisp sheets of currency coming hot off the presses to be checked, overprinted with the treasury seal, cut, stacked, and bundled for transport. The bureau makes a cool $20 billion worth of bills every year. An explanation of the process of making money is provided over a public-address system. The tour finishes in the gift shop, on the Maine Avenue side of the building, where bags of money can be bought at an enormous discount (too bad it's shredded). The bureau is open weekdays until 2 PM.

The strikingly modern, new *United States Holocaust Memorial Museum* (100 Raoul Wallenberg Pl. SW, between 14th and 15th Sts.; phone: 488-0400), adjacent, is nearly impossible to get into without advance tickets. You might, however, stop in to see some of its public areas, accessible without an entrance ticket. For more information, see the *Mall Area* under *Special Places* in THE CITY.

Walk down the bureau's steps and watch the Tidal Basin come into view across the street. Cross Maine Avenue to reach the footpath that encircles this peaceful, inviting body of water. At the entrance to the footpath is a boathouse (phone: 202-484-0206) where you can rent a paddleboat—a great way to spend a lazy summer afternoon.

Walk south (to the left) on the footpath. Glimmering in the distance at the foot of the Tidal Basin's placid water is our next stop, the *Jefferson Memorial* (phone: 202-426-6822). After crossing the Outlet Bridge, continue on the footpath up to the marble dome that is the southernmost of Washington's major monuments. This lovely area, surprisingly, is land reclaimed from the mud flats of the Potomac.

It is no secret that Thomas Jefferson admired the dome motif of Rome's *Pantheon:* He adopted it for his Monticello, Virginia, home, and he worked it into the design of the *University of Virginia* in Charlottesville. And so it is fitting that his memorial is also a dome. The 19-foot statue of our nation's third president—who was also the drafter of the Declaration of Independence and a secretary of state, botanist, architect, and general Renaissance man—stands firm in the rotunda, which is inscribed with some of his most compelling words. If you're interested in some reading material on Jefferson, try talking to the gregarious Jefferson scholar who works in the bookshop beneath the monument. The monument is always open, but sections will be blocked off for renovations until sometime next year.

After leaving the *Jefferson Memorial,* take the footpath that clings to the Tidal Basin leading to the Inlet Bridge, whose two bronze, human-headed fish sculptures spout water from their mouths. After crossing the bridge, stay on the path that is the right prong of this fork at the foot of *West Potomac Park* (the left is a not-so-spectacular stroll along the Potomac). If you are so inclined, *West Potomac Park* during the spring and summer is a relaxing spot to laze, picnic, and feed the squirrels against the backdrop of the Tidal Basin.

The undisputed main attraction in this area is the 600 Yoshino and Akebono cherry trees that were a gift to the American people by the Japanese government in 1912. During the 10 to 12 days in early April that they are in full blossom, the trees are absolutely gorgeous, causing traffic jams for miles. (See also *Quintessential Washington* in DIVERSIONS.)

Continue along West Basin Drive to the next fork in the road, and take the left prong as it curves back to Ohio Drive. Turn right on Ohio Drive to the northwest and continue to the *Lincoln Memorial* (also under renovation until 1996).

Though it is made of marble, like so many other buildings in Washington, something about the *Lincoln Memorial* (phone: 202-426-6895) is more inspiring and human than the rest. Perhaps it's the man. And perhaps it's the way sculptor Daniel Chester French depicted him—as a war-weary leader sitting pensively on his monumental throne. The two best speeches delivered by our articulate 16th president, the *Gettysburg Address* and the *Second Inaugural Address,* flank his statue. This Greek-style memorial, which resembles the *Parthenon* in Athens, goes a long way toward honoring this extraordinary man. Interestingly, Lincoln's hands form his initials, A and L, in sign language (French had just finished a memorial to Thomas Hopkins Gallaudet, the pioneer educator of the deaf, before he began work on the *Lincoln Memorial*). Also, it was on the steps of the *Lincoln Memorial,* above the *Reflecting Pool,* that Dr. Martin Luther King, Jr., delivered his moving "I Have a Dream" speech.

Walk down to the *Reflecting Pool* to confirm that Lincoln's statue is indeed reflected in this body of water. Now, walk to the left (north) of the *Reflecting Pool* to the somber *Vietnam Veterans Memorial* (phone: 202-426-6841). Architect Maya Lin's unorthodox design—two below-ground, polished, black granite walls forming an outstretched "V," with the names of all those killed or missing in the war etched in the stone—was fervently criticized at first; it is now widely admired by vets and former protesters alike. Critics were mollified by Frederick Hart's bronze sculpture of three soldiers and a flagpole nearby. Another statue, commemorating the women who served in Vietnam, is situated nearby as well. Few walk away from the site without being moved; it is always open. (See also *Special Places* in THE CITY.

Continuing east (toward the *Washington Monument*) through the *Constitution Gardens,* work your way north to Constitution Avenue. L'Enfant's original city plan envisioned a grand canal that would stretch roughly from where the *Lincoln Memorial* is now to the *Capitol Building* and then south to the Anacostia River. The French planner even envisioned the president riding from the *Capitol* to the *White House* on a barge. The canal, where Constitution Avenue is now, never captured the hearts and minds of sensible Washingtonians; before the Civil War, this putrid waterway (it was also prone to flooding) was filled in and converted to a street. At the corner of Constitution Avenue and 17th Street is a tiny and well-maintained stone building that was the home of the canal's lock keeper. It is the last stop on the *Mall* and Monuments walking tour.

Walk 2: Capitol Hill

The majestic building that sits firmly atop *Capitol Hill* appears to fit as naturally in its present location as the *Parthenon* atop Athens's *Acropolis.* It is hard to imagine the imposing edifice anywhere else. Nevertheless, the *Capitol* building's present location, at the crest of what used to be called Jenkins Hill and is now known as *Capitol Hill* (or simply "The Hill"), was the third choice of the men who founded America's capital city. James Madison favored Shuter's Hill, a mound west of *Old Town* Alexandria that is now the site of the *George Washington Masonic National Memorial* (see *Walk 7: Old Town Alexandria*). Thomas Jefferson agreed with Madison until he discovered another hill overlooking what is now Foggy Bottom. But President Washington, feeling that Virginia had received her full share of the honors in launching the new republic, insisted that the seat of government be on the Maryland side of the Potomac.

With these parameters in mind, Pierre L'Enfant, the city's original architect, set about surveying the area. When he laid eyes upon Jenkins Hill he remarked: "It's a pedestal waiting for a monument." Atop this pedestal now sit the *Capitol* building, the *Library of Congress,* the *Supreme Court Building, Union Station,* congressional office buildings, and one of the city's most charming residential neighborhoods.

The wisdom of Washington and L'Enfant's vision for *Capitol Hill* was probably lost on the first batch of congressmen who arrived in 1800 from Philadelphia, the former capital. There was only one sidewalk, made from chipped stone left over from the building of the *Capitol;* it cut the shoes of pedestrians in dry weather and covered them with white mortar when wet.

When some disgruntled representatives realized that the nearest tavern was in Georgetown, they moved there and commuted by coach to work. National newspapers echoed the grumblings of the new inhabitants of this remote village, which seemed more like a refugee camp than a national capital. One reported that *Capitol Hill* has "few houses in any place, and most of them are small, miserable huts." The national press began a campaign to encourage the government to move yet again, to a more populated and more civilized city. The campaign culminated in a resolution that was brought to a vote in Congress—and nearly passed.

This discouraging attitude made the members of the *Supreme Court* all the more sluggish in leaving their beloved Philadelphia. They were already reluctant to shack up in the *Capitol* building with a Congress that eyed the Court suspiciously: The first chief justice, John Jay, had resigned five years earlier because he thought the Court lacked the support needed to uphold its decisions.

The following walking tour of *Capitol Hill* takes approximately three hours, with only brief forays into the buildings on The Hill. (If you make

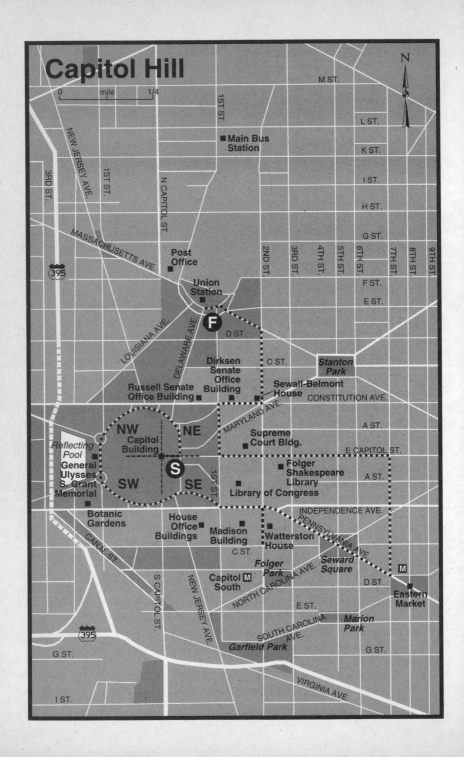

plans to visit them separately, try to allow at least a day—and note that federal properties in the nation's capital do not charge admission fees.) While you're on The Hill, consider just how far our national capital has come. And if by chance you wander too far toward the east, where crime is more prevalent, consider how far it has to go.

Our tour begins at the *Capitol* (First St. between Constitution and Independence Aves.; phone: 202-224-3121); to get there, take the *Metro* to Capitol South, then walk uphill on First Street. The East Front gives the most imposing view of this building, since L'Enfant mistakenly thought that affluent Washington would gravitate toward the east and the Anacostia River. The design of the *Capitol* is the result of Thomas Jefferson's desire for a Classical Greek–style structure. A competition was held in 1792, and the impressive design submitted by a physician named William Thornton was the winner; his award for setting the tone of the city's architecture was $500.

The *Capitol* in its early days, however, looked nothing like the imposing, dome-shaped structure seen today. When Congress arrived in 1800, the *Capitol* was a square two-story building. By 1807 a similar edifice had been built for the *House of Representatives*. The two buildings were connected by a wooden walkway—an arrangement that worked well until the British invasion of Washington in 1814. During the attack on the *Capitol*, Admiral Cockburn, a British officer, mounted the speaker's dais in the *House of Representatives* and called a mock session of Congress to order. The business was brief, putting the question to vote: "Shall this harbour of Yankee democracy be burned?" The roar of "ayes" from his men was unanimous, and the insurgents immediately set fire to the building, including a bonfire of written records and volumes from the *Library of Congress* (then housed in the *Capitol*). A sudden summer rainstorm saved the *Capitol* from total destruction.

Before advancing on the *Capitol*, notice the *Statue of Freedom* atop the dome. Though this 19-foot statue looks like an American Indian, the sculptor said he had a freed Roman slave in mind—and to prove the point, he topped off the figure with a liberty cap, the kind worn by such slaves. Jefferson Davis, then in charge of construction, objected to the antislavery implication and had the design changed. Davis went on to become the President of the Confederacy. A flag flying above the *House* (on the left, or south) or the *Senate* (on the right, or north) now means that the respective body is in session.

Enter the *Capitol*'s East Front up the steps where presidential inaugurals were historically held until Ronald Reagan decided to have his first inaugural on the West Front; George Bush and Bill Clinton then followed suit. It was here that Franklin Delano Roosevelt told Depression America that "the only thing we have to fear is fear itself" and John F. Kennedy urged Americans in the prosperous, early 1960s to "ask not what your country can do for you; ask what you can do for your country." It was also here that William Henry Harrison delivered, in a drenching downpour, the longest inaugural speech on record—only to die of pneumonia a month later.

The 10-ton bronze *Columbus Doors* lead the way to the *Rotunda,* the starting point for 40-minute guided tours of the *Capitol,* which include access to the visitors' galleries of Congress. Though this is America and you're free to wander about, even the savviest veterans of The Hill report getting gloriously lost in the complex labyrinth that is the hallowed halls of Congress. The tour is the best way to explore the *Capitol,* but you'll have to go it alone to ride the monorail between the House and Senate or to sample the famous bean soup in the *Senate Dining Room* (see *Quintessential Washington* in DIVERSIONS). The *Capitol* is open daily; the last tour is at 3:45 PM.

Return to the *East Front* of the *Capitol Building.* Ahead is East Capitol Street, which slices between the *Library of Congress* (on the right) and *Supreme Court Building* (on the left). Before wandering over to other branches of government, first inspect the *Capitol* grounds. The best way to approach is to turn left after descending the steps of the *East Front;* this is a popular broadcast spot for TV reporters and a setting for filming congress members' campaign ads. On the left, just past the *Senate* chamber and a guard post, is a path that winds downhill to the *Capitol's* western side. Follow the path as it bends to the left and pass the *Spring Grotto,* a charming little hideaway designed by Frederick Law Olmsted, creator of New York's *Central Park.* If the day is sultry, this stone grotto is a cool reprieve.

The path intersects with First Street and Pennsylvania Avenue at a traffic rotary (in Washington all roads lead to the *Capitol*). At its axis is the *Peace Monument,* a marble memorial to the sailors, marines, and naval officers who died in the Civil War. The figure of America cries on the shoulder of history; and written in America's book is a reference to Lincoln's *Gettysburg Address:* "They died that their country might live." Just off Pennsylvania Avenue is a short path leading to the spectacular *General Ulysses S. Grant Memorial,* a moving series of statues that is known for its realism and its condemnation of war. As you enter, the first group of statues is the *Cavalry Group,* featuring seven mounted men ready to charge (actually one is not so ready, as he is falling headlong off his horse into the mud). A 17-foot bronze of Grant, the commander of the Union troops, is in the middle, and the *Artillery Group* is to the south, depicting three horses pulling a cart with a cannon, and three men, each displaying a different face of battle.

This spot west of the *Capitol* affords perhaps the best perspective of the engaging structure; thanks to some impressive landscaping, the gentle slope up to the *Capitol Building* enhances its marbled stateliness. Broad flights of steps with intermittent marble terraces ascend this grassy slope, which was once used by neighborhood residents as croquet grounds. This part of the grounds used to be enclosed by an iron fence and gates that were shut in the evening by watchmen; congressmen working late would have to call the guard at the gates in order to exit. Since some chose a more expedient means of departure by smashing the gate locks with stones, the iron fence was finally removed.

The very best view of the city—from the terrace on the *West Front* of the *Capitol* overlooking the *Mall,* which gives way to the *Washington Monument,* the *Reflecting Pool,* the *Lincoln Memorial,* and beyond—illustrates what that flamboyant Frenchman who designed this city had in mind (see also *A Shutterbug's Washington* in DIVERSIONS). Take the steps up to that vantage point.

From here, walk south toward the *House of Representatives'* side of the *Capitol* and around again to the *East Front,* then take either of two paths around the egg-shaped park area on the southeast of the *Capitol.* Follow the path to First Street and the front of the *Jefferson Building* of the *Library of Congress,* the world's largest library. It began as a one-room reference collection for Congress, and was constructed in an American version of Italian Renaissance style, with the front façade a neck-craning 470 feet wide.

Grasping the breadth of its current literary holdings is like trying to calculate infinity. There are nearly 90 million items in the library, including around 6,000 books printed before the year 1500; one of only three remaining Gutenberg Bibles (the first great book to be published with moveable metal type); the world's finest collection of folk music recordings; and five Stradivarius violins, which are used for a concert series in the *Coolidge Auditorium* (First St. SE and Independence Ave.; phone: 202-707-5502). In the minute you spend standing before the *Jefferson Building,* seven more books are added to its stacks; it increases its holdings by 400 publications every hour.

The *Great Hall* features an enormous dome, columns, statues, murals, and carved balustrades (because of renovations, only guided tours are presently permitted inside the *Great Hall*). Another real treat is the *Main Reading Room,* a domed octagon that hovers over 212 reading desks and a veritable sea of reference volumes.

Since this library is widely used by researchers, there is an acute seriousness of purpose here. Adults are welcome to use the facilities, and visitors of all ages may tour the exhibit halls. At press time, the auditorium was undergoing renovation (scheduled for completion this year); meanwhile, classical music concerts are being held at the *National Academy of Sciences* (2100 C St. NW). Open daily, the library is at the corner of First St. SE and Independence Ave. (phone: 202-707-5000 for information).

Catercorner from the *Jefferson Building* are the *House* office buildings (*Rayburn, Cannon,* and *Longfellow*), three white marble structures named after former speakers of the House of Representatives. Around the corner to the left and across Independence Avenue is the *Madison Building* (101 Independence Ave. SE; phone: 202-707-8300), another *Library of Congress* annex. This white marble building primarily houses the library's extensive photo collection—more than 12 million items that span the history of photography. Upstairs on the sixth floor is the *Madison Building Cafeteria,* one of the city's best restaurant bargains, where generous portions of tasty soups, salads, sandwiches, and entrées are served in a handsome setting with a panoramic view of *Capitol Hill.* The lunchtime crowd is dense with congressional staffers, giving the constituent who pops in for lunch a feel for who is really deciding our fate.

At the corner of Second and Independence, just behind the Jefferson Building, is the rather austere, white Georgian marble John Adams Building, the first *Library of Congress* annex.

Cross the street and walk south down Second Street. On the left in the historic, Federal-era brick *Watterston House* is the *Cato Institute,* an independent public policy think tank. At the end of the block on the left is *Capitol Hill Suites* (200 C St. SE; phone: 202-543-6000), an intriguing former apartment building that has been converted into moderately priced luxury suites with fully equipped kitchens. Returning back up Second Street to Pennsylvania Avenue, take note on the right of a petite French bakery and café, *Le Bon Café* (210 Second St. SE; phone: 202-547-7200).

Turn right on Pennsylvania Avenue and make your way through the morass of dense shops along this thoroughfare. Take time to browse at the *Trover Shop* bookstore (221 Pennsylvania Ave. SE; phone: 202-547-2665). Then follow Pennsylvania Avenue as it veers off of Independence at Second Street.

The next several blocks are thick with shops, restaurants, pubs, and other commercial establishments serving the *Capitol Hill* crowd. Among the more interesting are *Taverna the Greek Islands* (307 Pennsylvania Ave. SE; phone: 202-547-8360), a Greek restaurant serving reasonably priced moussaka, souvlaki, and stuffed grape leaves; *Thai Roma* (313 Pennsylvania Ave. SE; phone: 202-544-2338), offering a unique menu of both spicy Thai and northern Italian dishes; and the *Hawk and Dove* (329 Pennsylvania Ave. SE; phone: 202-543-3300), a *Hill* treasure that is one of those dark, brooding bars filled cheek-to-jowl with an eclectic mixture of bureaucrats, congressional staffers, and barflies. Perhaps the most beloved *Capitol Hill* institution is the *Tune Inn* (331½ Pennsylvania Ave. SE; phone: 202-543-2725), which offers a hearty barbecue feast, greasy burgers, curly fries, and plenty of cheap beer. The help is notoriously surly—and patrons wouldn't have it any other way. Another colorful establishment is *Sherrill's Bakery* (233 Pennsylvania Ave. SE; phone: 202-544-2480), a throwback to your youth (if you're over 40), with wood-paneled booths, impatient waitresses, and amazingly inexpensive blue-plate specials. In the same block, *Moon Blossoms & Snow* (225 Pennsylvania Ave. SE; phone: 202-543-8181) is a terrific spot for browsers, with a variety of crafts and jewelry, as well as some clothing.

Continue down Pennsylvania Avenue through Seward Square, named after the former Secretary of State who purchased land from Russia for $7 million in a secret deal that became known as "Seward's Folly." As it turned out, Seward wasn't so foolish after all: That "big lump of ice" was mineral-rich Alaska. At the northwest corner of Pennsylvania Avenue and Seventh Street is *Bread and Chocolate* (666 Pennsylvania Ave. SE; phone: 202-547-2875), a popular tearoom that features soups, salads, French-influenced entrées, and delicious pastries.

Now walk one more block southeast along Seventh Street to the long green overhang of *Eastern Market,* the pavilion on the left, which shelters the stalls of the Virginia, Maryland, West Virginia, and Pennsylvania farmers who sell their produce, flowers, cider, and other wares outside. Inside are greengrocers and butchers hawking fresh foods, and the *Market Lunch* (phone: 202-547-8444), a densely populated luncheonette renowned for its hearty Saturday breakfasts, crab cakes on homemade fresh bread, and lines that snake out the door. The wildest and wooliest day to visit the market is Saturday. On Sundays, it mysteriously converts to a flea market, and it's closed Mondays.

In the immediate neighborhood, on the other side of Seventh Street, are several well-reputed antiques dealers. Perhaps the best is *Architectural Artifacts* (634 N. Carolina Ave. SE; phone: 202-546-2811); available by appointment for consultation only, it specializes in high-quality antique furniture without the highbrow atmosphere or prices. At the same location is a mini-market of dealers offering everything from Mission-style furniture to antique lamps and lighting fixtures. Another good antiques shop in the area is *Antiques on the Hill* (701 N. Carolina Ave. SE; phone: 202-543-1819).

Also on Seventh Street from *Eastern Market* are three good delis: *Prego* (210 Seventh St. SE; phone: 202-547-8686), which specializes in Italian food; *Misha's Place* (210 Seventh St. SE; phone: 202-547-5858), offering Eastern European cheeses and delicacies; and *Provisions* (218 Seventh St. SE; phone: 202-543-0694), which sells sandwiches and other take-out food to be enjoyed alfresco on a sunny DC day.

Two blocks up Seventh Street is East Capitol Street, the thoroughfare that separates the northeast quadrant of the city from the southeast. (It is crucial to pay strict attention to the quadrant designation in Washington since, for example, C Street NE is six blocks from C Street SE.) Turn left here amid some of *Capitol Hill*'s early residential architecture.

Five blocks ahead on the left is the *Folger Shakespeare Library* (201 E. Capitol St.; phone: 202-544-4600), a white marble building with nine bas-reliefs that feature various Shakespearean scenes. This library and theater, founded in 1930 by Standard Oil executive and Shakespeare aficionado Henry Clay Folger, contains the world's best collection of rare books, manuscripts, and research materials devoted to the Bard. The library is a handsome oak-paneled and barrel-vaulted Elizabethan palace that, along with its vast literary holdings, contains a model of London's *Globe Theatre.* The theater on the premises, which replicates the Shakespeare theater in Stratford-upon-Avon in England, hosts performances of Renaissance and medieval music, lectures, poetry, and fiction readings as well as the bard's plays; it is closed Sundays.

Return to East Capitol Street and turn left, facing the East Front of the *Capitol Building* head-on. After walking just over a block back to First Street, take a sneak preview of the *Supreme Court Building* on the right. Cross the intersection with care: The pandemonium wrought by droves of youngsters visiting here on field trips can easily distract even the most cautious pedestrian. Also, bus drivers delayed while unloading large groups of people on the *Capitol* steps tend to speed down East Capitol Street to make up for lost time.

It is appropriate that the massive *Supreme Court* edifice (First and E. Capitol Sts. NE) pays homage to ancient Greece, the birthplace of democracy, reason, and the Socratic method. The *Supreme Court* occupied seven different locations within the capital between 1800 and 1935 until it found a permanent home in this neoclassical building, designed by Cass Gilbert and completed in 1935. The main entrance, on First Street, is noteworthy for the 15 marble columns that support a pediment with the inscription "Equal Justice Under Law." This entrance is flanked by two seated statues representing "The Contemplation of Justice" and "The Guardian, or Authority, of Law."

Among the inside attractions are the *Great Hall,* lined with the busts of former chief justices; an exhibition of cartoon art depicting the *Supreme Court* and other *Court* photographs and memorabilia on display on the ground floor; courtroom lectures; and a film featuring the chief justice and several associate justices offering uncharacteristically candid descriptions of the inner workings of the *Court.* When the *Court* is in session, from October to April (two weeks on for oral arguments and two weeks off for deliberation and opinion writing), it is open to the public for hearings on Mondays and Tuesdays. Check the *Washington Post* or *Washington Times* for listings and times of cases to be heard. The building also has one of the best government cafeterias; it briefly closes to the public three times daily, from 10:30 to 11:30 AM, noon to 12:15 PM, and 1 to 1:10 PM. The *Supreme Court* is closed weekends (phone: 202-479-3395).

After descending the steps of the *Supreme Court,* a popular area for demonstrations, follow First Street to the right until reaching Constitution Avenue. The white marble building to the left of this intersection is the *Russell Senate Office Building,* one of three buildings containing the offices of senators, their staff, committee hearing rooms, and the offices of committee staff. The building to the right is the *Dirksen Senate Office Building.*

The general public is ordinarily invited to attend committee hearings for a close encounter with government activity (though many who frequent these hearings contend "inactivity" is a better characterization). Check the *Washington Post* or *Washington Times* for the daily schedule of hearings in such forums as the *Senate Foreign Relations Committee* and the *Senate Finance Committee.* Hearings that don't feature a financial scandal or a *Supreme Court* nominee generally draw an audience composed of congressional staff, lobbyists, aides to those testifying, and others with a stake in the proceedings. Nevertheless, ordinary folk have a civic right to attend, regardless of how boring the topic and how monotonous the questioning.

Located on the Constitution Avenue side, the guest entrances to the Senate Office Buildings are well marked. Committee protocol dictates that spectators form a queue outside the committee room well in advance. Lobbyists often leave their briefcases to hold their place in line as they go off for a cup of coffee or to use the phone.

Walk to the east (right from First Street) on Constitution Avenue from the *Dirksen Building* to the adjoining *Hart Senate Office Building*. This modern office complex is the newest of the Senate Office Buildings and contains an attractive, sunlit atrium with an assortment of modern statuary. As with all congressional office buildings, visitors must clear a metal detector before entering.

At the corner of Second Street NE and Constitution Avenue is the historic and stately *Sewall-Belmont House* (144 Constitution Ave. NE; phone: 202-546-3989), a museum of women's political achievements that is owned by the *National Women's Party*. The building has undergone so many additions and remodelings that it's a patchwork quilt of architectural styles. Nevertheless, part of it dates back to 1680, making it the oldest house on *Capitol Hill*. Albert Gallatin, Jefferson's and Madison's Secretary of the Treasury, is said to have hammered out the Louisiana Purchase in this house; and the only resistance to the 1814 British invasion of Washington originated here. The British responded by setting the house ablaze, damaging its front section. Displays—which cover the fight for women's suffrage—commemorate, among other noteworthy women, Alice Paul, author of the original *Equal Rights Amendment*. It is closed Mondays and weekend mornings.

Turn left on Second Street and walk past the driveway entrance of the *Hart Building*. Just two blocks up, hugging Massachusetts Avenue, is a cluster of restaurants and watering holes that are prime locations for Senate staffers' after-hours hobnobbing and alfresco lunches. The darling of this pack is the *American Café* (227 Massachusetts Ave. NE; phone: 202-547-8500), part of a beloved local chain that serves inventive American cuisine and features a bustling outdoor patio in the summer. Across the street is *Bob's Famous Homemade Ice Cream* (236 Massachusetts Ave. NE; phone: 202-546-3860), serving "designer" ice cream by Bob, who once had a high-powered Washington law practice. Also on this block is *La Brasserie* (239 Massachusetts Ave. NE; phone: 202-546-6066), which features excellent nouvelle and classic country fare, such as rabbit and quiche.

A left up Massachusetts Avenue, to the northwest, is *Union Station* (50 Massachusetts Ave. NE; phone: 202-371-9441), Washington's recently renovated railway terminal. The exterior of the Beaux Arts building has been restored to its original state, with statues aplenty, gold leaf, and columns, plus an overwhelming grand façade (adorned during the *Christmas* season with wreaths larger than many Pacific atolls). The new *Union Station* serves its original purpose as a train station, but its transportation function seems almost secondary to its over 100 upscale shops, food court, movie theater, and spectacular barrel-vaulted interior. Here too—unless you take a jaunt to one of Washington's most spirited Irish pubs, the *Irish Times* (14 F St. NW; phone: 202-543-5433) or the *Dubliner* (520 N. Capitol St. NW; phone: 202-737-3773)—is the end of the line on the *Capitol Hill* walking tour.

Walk 3: Downtown

Anchored by the *White House* and *Lafayette Square* (often called *Layfayette Park*), Washington's downtown area contains a patchwork quilt of sites that are of interest to tourists. Perhaps because the area is not a traditional urban downtown of towering office buildings and apartment complexes (a city building code forbids erecting any buildings higher than the *Capitol* and the district's monuments), it's not clear just where downtown DC begins and ends. The most accurate statement that can be made about this densely developed area is that it begins where others end: Downtown is bordered by the *Mall* to the south, Foggy Bottom to the west, *Capitol Hill* to the east, and a sliver of Adams Morgan to the north.

Downtown is home to Washington's toniest shops, especially along lower Connecticut Avenue, the capital city's Rodeo Drive. Several blocks to the south is K Street, an area of impersonal buildings known as "Lawyers' Canyon," which houses the highest concentration of lawyers anywhere in America. The country's chief executive is a resident of downtown; also here are the historical homes, museums, churches, hotels, and green spaces that surround the *White House*. Pennsylvania Avenue (known among locals as "the Avenue"), which connects the *Capitol* with the *White House* and serves as the ceremonial parade route for inaugurals and other national events, forms the downtown's southern border. To the north are take-out restaurants, colorful shops, and the distinctly Asian feel of Chinatown. Also carving out a niche are the hip music clubs, art galleries, and bohemian ambience of the area just east of the *Washington Convention Center,* the city's premiere exhibition and entertainment complex.

The logical starting point for a tour of downtown, a walk that should take approximately four hours, is the familiar white residence at 1600 Pennsylvania Avenue which must have as high (if not higher) a turnover as any Washington residence: the *White House.* The nearest *Metro* stations are McPherson Square and Farragut West.

Many interesting anecdotes accompanied George Washington's tireless efforts to secure land for the capital city from District landowners reluctant to part with their plots. Some of the most stubborn resistance came from the previous owner of the land on which the *White House* and *Lafayette Square* now sit, a canny Scot named David Burns. It is said that Burns held out so long that Washington had to appeal to him in person. After pointing out the financial windfalls Burns stood to gain from selling his coveted land, Washington added: "But for this opportunity, Mr. Burns, you might have died a poor tobacco planter."

"Aye," replied the unflappable Scotsman, "and had ye no married the widow Custis"—Custis was the name of Martha Washington's first husband, who left her rather well off—"ye'd ha been a land surveyor the noo,

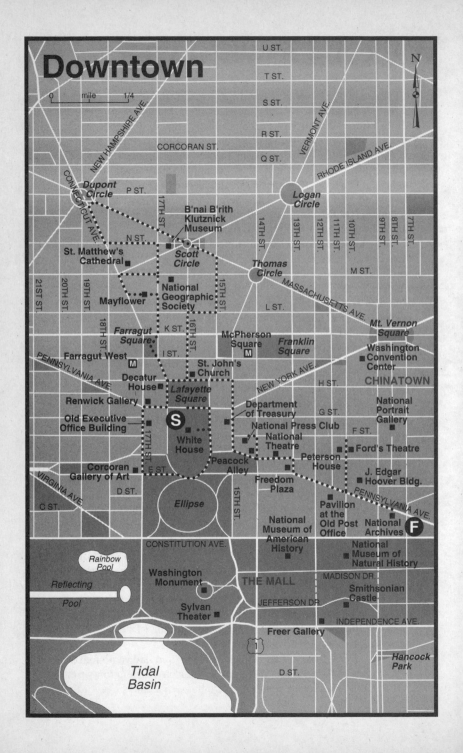

and a mighty poor one at that." Despite his reluctance to sell, Burns finally came to realize that if he didn't accept Washington's offer his land would be seized for the public good, and do him no good at all.

This elevated spot overlooking a bend in the Potomac, with a view of Alexandria to the south, was chosen for what was originally called the *Presidential Palace*. It was designed by James Hoban, an Irish architect who modeled the house after Dublin's *Leinster Hall*. The president's residence and office was not originally white, having been built with a sort of pinkish Virginia sandstone. It was only after the British set fire to it during their invasion of the capital in 1814 that the palace was painted white (to cover the damage). Over the years, the *White House* has undergone a number of renovations and reconstructions before evolving into the house we know today.

Start with a stroll through *Lafayette Park* (officially known as *Lafayette Square*). Chances are you'll pass an assortment of demonstrators attempting—perhaps quite rambunctiously—to catch the president's eye. Approaching the *White House* from the north, you'll reach the *Main Portico* on Pennsylvania Avenue. This is the First Family's front door, although it's rarely used except by tourists. From this side, this esteemed residence appears tranquil, small, and as white as freshly laundered linen. The tall, black wrought-iron fence is a striking contrast to the white façade—an imposing reminder that, though this is a free country, uninvited guests are frowned upon. This scene is especially pleasing in the evening when the bustle of Pennsylvania Avenue has died down and the trickle from the *White House* fountain can be heard. After crossing Pennsylvania Avenue, walk to the left along the sidewalk toward the east side of the *White House*.

When you reach the open gate on the east side (it is always overseen by a watchful guard), turn right into *East Executive Park*. This thin strip of green space features a series of lovely shrubs and fountains that cut a path between the *White House* and the rather self-important *Department of Treasury* building on the left. The first gate within the park on the right (known as the East Gate) is the entrance for *White House* tours (phone: 202-456-7041).

Tours of the *White House* focus on the lower floors' majestic public rooms. Tourists are not permitted entrance to the offices, kitchen, pressroom, or private living quarters of the president, located on the upper floors. At the start, visitors are led past the *Library* and the *Vermeil Room*, with its extensive collection of gilded silver; into the *China Room*, for a glimpse of the china chosen by past presidents and their wives; and on to the *Diplomatic Reception Room*, a Federal-period parlor where foreign diplomats present their credentials to the president and where Franklin D. Roosevelt delivered his legendary "fireside chats."

The next floor up is the *State Floor*, on which the *East Room*, the largest room in the *White House*, is situated. Here, press conferences, receptions, and other ceremonies are held under elaborate glass chandeliers dating from 1902. Seven presidents have lain in state here, and the *Harlem Globetrotters* played a game of basketball on this parquet floor during the Carter administration. The other rooms on this floor that are part of the *White House* tour include the *Green Room,* a reception room that was Thomas Jefferson's dining room; the *Blue Room,* furnished to represent the period of James Monroe and often thought to be the building's most beautiful; the *Red Room,* beloved of First Ladies; and the *State Dining Room,* which seats 140 guests. Carved into the fireplace mantel is a quotation by former President John Adams: "I Pray Heaven to Bestow the Best of Blessings on This House and All that shall hereafter Inhabit it. May none but Honest and Wise Men ever rule under this roof." Regardless of how one rates the results of this blessing, Adams's sentiments are unimpeachable. The tour ends on the *Main Portico* facing Pennsylvania Avenue.

The *White House* tour is a favorite tourist attraction. To avoid the crowds, the best strategy is to call your senator or representative in advance for a guided VIP tour, held early in the morning before the *White House* is open to the general public. Call far in advance for spring and summer tours. Otherwise, the *White House* is open Tuesdays through Saturdays from 10 AM to noon only. Tickets can be obtained at the East Gate in the *East Executive Park.* From *Memorial Day* to *Labor Day* tickets with a specific time are issued beginning at 8 AM from a booth on the *Ellipse* just south of the *White House.* There is no admission charge.

After exiting the executive residence, return to *East Executive Park* and continue along the east side of the *White House.* Pass through another gate to where East Executive Avenue meets E Street. Straight ahead are the *Ellipse* and the *Washington Monument.* It is on the north section of the *Ellipse* that the national *Christmas* tree is placed each year, drawing a festive crowd for its lighting by the president. Also on the 32-acre *Ellipse* are a number of softball fields.

The view from the south side of the *White House* is perhaps the best and most familiar. It was here that we saw President Kennedy scooping up his children after returning from a journey, and George and Barbara Bush leading Millie to the helicopter that would whisk them off to Kennebunkport or Camp David. And it was here that President Nixon boarded the presidential helicopter one last time after resigning his post in 1974.

Continue around the south lawn, hugging the sidewalk just outside the black iron fence. The 18-acre spot of greenery that surrounds the *White House,* known as *President's Park,* is home to more than 80 varieties of trees that have been planted over the years by almost every presidential family. The giant elm within the central oval (on the south side) was planted by John Quincy Adams—a seedling from his home in Massachusetts. There is Andrew Jackson's magnolia from Tennessee, planted as a memorial to his wife. Gerald Ford's white pine and Richard Nixon's giant sequoia can be seen within the central oval. Even Amy Carter's tree house has survived two Republican administrations, shielded by a huge silver Atlas cedar.

A favorite section of the *White House* grounds is the *Kennedy Rose Garden,* a re-creation of an 18th-century garden that was planted in 1913; these sumptuous flower beds bear the Kennedy name because JFK commissioned a re-design of the garden in 1962. Within the garden are osmanthus, boxwood hedges, tulips, chrysanthemums, and a number of other plantings. One can romp through the rose garden only during *White House* garden tours in mid-April and mid-October and during the annual *Easter Egg Roll,* when the *White House* grounds are deluged by children eight and under, bearing hard-boiled eggs and boundless energy (for more information, call the special events line at 202-456-2200; for regular tours, call 202-456-7041).

After rounding the south lawn to the gate of *West Executive Drive* (closed to the public), follow E Street to 17th Street. On the right is the rear of the *Old Executive Office Building (OEOB),* an extravagant French Second Empire structure that is one of Washington's most recognizable buildings (see below). On the left is a memorial obelisk dedicated to the army's *First Infantry Divisions* that served in World War II and Vietnam. Across the street is the *Corcoran Gallery* (see *Walk 5: Foggy Bottom*). Turn right at 17th Street for a short jaunt back up to Pennsylvania Avenue.

Notice the *Federal Deposit Insurance Corporation (FDIC)* across from the *OEOB* (Washingtonians love to speak in acronyms). The *FDIC* is the government agency that satisfies the claims of depositors when banks fail; unfortunately, the agency has been very busy of late. Also on the left, before Pennsylvania Avenue, is the *Office of the US Trade Representative,* which is responsible for setting trade policy and negotiating trade treaties with other nations. At Pennsylvania Avenue, turn right.

This stretch of sidewalk offers a better view of the *OEOB.* Formerly hosting the Navy and the War and State Departments and now used for the offices of senior-level White House officials, this almost whimsical-looking structure was so disliked by sober Washingtonians at the time of its completion that nobody wanted to pay the architect, Alfred Mullett, his fee. Today, people either love or hate the busy architectural creation—with a large contingent representing the latter category. Notice the two five-inch brass trophy guns next to the front entrance. They were captured from the Spanish in Manila Bay by the US Navy as America successfully fought the Spanish for control of the Philippines, in 1898. A tour of the building's Victorian interior, various libraries, and treaty rooms requires some planning, but is highly recommended. Reservations for Saturday tours should be made two weeks in advance on weekday mornings between 9 AM and noon (phone: 202-395-5895). There is no admission charge.

Across the street in a distinctive Second Empire–style building is the *Renwick Gallery,* the *Smithsonian Institution*'s showcase for American designs, crafts, and decorative arts (phone: 202-357-2531). The second-floor galleries, made up of the *Octagon Room* and the *Grand Salon,* have a Victorian parlor from the late 19th century and include several oil paintings as big as highway billboards. Ease back into one of the sofas and take it all in. Many of these paintings are from the collection of William Corcoran, for whom the structure was built. However, Corcoran's collection grew so large that it had to be moved down the street to its present location on 17th and E Streets (phone: 638-3211). The *Renwick Gallery* is open daily; there's no admission charge.

Walking back toward *Lafayette Square* (opposite the *White House*), notice the cluster of early-19th-century townhouses on the left. The *Blair-Lee Houses,* the historic name of the four combined townhouses which today are referred to together as *Blair House* (1651-1653 Pennsylvania Ave. NW), are brimming with history—but, alas, are open only to official guests of the president. Robert E. Lee was offered command of the Union army here by Abraham Lincoln (he refused); and when the *White House* was deemed unsafe for human habitation, Harry Truman lived in *Blair House* during the renovations.

Back to *Lafayette Square.* This pleasant park was designed by Pierre L'Enfant as the president's front yard. Thomas Jefferson, however, decided 80 acres were enough (and perhaps a bit too much to mow) and deeded much of the executive mansion's front yard to the city for use as a public park. Though named after George Washington's faithful sidekick, the real star of this park is the Andrew Jackson equestrian statue, around which everything else in the park revolves. The Marquis de Lafayette's diminutive statue, depicting the fiery Frenchman asking the French people to support the American Revolution, is on the southeast corner. Other monuments in the park include ones commemorating Major General Comte de Rochambeau, another Frenchman who distinguished himself in the American Revolution at Yorktown; Brigadier General Thaddeus Kosciusko, the Polish-born hero responsible for the fortifications at *West Point;* and Baron von Steuben, a Prussian who organized, trained, and drilled the army, beginning at Valley Forge.

The row of townhouses along Jackson Place are attractive, and their proximity to the *White House* is no coincidence. The *Carnegie Endowment for International Peace* once occupied No. 700; the *President's Drug Advisory Council* (no longer in existence) was once at No. 708; and a public service organization that owes its name to a much-mocked line from an acceptance speech at a presidential convention, the *Points of Light Foundation,* is at No. 736. On the corner is the *Decatur House* (748 Jackson Pl. NW; phone: 202-842-0920), one of the original homes built along *Lafayette Square.* This early-19th-century townhouse was built by the naval hero Commodore Stephen Decatur, who coined the line: "Our country! In her intercourse with foreign nations, may she always be in the right; but our country, right or wrong." Tours of the spiral staircase, handsome woodwork, and Federal-period furniture are conducted every 30 minutes. The home's second-floor ballroom is a real treat. There is a small admission charge to tour the house, which is closed Mondays.

To the right on H Street is the *US Chamber of Commerce Building.* Yet another of the city's ubiquitous Roman monstrosities, this one is distinguished by the flags of many nations. Formerly on this site facing *Lafayette Square* was a mansion in which Daniel Webster lived while he was Secretary of State. A bit farther down H Street on the other side of 16th Street is the charming, yellow *St. John's Church* (16th and H Sts. NW; phone: 202-347-8766), also known as "the Church of Presidents," since every president since James Madison has attended services here (see *Historic Churches* in DIVERSIONS).

Return to Connecticut Avenue, on the northwest corner of *Lafayette Square,* and turn right. This leads to Farragut Square; surrounded by office buildings and *Metro* stops, it is one of the city's busiest areas. Crowds of professionals flood this tiny park around lunchtime, and the city's fearless bike couriers congregate here when not making their deliveries. On the square is the *Map Store* (1636 I St. NW; phone: 202-628-2608), which sells cartography covering every inch of the globe. Just before Farragut Square is the *Bombay Club* (815 Connecticut Ave. NW; phone: 202-659-3727); a good Indian restaurant, it is a favorite among the local professional crowd for its central location and its kebab platter and green chili chicken.

After walking through Farragut Square, follow 17th Street due north for one block. At the corner of 17th and L Streets is the *Capitol Coin & Stamp Co.,* a wonderfully cluttered little shop that has a comprehensive assortment of political memorabilia (campaign buttons, posters, recorded speeches, photos, and presidential china) in addition to its staple of rare coins and paper money (phone: 202-296-0400).

In the next block on the left is the sumptuous, yellow-brick-and-limestone *Stouffer Mayflower* hotel (also see *Checking In* in THE CITY) with its ornate lobby. Along the way to the ritzy section of Connecticut Avenue is a display of photographs documenting the dignitaries—including Queen Elizabeth, de Gaulle, Churchill, the Shah of Iran, and Will Rogers—who have chosen the *Mayflower* for their Washington stay. After reaching the other end of the lobby, note the hotel's resident *Cartier* shop, which sets the tone for what will be encountered on Connecticut Avenue. Walk to the right up Connecticut. There are a number of pricey emporia over the next several blocks.

Walk up to where Rhode Island Avenue and M Street split off of Connecticut Avenue and turn right on Rhode Island Avenue. The red brick cathedral with the green dome and intriguing mosaic over the entrance is *St. Matthew's Cathedral,* the seat of Washington's Catholic archbishop. But this Renaissance-style cathedral's most familiar association was with President John F. Kennedy. This is where Kennedy frequently worshiped and where his funeral mass was held (an inscription marks the spot of the casket). The church is open daily (phone: 202-347-3215). In the next block is the *National Geographic Society Explorers Hall* (17th and M Sts. NW; phone: 202-857-7588), the world headquarters of the society that funds global exploration and publishes the enormously popular journal. Also within *Explorers Hall* are a number of items of interest to tourists, including the sled Admiral Robert Peary used to reach the North Pole; dioramas depicting the lives of Southwest American cliff dwellers; and the 11-foot, hand-painted, freestanding globe that has become the symbol of the *Society*. There's also *Geographica,* an interactive center for the study of geography, and a publication desk, which has a world class selection of maps, atlases, and photography books. *Explorers Hall* is open daily, and there is no admission charge.

From *Explorers Hall,* turn right on 17th Street and cross Rhode Island Avenue. On the right is the *B'nai B'rith Klutznick Museum* (phone: 202-857-6583) which contains one of the largest Jewish history collections in the US. Among the items on display are thousand-year-old coins and a 16th-century Torah wrapper. It's closed Saturdays and Jewish holidays; voluntary donations are accepted.

From here a left on N Street is like stepping into a different era. *Washingtonian* magazine calls this the best block in the city. The chaos of the surrounding thoroughfares is left behind amidst the elegance of this charming, tree-lined street. On the left is the *Iron Gate Inn* (1734 N St. NW; phone: 202-737-1370), a former 19th-century stable now dedicated to Mediterranean fare. For ambience, this place can't be beat: The original horse stalls and hay racks have been converted into dining booths, and the original fireplace is still intact. General Nelson Miles, one of the youngest generals ever—and a former owner of the buildings—is said to haunt the place. The outdoor terrace is the crowning glory of the restaurant, with a grape arbor overhead and a clear view of the dome of *St. Matthew's Cathedral.* On any given night you may find one or several of Washington's political pundits (from "Face the Nation," the "Capitol Gang," or the "McLaughlin Group") dining here. It is also a favorite of controversial biographer Kitty Kelley.

Across the street is the *Tabard Inn,* the oldest continuously operating hotel in Washington. Named after the famous hostelry in Chaucer's *Canterbury Tales,* it has a dimly lit, creaky-floored parlor filled with overstuffed sofas and chairs, antiques, and oil paintings. The inn's casual, crowded restaurant (see *Eating Out* in THE CITY) uses fresh farm produce shipped direct from Middletown, VA. Next door is the *Canterbury,* an elegant and comfortable hotel that is on the site of the *Little White House*—the residence of Teddy Roosevelt; for details, see *Checking In* in THE CITY.

Follow N Street west back to the bustling intersection of 18th Street, Connecticut Avenue, and N Street. Before heading up Connecticut to Dupont Circle, have a look into *Rand McNally* (1201 Connecticut Ave.; phone: 202-223-6751), one of the more fascinating shops on Connecticut Avenue. This wood-paneled enclave is a veritable universe of maps, globes, travel literature, and sundry knickknacks with the globe motif.

Now, make an about-face and follow Connecticut Avenue into Dupont Circle, which has been many things to many people through the years. Presently, it is a premier residential and commercial center and the nucleus of Washington's arts community, gay community, and local avant-garde. The circle is graced by the *Dupont Fountain;* it replaces a statue of Civil War Admiral Samuel Francis Dupont which was taken back to Delaware in the early 1900s by the Dupont family. Dupont Circle's benches, when not overrun by rogues and scalawags, are the domain of musicians, chess players, and political demonstrators. There is such a brimming cornucopia of shops, cafés, and galleries in this area that to do them justice would require a lengthy scroll. Certainly one stop should be at *Kramerbooks & Afterwords* (1517 Connecticut Ave. NW; phone: 202-387-1462 for the café; 202-387-1400 for the bookstore), a bookstore and café that is open all night on Fridays and Saturdays and until 1 AM Sundays through Thursdays. Otherwise, spend some time wandering the area before exploring Massachusetts Avenue and the northern reaches of this downtown walking tour.

Massachusetts Avenue leads southeast from Dupont Circle to Scott Circle, which interrupts 16th Street in its path to the *White House.* Along the stretch of Massachusetts between 18th and 17th Streets on the right is the *School of Advanced International Studies (SAIS),* the arm of Baltimore's *Johns Hopkins University* for graduate students specializing in foreign relations. Also in this block are several embassies and embassy chanceries: the *Chilean Chancery,* the *Turkish Chancery,* and the embassies of Trinidad and Tobago and Peru. Pass by the statue of the great legislator Daniel Webster on the right.

The confusion visible ahead is the intersection of Massachusetts and Rhode Island Avenues. On the right is the former headquarters of the *National Rifle Association (NRA).* One of the strongest lobbying associations in America, the *NRA* is known for fighting any form of restriction on the right of Americans to bear arms; the relevant passage in the *Constitution* appears on the building's front. Continue down Massachusetts Avenue through the circle, pausing for a few moments on the bridge spanning 16th Street. Look to the south down 16th Street: The *White House* can be seen in the distance, *Lafayette Square* is in the foreground, and the *Washington Monument* is in the background. With cars bounding up an incline to a traffic light in the immediate foreground, this is one of those Washington street scenes wrought with balance and symbolism.

Cross over the intersection of Massachusetts Avenue and 15th Street. The *Madison* hotel will be seen on the right; it's worth a short detour to stroll through its public rooms, rich with antique treasures. In the lobby is a rare Chinese Imperial altar table, black lacquered and inset with a porcelain plaque; and a Louis XVI palace commode, cartel clock, and gold leaf girandole mirror. This spot is a favorite of visiting heads of state, and features a top-security floor once favored by Russian delegations. (Should hunger strike at this point, note that there are two restaurants at the hotel, one of which serves afternoon tea; for more details see *Checking In* in THE CITY).

Go left out of the *Madison* and continue down 15th Street. Across the street are the offices of one of America's most respected newspapers, *The Washington Post* (1150 15th St. NW; phone: 202-334-7969). Its dogged investigative coverage during Watergate—a scandal that the *Post* was largely responsible for breaking to the American people—and its publication of the Pentagon Papers boosted the newspaper into national prominence. Free 45-minute tours through the building include the newsroom, pressroom, and museum; tours are offered Mondays from 10 AM to 3 PM.

At L Street turn right and go back one block to 16th Street, and then turn left (toward the *White House*). There are several points of measured interest in this next block. The *Jefferson* hotel, with its Federal-style façade, sits proudly on the right. The hotel's *Hunt Club* is a preferred venue for an early evening cocktail (see *Checking In* in THE CITY). On the opposite side of the street is the stately *Russian Embassy,* a charming, old, ivy-covered stone building that is much more active now than when its Soviet diplomats adopted the bunker mentality for the Cold War.

On the corner of the next block you will pass the *Capital Hilton.* Soon afterward, on the right, is *Tuckerman House,* a late-19th-century Romanesque dwelling just off 16th Street at 1600 I Street. Farther along 16th, near H Street (but before you reach *Lafayette Square*), is the *Hay-Adams,* thought by many to be Washington's best hotel.

After reaching *Lafayette Square* again, turn left on H Street. At the corner of H Street and Madison Place is the *Dolley Madison House* (not open to the public). Part of the original square, it was the home of the widowed former First Lady until she died in 1849. The building is now part of the *Claims Court* complex.

Cross Madison Place, remaining on H Street until reaching 15th Street. Notice the *Southern Building* just across the intersection, designed in 1912 by the renowned American architect Daniel Burnham. Burnham displayed great restraint with this building, seeming to channel his creative energies instead into its wildly decorative cornice. The *Southern Building* is now an office building. Walk down 15th Street (to the right).

On the left is *Prime Plus* (727 15th St. NW; phone: 202-783-0166), a restaurant featuring new American food such as grilled venison, and a slew of salmon dishes. The pre-theater dinner at this rather formal restaurant (it's within a short walk of the *National Theatre*) is first-rate. Farther down 15th Street is the modern incarnation of a true Washington institution, the *Old Ebbitt Grill* (675 15th St. NW; phone: 202-347-4801). Since its founding in 1856, the *Old Ebbitt* has been wandering around Washington like a nomad in one form or another—it has been a boarding house, a saloon, and a restaurant. The *Clyde's* restaurant chain acquired it in 1970, along with its collection of antique beer steins and animal heads (reputedly bagged by Teddy Roosevelt). It then became the *Old Ebbitt Grill,* and it has prospered ever since. Stop in for for breakfast, Sunday brunch, dinner, or just a gander at the big game hanging on the walls.

The Italian Renaissance building that sits on the corner of the next block down (Pennsylvania Avenue) is the *Washington* hotel (see *Checking In,* THE CITY), a grand matron of Washington hostelries. Possibly every 20th-century American president and scores of national and international dignitaries have stayed here. One of its best features is its rooftop terrace, the *Sky Terrace,* which offers great views of the *White House,* the *Treasury,* and the *Mall* area—a delightful backdrop at cocktail time.

Turn left at Hamilton Place onto Pennsylvania Avenue. Ahead towers one of Washington's cherished landmarks: the *Willard Inter-Continental* hotel. The intricate craftsmanship that went into this imposing marble Beaux Arts building is awe-inspiring, as is its roster of past guests—it has served as the temporary home for 10 presidents-elect. Have a look at *Peacock Alley,* the opulent, block-long hall with marble columns that connects the hotel's two entrances, where the term "lobbyist" was supposedly coined. Before the canopied entrance, but still in the *Willard* complex, is the *Occidental Grill* (see *Eating Out* in THE CITY), a watering hole for power brokers. Its grilled swordfish is a staple in the diet of our nation's legislators. The upscale shops in the *Willard* complex also are worth a look. And venture over to the appealing tuft of green in front of the hotel. *Pershing Park* has a glimmering pool that becomes a skating rink in the winter, a cluster of trees, and a kiosk. Beyond this park is the *District Building,* an overblown Beaux Arts affair that once housed the administration of the District of Columbia.

Walk through the passageway that houses the shops of the *Willard* complex and turn left on F Street. On the right side of the next corner is the *National Press Club Building* (14th and F Sts. NW; phone: 202-783-9090), the forum where the press hosts (and roasts) famous speakers, from foreign heads of state to American presidents and musicians. With the recent installation of shops formally called *The Shops at National Place,* it has become a consumer spending destination as well. After returning to the street, follow 14th Street back down to Pennsylvania Avenue. On the left is *J.W. Marriott,* the flagship of the international hotel chain.

Just past the *Marriott* is the *National Theatre.* First established in 1835, the *National* is one of the oldest continually operating theater organizations in America. Nevertheless, it wasn't until a comprehensive renovation in 1984 that the theater's earlier glory was recaptured. Since then, performances have included such classic musicals as *My Fair Lady* and *Annie Get Your Gun.* (Also see *Theater* in THE CITY.) Around the corner from the *National,* on 13th Street, is the recently renovated *Warner Theater,* which began as a venue for vaudeville, later became a movie house, and now stages concerts and some plays.

Return to Pennsylvania Avenue via 13th Street on the east end of an intriguing, block-long plaza known as *Freedom Plaza.* It is here that

Pennsylvania Avenue comes into full view. This street has borne witness to the emotional roller coaster ride of American history, including such memorable processions as the victory parade following World War I, in which Union and Confederate veterans marched together for the first time; the parade led by Dwight D. Eisenhower after victory in World War II; and the slain John F. Kennedy's funeral cortege, led by a riderless horse. The street has hosted demonstrations of angry farmers, African-Americans, women, and many other groups that felt betrayed by Washington. And it is along this path that the president rides—or walks, in the case of Presidents Carter and Clinton—between the *Capitol* and the *White House* on inauguration day.

It was one of those inauguration journeys that contributed to the avenue's rebirth, after its post–World War II decline. Looking out upon a combat zone of liquor stores, abandoned buildings, and downtrodden masses, President Kennedy commented to an aide on the deplorable state of the avenue. And, setting the tone for the New Frontier, he added: "Fix it."

Pennsylvania Avenue's renaissance was inspired by Kennedy's conviction, and the conviction of many others to follow, that this American Champs-Elysées must be transformed. A centerpiece of the redevelopment is the *Old Post Office* building, the gorgeous Romanesque edifice at 12th Street, with the clock tower. In addition to the government offices that remain on the upper floors, the building's pavilion has been converted into the city's most dazzling indoor mall, known as the *Pavilion at the Old Post Office* (12th St. and Pennsylvania Ave. NW; phone: 202-289-4224); even for non-shoppers, it's definitely worth a look inside. Directly behind the *Old Post Office* is the dreaded *Internal Revenue Service (IRS)*.

Proceed past the *Pavilion at the Old Post Office* to 10th Street. A slight (one-and-a-half-block) diversion up 10th Street from Pennsylvania Avenue leads to the infamous *Ford's Theatre* (511 10th St. NW; phone: 426-6924; 347-4833 for theater tickets) on the right, where President Lincoln was assassinated. After that fateful night in April 1865, the theater was closed for 100 years. It was reopened in the late 1960s, and today hosts professional productions of contemporary plays. The box in which Lincoln sat when he was shot is draped with a flag. In the basement is a collection of personal mementos of the slain president and his assassin, including the murder weapon, the suit of clothes that Lincoln wore when shot, and the flag that was draped over his casket. (Also see *Theater* in THE CITY.) Across the street is the *Peterson House* (516 10th St. NW; phone: 202-426-6830), the house in which Lincoln died. Self-guided tours are available of the house's first floor, which is decorated in period furnishings and is the only area open to the public. It's open daily; no admission charge.

Farther up 10th Street and to the right on F Street are a number of progressive music clubs, including the *9:30 Club* (930 F St. NW; phone: 202-393-0930), in a dilapidated storefront; and the *Fifth Column* (915 F St. NW; phone: 202-393-3632), a three-story dance club and art gallery.

If you're not in the mood for high-decibel music, return to Pennsylvania Avenue for the completion of this downtown walking tour. The ultra-institutional building on the left, just across from the monolithic *Department of Justice,* is the *J. Edgar Hoover Building,* headquarters of the *Federal Bureau of Investigation (FBI).* One of Washington's favorite tours is conducted here. It includes a visit to high-tech laboratories and exhibitions chronicling the *FBI's* history from the Dillinger days to the present, plus a popular firearms demonstration by a special agent. Free tours are offered weekdays; enter on E St. (phone: 202-324-3447).

And, finally, diagonally across Pennsylvania Avenue toward the *Capitol* is a stout building that marks the end of this walking tour of downtown. The *National Archives* (open daily), in addition to being our nation's file cabinet and safe deposit box, is the resting place of the great documents that are the cornerstone on which our republic was founded: the *Declaration of Independence,* the *Bill of Rights,* and the *US Constitution.* (Also see *Quintessential Washington* in DIVERSIONS.)

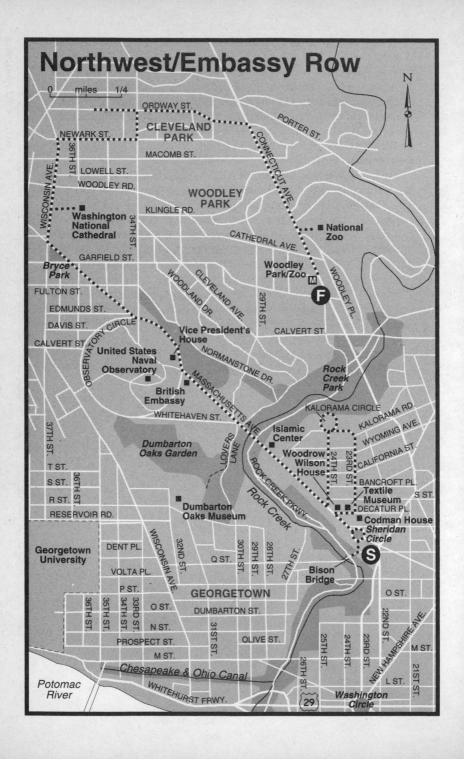

Walk 4: Northwest/ Embassy Row

As downtown Washington developed, this leafy precinct of the city became a residential haven for members of the upper crust who sought to distance themselves from their harried offices during their off hours—while remaining within a croquet shot of civilization. The northwest quadrant of DC was, until well into this century, the city's backyard. Development was slow. For most of the 19th century, Northwest (now recognized by its capital letter) was an enormous picnic ground crisscrossed by dusty, desolate paths. Its gently rolling hills were an ideal place to cavort, throw a spread, and ignore, if only for an afternoon, the enormous in-basket of the nation's business.

President Grover Cleveland, in a tradition set by President Martin Van Buren, "summered" on the higher ground of Northwest, west of *Rock Creek Park.* He was so taken with the cool breeze that comes with the elevation that, during his administration, he bought a country house to escape the fabled heat and humidity of the District. (Washington summers are characterized by an oppressive stickiness that has caused many presidents to flee the *White House* for long stretches during the hottest months.)

Though Cleveland wanted to keep his anonymity, his neighbors welcomed his arrival with fanfare, naming the area *Cleveland Park* (more about this later). The president's name lent a certain cachet to the area—the first iron truss bridge was built over Rock Creek, allowing trolley cars to cross—and the rush for development was on. Northwest is now home to a historic residential district, the sprawling *National Zoo*—where one of Washington's most popular residents, Hsing-Hsing the panda, lives—and the *Washington Cathedral,* the city's highest building, on Mount St. Albans.

A row of dazzling Beaux Arts dwellings and masterful mansions emerged northwest of Dupont Circle. Custom-built for lavish living and entertainment, each is a testament to the carefree era before FDR applied the brakes of regulation to the runaway freight train of free enterprise. This area is known as Kalorama, the name of the area's first estate and country house, built in 1807 by businessman and diplomat Joel Barlow (US Consul to Algiers from 1795 to 1797). The name "Kalorama," a Greek word meaning "beautiful view," is apt, since the area looks out across the capital and the Potomac River to northern Virginia.

The stock market crash of 1929 and the ensuing Depression severely depleted the bank accounts of many of these proud homeowners. A number of the palatial mansions were divided into apartments or sold intact for use as embassies. In fact, the influx of foreign delegations was so pervasive that today the corridor along Massachusetts Avenue is known as Embassy Row.

It is from Sheridan Circle, the heart of Embassy Row, that this walking tour begins (the closest *Metro* stop is Dupont Circle). *Cleveland Park* represents the outer limits of this rather long walking tour, which will require about five hours.

Sheridan Circle is just a few blocks northwest of Dupont Circle, up Massachusetts Avenue. This main thoroughfare slices diagonally through three blocks between Dupont and Sheridan Circles. Though it was not conceived by Pierre L'Enfant, it represents everything the French city planner revered in a circle: a small, prim park, from which radial avenues branch off in all directions, with a monument at the center. The statue's sculptor, Gutzon Borglum (who also carved the presidential portraits on Mount Rushmore), featured the circle's namesake, Union Army General Philip Sheridan, sitting atop his favorite horse.

Begin to orbit the circle along the outside sidewalk, noting the subdued splendor of the architecture of the surrounding mansions. The circle's present-day tranquillity belies a violent turn of events here on September 21, 1976, when Chilean Ambassador Orlando Letelier and his aide, Ronni Karpen Moffitt, were killed by a remote-controlled car bomb. The Chilean secret police and army officials were later implicated in the assassination. A small memorial to the pair rests on the outside curb of the southeast quadrant of the circle. Walk just short of one revolution around the circle and note the *Turkish* and *Romanian Embassies* with their mammoth antennae perched on top.

You may want to take a jaunt down to Q Street, in the direction in which General Sheridan seems to be gazing. Spanning Rock Creek and leading into Georgetown is the impressive Dumbarton Bridge. It's more commonly called Bison Bridge because of its four sculpted bison (bison are the creatures that paleontologists say some native Americans drove over cliffs in herds). From here you can see the *Washington Monument* poking above buildings on the left; the spires of the *Washington Cathedral* are visible on the right. The perpetual hum of Rock Creek Parkway traffic is underneath.

The bridge's arches are supported by copper Indian heads in full headdress, sculpted by Glenn Brown from a life mask of the Sioux chief Kicking Bear. Don't attempt to dangle over the side to find them (remember what happened to the bison); they are more safely visible from the green handrail just to the right before reaching the bridge, or from Rock Creek Parkway, below.

Head back to Sheridan Circle, noticing the stately *Turkish Embassy* on the left, a villa originally built for Edward Everett, the inventor of the bottle cap. Fortunately, Massachusetts Avenue separates the Turkish and Greek embassies, otherwise at uncomfortable proximity considering the two countries' historical animosity toward one another. Meanwhile, the *Embassy of Cyprus,* the Aegean island that has long been the focus of dispute between these two countries, lies equidistant from the Turks and the Greeks on R Street. On the right is the attractive *Romanian Embassy* and an adjoining chancery building.

After reaching Sheridan Circle, walk left on the outer sidewalk. On the left is the Mediterranean-style *Barney Studio House* (2306 Massachusetts Ave.; no longer open to the public). At the turn of the century, artist Alice Pike Barney complained that America's capital city was a cultural wasteland—and decided to do something about it. Her home, the second to be built on Sheridan Circle, became a meeting place for Washington's cultural elite.

After rounding Sheridan Circle to the left, start up Massachusetts Avenue to the northwest. This is Embassy Row's main street. Though security is tight and the limos, blue suits, and attaché cases are aplenty, stroll through this neighborhood slowly; enjoy its splendid and occasionally eclectic architecture, its cosmopolitan feel, its United Nations of national banners, the aromas of a cornucopia of cuisines, and, perhaps, pedestrians sporting a turban, an African gown, or exotic footwear or jewelry from the far reaches of the globe. Embassy Row is truly a global village.

On the right when heading up Massachusetts Avenue are the *Chilean, Haitian,* and *Pakistani Embassies.* Before going right on Decatur Street, notice the *Cameroon Embassy* (2349 Massachusetts Ave.). This ornate mansion—with a cone-shaped turret, extraordinary detail, and a fleet of limousines out front—is one of the most impressive buildings on Embassy Row.

Walk down Decatur Place about a block to a delightful stone and concrete staircase, framed by gas lamps on either side and crowned by a quietly trickling lion's head fountain. The staircase is known as the *Decatur Terrace Steps* (also referred to by some area residents as the "Spanish Steps" because of its vague resemblance to the *Piazza di Spagna* staircase in Rome).

But before heading up the steps, have a look at the mansion to the immediate right. This is the *Codman House* (2145 Decatur Pl.), built in 1907 as a Washington residence for Miss Martha Codman, unmarried until the age of 72, when she wed a Russian tenor who was half her age. Codman was "of Boston and Newport"—a delightful designation that was the seal of good breeding in her day. Codman House is a deep-red brick, four-story townhouse with stone panels of festoons between the second- and third-floor windows. The house was later sold to Dwight Davis, who, aside from being a former Governor of the Philippines, is best remembered for donating the *Davis Cup* to the sport of tennis. Scheduled for "condo-ization" in the late 1970s, the house was fortunately bought by a neighbor and now is in the safe harbor of the *National Register of Historic Places.*

Climb the steps to S Street. Ahead is the exclusive Kalorama district. Architecture buffs should walk the length of 23rd Street to 2122 Kalorama Road, a Tudor mansion built in 1911 for the mining magnate W. W. Lawrence. One of the more spectacular buildings in this posh area, it is now the residence of the French ambassador. Proceed left down Kalorama

Road to Kalorama Circle for a real *kalorama,* in the Greek sense, down into *Rock Creek Park* (for more on the park, see *Special Places* in THE CITY. Return to S Street via 24th Street.

The first of two museums to the left, the *Woodrow Wilson House* (2340 S St. NW; phone: 387-4062), is where Wilson chose to live after he left office. (Most 20th century US presidents left town after their years of what Thomas Jefferson called "splendid misery" as the nation's chief executive.) The Georgian Revival house in which the 28th president and his wife lived after Wilson's second term—during which he led the country through World War I—is now a museum. Several doors down from the *Woodrow Wilson House,* on the same side of the street, is the *Textile Museum,* a great temple to the art of weaving; for more details on both museums, see *Museums* in THE CITY.

Return past the *Woodrow Wilson House* to Massachusetts Avenue. On the left at the intersection is a statue of the Irish patriot *Robert Emmett,* dedicated in 1966 to mark the 50th anniversary of Irish independence. Make a right on Massachusetts, the broad avenue that will lead past the *Japanese Embassy,* the *British Embassy,* the vice president's home, and up Mount St. Albans to *Washington National Cathedral.* Street signs in this neighborhood include the names of the embassies located on the adjoining side streets.

Just past the intersection with California Street, the *Japanese Embassy* is on the left. (Try to ignore the gray, colossal, and rather ugly administrative building next door.) The plans the American architects conjured up for this neo-Georgian embassy house, with its cobblestone courtyard surrounded by a row of trees and concave arch above the balcony that suggests the rising sun, were approved by the emperor himself.

Farther up Massachusetts Avenue on the right is another architectural style from yet another corner of the globe. The handsome *Islamic Center,* a.k.a. "the Mosque" (2551 Massachusetts Ave; phone: 202-332-8343), provides a place of prayer for the diplomatic missions in Washington that represent nearly 40 predominantly Islamic countries. The faithful are called to prayer five times a day. Anybody is invited into the mosque, which faces Mecca; its lush interior is replete with thick Persian carpets (there are no chairs) and intricate Turkish tiles that grace the walls. Visitors must keep with custom, though, for this is a house of worship. No shoes (leave them at the entrance), shorts, short sleeves, or bare female heads (head coverings are provided). It's open daily, and tours can be organized upon request.

After crossing over Glover Bridge, which spans *Rock Creek Park,* note a series of Latin American embassies on the left. The most striking—some would say appalling—is the *Brazilian Embassy.* This strange building looks like a top-heavy ice cube that somehow keeps from melting.

The *British Embassy* is not far along on the left. With its Queen Anne architecture and stately English country house look, it is the quintessential diplomatic residence, complete with a fire-engine red British telephone booth in front of the embassy annex next door. A statue of Winston Churchill, flashing a "V" for victory along with an impish grin, extends greetings and salutations. Interestingly, this statue places the former British prime minister with his right leg on American territory and his left in the United Kingdom. Sir Winston considered the idea smashing; after all, his mother was an American, his father a Brit.

Across the street is a garden and fountain dedicated as a memorial in May 1991 to the Syrian-born poet and philosopher Kahlil Gibran. His book *The Prophet,* which has sold millions of copies, is a moving contribution to cultural and religious understanding. Among the passages inscribed in stone is this one: "We live only to discover beauty. All else is a form of waiting." If you have never before stopped at this memorial, sit on the circular bench and take a few pensive moments to drink in the poet's poignant prose.

Continue up Massachusetts Avenue to the visitors' entrance to the *United States Naval Observatory* (34th St. and Massachusetts Ave. NW; phone: 202-653-1543)—an often overlooked Washington attraction. In addition to maintaining the plush, pastoral surroundings, the work of the observatory is to provide the most accurate time and astronomical information for air, space, and sea navigation. Tours include a look at the clocks that keep the most accurate time on the planet (a good place to set your watch) and the telescopes that track planetary positions. Due to the sensitivity of some of the instruments, Massachusetts Avenue gives the *Naval Observatory* a wide berth, ensuring that the occasional rumbling dump truck won't send the world's navigation into disarray. It's closed on federal holidays and *Christmas;* there's no admission charge.

Follow Massachusetts Avenue uphill as it rounds the *Observatory* grounds. The vice president's house comes into view on the left—a late Victorian mansion with a turret, dormers, and a surrounding porch the size of a Tennessee soybean field. Completed in 1893 and first occupied by the superintendent of the *Naval Observatory,* it became the home of the Secretary of the Navy in 1928. It wasn't until 1974 that it was officially designated the residence of the VP. Since Nelson Rockefeller preferred to live in his own rather comfortable area home, Walter Mondale was the first vice president to live here full-time. The house has had until recently a reputation for a terribly leaky roof, which was brought under control only after hundreds of thousands of dollars were spent on repairs during the Bushes' and Quayles' stays here.

After passing the enormous anchor at the employee entrance of the *Naval Observatory,* you will reach Wisconsin Avenue, which begins the climb up Mount St. Albans toward *Washington National Cathedral.* The chunk of terra firma at the intersection of Massachusetts and Wisconsin Avenues was once thought to yield the best view of the capital city, according to James Bryce, a British ambassador in the early part of this century. (That was before a cluster of rather unseemly townhouses took root.) When a glowing magazine article that he wrote about the spot was recently uncovered, a triangular park was named for him here. *Bryce Park* is an excellent place to rest after making the gradual—but persistent—climb to the District's highest point.

Before venturing into the *Washington Cathedral,* you may want to explore one of several good restaurants in the next block of Wisconsin Avenue. First up on the left is *Primavera* (3700 Massachusetts Ave.; phone: 202-342-0224), a rather pricey Italian place with both indoor dining and a courtyard. Recommended dishes include fried calamari, swordfish, and *tiramisù.* Much less expensive and certainly less formal is the *Zebra Room* (3238 Wisconsin Ave.; phone: 202-362-8307), which, true to its name, is clad in zebra wallpaper. The *Zebra Room* has featured half-price pizza every Tuesday and Thursday evening since the early 1960s and is usually packed with a loyal clientele. A memorial plaque for a late customer tells it all: "Every Tuesday night he enjoyed beer, his friends, and pizza here. In that order." Across Macomb Street is the *Cactus Cantina* (3300 Wisconsin Ave.; phone: 202-686-7222), offering laudable Tex-Mex food in a festive, neon-saturated environment. For classic Thai cuisine, try *Thai Flavor* next door (3709 Macomb St.; phone: 202-966-0200).

Now, return down Wisconsin Avenue to the pièce de résistance of the Northwest walking tour: the *Cathedral Church of St. Peter and St. Paul,* better known as the *Washington National Cathedral* (Wisconsin Ave. at Woodley Rd.; phone: 202-537-6200). For more on this dramatic, twin-towered Gothic cathedral that is the closest thing the US has to a national church, see *Historic Churches* in DIVERSIONS. You may want to allow at least an hour to see the *Space Window, Bishop's Garden,* and other treasures here.

Afterward, amble several blocks up Wisconsin Avenue to Newark Street and turn right. This area is the *Cleveland Park Historic District,* one of the District of Columbia's loveliest neighborhoods, now home to well-to-do lawyers, bureaucrats, and journalists (the city's three main professions). It was on Newark Street that President Grover Cleveland built a country house (now long gone). By the turn of the century, *Cleveland Park* became a full-time suburban community, attracting several noteworthy architects who built the gorgeous, large frame houses with front and back porches, an occasional turret, and gazebos that can still be seen today.

Walk down to 3501 Newark Street. This farmhouse, built by General Uriah Forrest, dates from 1740. Known as *Rosedale,* it is where George Washington and Major L'Enfant dined when they were working on the boundary plans for the 10-square-mile federal district.

Turn left on 34th Street, and left again on Ordway Street. On the right is a bizarre dwelling (3411 Ordway) designed by architect I. M. Pei as a favor to his friend and business partner, William Slayton; it's hard to see from the street, but in any event not everyone considers it a pleasant thing to look at. A cluster of houses at the end of the block, built by the Faulkners, a family of architects, is worth a look.

Return down Ordway Street east to Connecticut Avenue. Go right on Connecticut; the next block features a number of pubs, restaurants, and bookstores, as well as the *Cineplex Odeon Uptown Theater* (3426 Connecticut Ave.; phone: 202-966-5400). Just "the *Uptown*" to locals, the theater features blockbuster classics such as *Gone With the Wind, Lawrence of Arabia,* and other epics where they were meant to be shown—on the big screen. Farther down the street is *Ireland's Four Provinces* (3412 Connecticut Ave.; phone: 202-244-0860), a cavernous drinking haunt with Gaelic musicians, *Harp* beer on tap, and plenty of corned beef and cabbage. Across the street is *Roma* (3419 Connecticut Ave.; phone: 202-363-6611), an Italian restaurant with a Romanesque courtyard, bubbling fountain, and tables shaded by a grape arbor. Weather permitting, request to sit outside. *Vace* (3315 Connecticut Ave.; phone: 202-363-1999), farther down Connecticut, is an Italian deli with fresh pasta, sauces, pizza, and the wine to wash it all down.

Continue down Connecticut Avenue past the DC branch library on the right to the last stop on the Embassy Row/Northwest walking tour. Several blocks down on the left—the signs will guide you in—is the *National Zoological Park,* better known as the *National Zoo.* A continuation of *Rock Creek Park* (where Teddy Roosevelt used to take his strenuous walks), the expansive, 163-acre zoo is a Washington treasure. Its enormity gives its 4,000 residents plenty of room to move about over land and water that simulate their natural habitats. There are elephants, giraffes, gorillas, jaguars, but now only one panda left of the famous pair donated by the People's Republic of China; Hsing-Hsing's mate, the female Ling-Ling, died in late 1992. However, you may want to see how the young elephant, Kumari, is sizing up; she is the *National Zoo*'s first ever elephant calf, and was born in December 1993. She weighed about 300 pounds in the early spring of 1994, but still had a way to go to catch up to mother Shanthi, who just before delivering weighed a whopping 8,900 pounds! (Shanthi gained 1,000 pounds during her 22-month pregnancy.) For more on the zoo, see *Special Places* in THE CITY.

To return to the vicinity of where the walk began, turn left after exiting the zoo on Connecticut Avenue. Several blocks on the right is the *Woodley Park/Zoo* metro stop on the red line, just one stop from Dupont Circle.

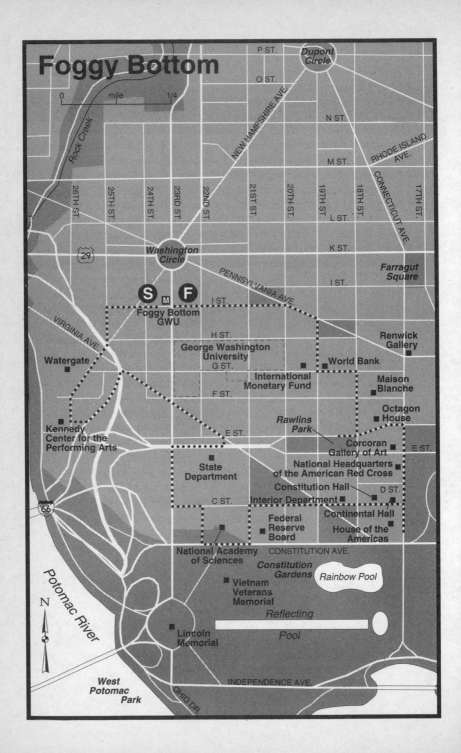

Walk 5: Foggy Bottom

America was spared a potentially embarrassing misstep when Thomas Jefferson's idea of locating the *Capitol* building on a bump of land rising out of a malarial swamp was ignored. According to the early plan for the city, the ordinarily lucid Jefferson originally intended to place the *Capitol* in a town named Hamburg, also known as Funk (it was founded by a German immigrant named Funks): Congress narrowly escaped being dubbed Hamburgers or Funksters.

This mosquito-ridden community on the Potomac in the District's southwest was later known by the less appealing but well-deserved nickname Foggy Bottom. It may have been Jefferson's intention to discourage legislators from meddling in the affairs of the executive branch by plopping them down in an inhospitable district to tend to mosquito bites and soggy shoes. Or maybe he just hadn't ventured over to Jenkins Hill, the lovely spot where the *Capitol* was finally situated. We'll never know.

Foggy Bottom, the mention of which usually causes visitors to chuckle, earned its memorable name from the omnipresent bank of "fog" that hung over this low-lying area when it was the city's industrial center. In contrast to the marble monuments, museums, and government offices that fill the area today, it was then home to a glass factory, a coal depot, a brewery, and wharves. The brewery spewed forth enough beer to make its founder, Christian Heurich, a millionaire many times over, and the factories spewed forth enough smog and foul stench to ward off middle class development until after World War II. Throughout the 19th century, Foggy Bottom was home to Irish, Italian, and German immigrants who were starting anew in this once-grim enclave of the New World.

The factories eventually moved away, and Foggy Bottom began to emerge from its proletarian squalor. The building of the new *State Department* after World War II cleared the way for a process of gentrification, and many of the small but charming row houses that comprise the *Foggy Bottom Historical District* (an area clearly marked with signs) were saved from the wrecker's ball.

Foggy Bottom is now dominated by the imposing structures of the *Kennedy Center,* the *Watergate* complex, and *George Washington University*, and offers excellent views of the Potomac, especially from the *Roof Terrace* of the *Kennedy Center.* The broad avenues are home to numerous government buildings, shops, and restaurants. Our three-and-a-half-hour walking tour of the area begins on the plaza area of the Foggy Bottom/GWU *Metro* station.

To the south and east of the *Metro* station is *George Washington University (GWU).* George Washington had hoped that a national university equal to *Oxford* and *Cambridge,* endowed with funds from his stock in the

Potowmack Canal Company, would be founded after his death. Congress couldn't decide what role government should play in the university and, in making no decision, forfeited Washington's stock. Instead, the non-sectarian *Columbian College,* founded by the Baptist Church in 1821, became *George Washington University* a century later. The renamed university moved to Foggy Bottom and become instrumental in the area's redevelopment, snatching up and restoring many of Foggy Bottom's fine old homes (*GWU* is the second-largest landholder in Washington next to the federal government). Adjacent to the campus, on 23rd Street, is the *GWU Hospital* (901 23rd St. NW); Ronald Reagan was rushed into surgery here after being shot in March 1981.

Begin walking down I Street to the right. After crossing 24th Street and New Hampshire Avenue, notice some of the colonial-style, wooden homes of the factory workers located on this tree-lined street. Lumped into the *Foggy Bottom Historical District,* they have gone markedly upscale as the neighborhood has been gentrified and university professors and administrators have moved in. Turn left on 25th Street, where a row of some of the most charming houses can be seen on the left side of the street between Nos. 813 and 803.

Before crossing the traffic circle at Virginia Avenue, note an otherwise ordinary and rather humdrum *Howard Johnson Motor Lodge* to the right. It figures prominently in the notoriety of the *Watergate* complex, the serpentine, upscale residential monstrosity across the street. From Room 723 at *HoJo's,* President Richard Nixon's aides G. Gordon Liddy and E. Howard Hunt monitored the break-in by five men at the *Democratic National Committee Office* on the sixth floor of the *Watergate* building (you'll find a doctor's office there now). Their actions and bungled cover-up, which led to the eventual resignation of the late Nixon, are firmly etched in the nation's conscience along with the *Watergate* name.

The *Watergate* office/apartment complex is one of the choice addresses of Washington's power elite. (It gets its name from the steps leading up from the river behind the *Lincoln Memorial.*) Also in the complex are the *Watergate* hotel, with contemporary-style rooms and balconies that open up on the Potomac for spectacular sunrises (see *Checking In* in THE CITY); one of the capital's better (and pricier) restaurants, *Jean-Louis* (see *Eating Out* in THE CITY), a stronghold of nouvelle cuisine run by top Washington chef Jean-Louis Palladin; Palladin's newer and more reasonably priced *Palladin* (phone: 202-298-4455); and a collection of exclusive shops.

After exploring the *Watergate,* cross the traffic circle—which is anchored by a statue of Benito Juárez, the 19th-century Mexican revolutionary hero and president—to enter the *John F. Kennedy Center for the Performing Arts* (usually just called the *Kennedy Center*). Though the building has been criticized for being dull and unadorned, it affords a panoramic view from its roof terrace. More importantly, the center put a hitherto absent Washington, DC, on the cultural map with high-caliber opera, theater, film, ballet, musicals, and concerts (phone: 202-416-8341). For more on the *Center,* see *Theater* in THE CITY, and *Quintessential Washington* ("A Kennedy Center Opening") in DIVERSIONS.

After walking through the *Hall of States* and the *Hall of Nations,* two grand halls that separate the *Kennedy Center's* major theaters, exit the building from the east. To avoid the phalanx of streets ahead, take the paved path that circumvents them and leads northeast to Virginia Avenue, a major thoroughfare that slices through Foggy Bottom. To get to the path, follow the sign with a trolley on it labeled "Columbia Plaza Path and Tram."

Head to the right down Virginia Avenue for several blocks, to E Street and an equestrian statue of Bernardo Gálvez, Spain's Governor of Louisiana in 1776. Dedicated in 1976, in commemoration of our *Bicentennial,* it conveys appreciation to Spain for its unwavering support in the struggle for American independence.

Across the street is the State Department, confined to a remarkably uninspiring, stolid building with all the charm of a Midwestern post office. This is where our country's (some would say equally stolid) foreign policy is made. Our government's first Cabinet department, the *State Department* was founded in 1789. Before decamping to Foggy Bottom (the *State Department* itself is sometimes referred to as Foggy Bottom), it was housed in the *Old Executive Office Building,* one of the capital city's more impressive structures, located near the White House.

Behind the *State Department's* undistinguished exterior are the splendidly furnished, artistically excellent *Diplomatic Reception Rooms.* Located on the eighth floor, these stately salons contain an outstanding collection of 18th- and 19th-century American art and furniture, much of which is historically significant. Foreign diplomats are received here—as are visitors who have the foresight to make a reservation for a tour. Call a week in advance to schedule a weekday tour. There is no admission charge (phone: 202-647-3241).

Moving counterclockwise, circle the *State Department* building by taking a left on 23rd Street and a left on C Street; then turn right on 22nd. The *Constitution Gardens* and *Vietnam Veterans Memorial* are ahead. The white, Greek-style building on the left is the *National Academy of Sciences,* an organization that got its start during the administration of Abraham Lincoln and functions as a link between science and government. The *Academy* can mobilize thousands of scientists in a nanosecond to provide scientific information to the government or synthesize conflicting information for lawmakers. Though the inside of this building is rarely visited by tourists, its *Great Hall,* dome, and Foucault pendulum (which represents the earth spinning on its axis) are worth a look. It's closed weekends; there is no admission charge (phone: 202-334-2000).

The well-groomed grounds of the *National Academy of Sciences* are nice for a stroll. Of particular interest is the *Einstein Memorial,* in the back of the building on the southwest corner. A path that plunges into a clump of bushes leads the way to the larger-than-life statue of Albert Einstein. The pensive genius sits, tousled hair and all, with a tablet that contains mathematical equations summarizing three of his most important scientific contributions: the photoelectric effect, the theory of general relativity, and the equivalence of energy and matter. The statue was sculpted in the characteristic "mashed potato" style of Robert Berks. Children love to sit in Einstein's lap.

Walk out to Constitution Avenue, formerly B Street and before that a putrid canal that extended from the Potomac to the *Capitol Building*. Turn left on the sidewalk. A few paces will lead to 21st Street; turn left again.

The deeply conservative building on the right is home to the *Federal Reserve Board*. The conduit for the nation's cash, the *Fed* determines the nation's monetary policy (interest rates, cash flows, and so on) and wields enormous clout in financial circles. The *Fed's* board ordinarily meets on Wednesdays at 10 AM, and anyone interested can hear abstruse disputations on banking and regulatory matters—the meetings are usually open to the public. (For a list of the topics to be discussed, call 202-452-3206.) A 45-minute tour, complete with a film that explains the *Federal Reserve,* is given on Thursday afternoons; other tour times can be arranged by appointment for groups of 10 or more (phone: 202-452-3149). The building contains a respectable collection of 19th- and 20th-century paintings and sculpture in a gallery that is open weekdays from 11:30 AM to 2 PM only (phone: 202-452-3000). There is no admission charge to the *Fed*.

Turn right on C Street and walk between the old (on the right) and new buildings of the *Federal Reserve*. C Street curls around to the left in front of the *Office of Personnel Management,* an agency that sets government personnel policy and manages (so to speak) the civil service.

Directly across Virginia Avenue is the continuation of C Street. To the right is an attractive statue of Simón Bolívar, the liberator of much of South America. Spanning two blocks, the building on the left is the *Interior Department.* The *Interior Department Museum,* housed in the same building, contains exhibits covering the breadth of the *Interior Department's* purview, which includes the *National Park Service,* land reclamation, geological surveys, Indian affairs, land management, wildlife preservation, and a dense forest of other duties. The centerpiece of the museum is its portrayal of the opening of the Wild West, illustrated by bounties, patents, paintings, photos, and original land grants. Also on display and for sale is an impressive collection of Indian crafts and artifacts. The museum is closed weekends; no admission charge (phone: 202-208-4743).

Continue down C Street across 18th Street toward the *Ellipse,* which is straight ahead. On the left is the Romanesque *Constitution Hall.* Built in 1930 by John Russell Pope, this was the city's premier concert venue until the *Kennedy Center* stole the scene. Seating 4,000, it has attracted such renowned performers as actor Stacy Keach and pianist André Watts.

Toscanini thought the concert hall's acoustics were remarkable. Watch the newspapers for concert announcements (phone: 202-638-2661).

The ornate Beaux Arts building on D Street between 18th and 17th Streets is the headquarters of the *Daughters of the American Revolution (DAR)*, an elite group of women who trace their lineage back to the American colonies' struggle for independence. The building, known as *Continental Hall*, has a vast portico supported by Ionic columns, and houses the *Daughters of the American Revolution Museum* (see *Special Places* in THE CITY).

After reaching 17th Street, see an unsung but noteworthy tourist destination housed within the majestic Beaux Arts building on the right. The *House of the Americas*, formally called the *Pan American Union Building*, faces 18th Street as well as Constitution Avenue; it's made of white Georgian marble and black Andean granite. This is the headquarters of the *Organization of American States (OAS)*. Dating back to 1890, the *OAS* is the oldest international political organization with which the US has been steadily associated (main phone: 202-458-3000; 202-458-3751 for tour appointments). Directly behind the main building is the *Art Museum of the Americas*, featuring paintings and sculpture; it's closed Sundays and Mondays (phone: 202-458-6016). See *Special Places* in THE CITY for more details on both.

Now retrace your steps up 17th Street. Just past *Continental Hall* on the left, in a building as white as hospital sheets, is the *National Headquarters of the American Red Cross*. The American branch of this international organization was founded in 1881 by Clara Barton in an attempt to humanize an increasingly hostile world. The administrators who work here coordinate the more than 3,000 *Red Cross* chapters across the country, which provide vital services ranging from disaster relief and blood banks to children's swimming lessons. The *Red Cross* is known best for its brave and selfless service tending the wounded through the Civil War, the two World Wars, and countless other conflicts. The centerpiece of the building is an enclosed marble atrium commemorating the women who ministered to the Civil War wounded. A century of *Red Cross* uniforms is on display, as is a retrospective of recruitment posters; a trilogy of Tiffany stained glass windows brightens the lobby on the second floor. Altogether, it's worth a look. It's closed weekends; there's no admission charge (phone: 202-737-8300).

Continue the trek up 17th Street. The next point of interest is the *Corcoran Gallery of Art*, just past E Street on the left. The Beaux Arts building that houses this fine American collection has flourishes of the clean lines characteristic of American architecture (it was Frank Lloyd Wright's favorite building in Washington). It's closed Tuesdays (phone: 638-3211; also see *Special Places* in THE CITY).

The oval, northern edge of the *Corcoran* is rimmed by New York Avenue, which slashes back to the southwest. Follow New York to the corner of 18th Street. On the right is the handsome *Octagon House*, an

18th-century building that was spared sacking and burning by the British during their invasion of Washington in 1814. (*Octagon House* is a misnomer, since it has only six sides; nobody seems to know how it got its name.) President James Madison and wife Dolley took refuge here until 1815, the year the *Treaty of Ghent* was signed with Britain, ending the War of 1812. The *American Association of Architects,* whose headquarters are adjacent to *Octagon House,* saved the house from deterioration almost a century ago; they also periodically restore it. Tours are available. It's closed Mondays; donations are suggested (phone: 638-3105). For more details, see *Special Places* in THE CITY.

A just reward for following this walking tour awaits the tuckered-out tourist in *Rawlins Park,* just past 18th Street on the left. This park is soft and inviting, despite being named after Ulysses Grant's hard-bitten chief of staff and, later, secretary of war. The park's two pools are home to goldfish and, when the season is right, blooming water lilies. Lingering about on spring days amid the tulip-tree magnolias is a favorite pastime of visitors and locals alike.

After relaxing in the park, return to the *Octagon House* and head north up 18th Street. Cross F Street; *Maison Blanche* is on the right. This pricey French restaurant has long been a favorite of newspaper columnist and humorist Art Buchwald (see *Eating Out* in THE CITY). Where 18th Street meets G Street one block past *Maison Blanche,* turn left. Then turn right on 19th Street.

Towering over both sides of this shady thoroughfare are the headquarters of the twin pillars of world finance and development, the *International Monetary Fund (IMF)* and the *World Bank.* Both institutions, which received more than their share of bad press during the Third World debt crisis in the mid- to late 1980s, were established as the foundation of the postwar economic order in 1944 by Britain, the US, and their wartime allies. Though their roles have changed dramatically since then, they remain two of the most powerful institutions in the world, controlling tens of billions of dollars and the economic policies of the countries that receive their loans. Until recently their roles were clearly defined: The *IMF* would provide low-interest loans in exchange for the recipient adopting a package of monetary policies, and the *World Bank* granted loans for specific project development. But lately these duties have blurred. Some banking experts contend that the two institutions will eventually merge into one.

Strolling around this area at lunchtime, you will hear a veritable Tower of Babel of languages spoken, reminding you that that these are truly global institutions. Drop in on the *IMF Visitors' Center* (700 19th St.; phone: 202-623-6869), which features an art gallery, crafts from Third World countries, a film series, a library, a reading room, and a lecture series on international economic issues. It's closed weekends; there's no admission charge.

Just a quarter of a block past H Street, 19th Street meets Pennsylvania Avenue. But this tour does not head in the direction of the influential residents at No. 1600 who make this street famous (see *Walk 3: Downtown*). Instead, follow Pennsylvania Avenue left as it turns to the northwest. Walk through the canyon of "federal buildings" (a handy, catch-all description that amateur Washington tour guides employ when they are stumped by the identity of yet another marble building).

At the corner of Pennsylvania Avenue and 20th Street is *Dominique's,* a Washington restaurant known for exotic game dishes like rattlesnake and alligator, and a chocolate truffle dessert named after Elizabeth Taylor (phone: 202-452-1126). This is also the corner where I Street veers off to the left, parallel with the other alphabet streets; the first block of attractive townhouses here is known as "Lion's Row." It underwent a brilliant renovation in the early 1980s that preserved the brick façades. A petite mall within a couple of the townhouses contains several shops (*Ciao,* a sandwich shop; *Tower Records;* a newsstand; the *Gap;* and so on). Also, a one-block stroll across Pennsylvania Avenue brings the walker with an appetite for Italian food to *Primi Piatti* (2013 I St. NW; phone: 202-223-3600), an establishment that specializes in simple, delicious pasta dishes.

A short stroll down I Street leads to the Foggy Bottom *Metro* station and the conclusion of this tour.

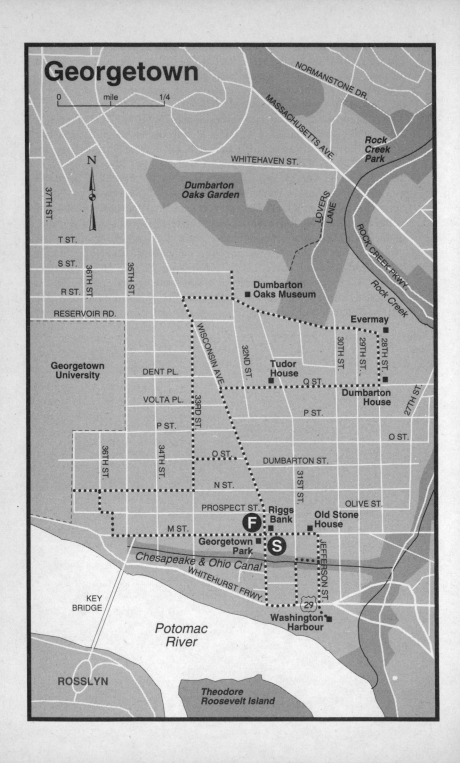

Walk 6: Georgetown

Though Washingtonians are quick to claim the historic area in west Washington as their own—the municipal government in its ravenous search for revenue is particularly proprietary on this score—the people of Georgetown would rather be left alone.

Formerly a booming Maryland tobacco port and now Washington's oldest neighborhood, Georgetown is home to the city's stateliest Federal-era architecture. Georgetown became part of the federal territory in 1790 when it was incorporated into the newfangled District Territory by George Washington and city architect Pierre L'Enfant, but it remained an independent town.

Then the Potomac began filling in with silt, and in the years of decline that followed, Georgetown lost its pre-eminent port status to Alexandria (Virginia) and Baltimore (Maryland). Georgetown was finally swallowed whole by the capital city in 1871, as the town was a seething hotbed of secessionist fervor throughout the Civil War, and the federal city couldn't risk keeping a heretic on its flank.

Initially, it was hoped that this acquisition would stave off Georgetown's economic power slide. Instead, because of suburban flight, the District itself entered an era of decline, and Georgetown found itself aboard a sinking ship. Furthermore, as part of the District of Columbia, the town lost its congressman and its right to vote for president. Adding insult to injury, against the vehement protests of the locals, colonial street names such as Water Street, Fishing Lane, and the Keyes were turned into the anonymous and impersonal alphabet soup of street letters to conform with L'Enfant's plan and the rest of the city. The neighborhood was brought to its knees.

In desperation, Georgetown attempted to regain its slumping property values and escape the creeping blight of the District by asking Maryland to take the town back, as Virginia had done with Alexandria in 1843. No such luck. "Georgetownians," in response, hunkered down like Herefords in a snowstorm. Ironically, it was the fanatics of 20th-century federalism, the New Dealers, that discovered this historic district and breathed life back into its decaying mansions, crumbling townhouses, and bumbling business district. It got a new lease on life in the 1940s when New Deal administrators came looking for homes, and the area began to boom.

Today, with its world class university and brimming cornucopia of shops, colonial architecture, fine restaurants, and thriving nightlife, Georgetown has clearly benefited from its association with Washington and the federal government. But the average Georgetown resident won't admit it. Fiercely independent, the people of Georgetown still cling to their district's old name. Never mind that it was named not after King George II, as some contend, but after one George Boone, a simpleton farmer who happened to purchase a chunk of land here in the early days: Residents refuse to accept their community being called West Washington—the district's official label—and are known to use Georgetown, DC, for their postal address. Much to the chagrin of tourists, local residents also rejected the construction of a *Metro* route through their community, and they refused to allow DC lottery tickets to be sold in Georgetown (indeed, property owners and trust-fund beneficiaries in this wealthy district don't need to win a lottery).

Georgetown's sequestered geography has helped it maintain its separate-and-better status. Rock Creek is an ideal buffer zone between the rest of Washington and Georgetown, which is flanked by the Gothic campus of *Georgetown University* to the west and the Potomac to the south. There is no threat to the north, where Georgetown gives way to the posh Cleveland Park residential area. In fact, Wisconsin Avenue is the only thoroughfare that makes its way into Georgetown unencumbered by parkland or greenery. A word: It's fair to say that certain stretches of this avenue have succumbed to the tackier side of tourism, and human gridlock is not unknown on a clear day.

Our walking tour of Georgetown begins at the intersection of M Street and Wisconsin Avenue, a bustling corner around which all of Georgetown revolves. The crush of pedestrians on weekends here is almost as dense as during a papal visit or at a *Redskins* game at *RFK Stadium.* Though the golden-domed building on the northeast corner looks as if it might have some historical significance, it doesn't. It is the *Riggs Bank,* which is a useful landmark and a reliable meeting place; gracing its tower is a trusty clock.

On business days, libating lobbyists, politicos, and other serge-suited power brokers can be seen from the street dining in the clubby atmosphere of *Nathan's* (3150 M St.; phone: 202-338-2000), a popular Georgetown dining spot with a good Italian kitchen specializing in fresh pasta and seafood dishes. The front bar's understated atmosphere and impressive selection of champagne draw a sophisticated crowd.

Just up Wisconsin Avenue—one of the few remaining streets that predate L'Enfant's master plan for the capital city—is the *American Café* (1211 Wisconsin Ave.; phone: 202-944-9464), a DC institution. Founded in 1977, this flagship restaurant has thus far spawned 18 franchises from Richmond to Baltimore. No visit to Washington is complete without a lunch stop here. Try the mushroom pesto lasagne, Baja flour-tortilla rolls, or tarragon chicken salad.

Begin walking east on M Street (in the direction of the *Riggs Bank* side of Wisconsin Avenue). If you need to stock up on smoking supplies, or simply enjoy a quick jaunt through a tobacco store to take in a complexity of aromas and view the intricate tobacco paraphernalia, nose your way into *Georgetown Tobacco & Pipe Stores* (3144 M St.; phone: 202-338-5100). The late Egyptian President Anwar Sadat used to smoke out this shop during his Washington visits for its special blend of pipe tobacco. Near the corner of M and 31st Streets is *Bistro Français* (3128 M St.; phone: 202-338-3830), an authentic French bistro with reasonably priced *boeuf* in a romantic setting that gives francophiles a taste of *la belle France*—without the hefty airfare.

Across the street is *Old Glory* (3139 M St.; phone: 202-337-3406), the restaurant and pub where one is most likely to have a sighting of Elvis in the Washington area. The staff swear up and down that "the King" frequents the place—which serves excellent burgers, barbecued ribs, and beer along with fancier items—and that he hunches down on the end barstool, where he savors a sassafras and his anonymity. Even if the rock legend does not waddle in while you're there, a gaudy ceramic likeness of his majesty sits behind the bar, keeping the faith alive.

Continue down M Street to a two-story stone cottage on the left. This is the *Old Stone House* (3051 M St.; phone: 202-426-6851), which is thought to be the only surviving pre-Revolutionary building in the District. Built by Pennsylvania cabinetmaker Christopher Layman in 1764, this house has been many things to its residential and commercial occupants over the years. Currently, the registered historical site's proprietor is the *National Park Service,* which keeps the house's furnishings—including solid beds, simple tables, and spinning wheels—true to its 18th-century colonial heritage. After inspecting its interior, walk around to the house's subdued garden, rich with fruit trees. It's closed Mondays and Tuesdays, and there is no admission charge.

Now cross M Street to Jefferson Street. For some time, the area south of M Street (formerly Bridge Street, it was named after the bridge that spanned Rock Creek to the east) was a working class neighborhood, home to the manual laborers, tradesmen, and merchants of this once-thriving port and industrial city. Today these once-modest dwellings—most of which have undergone major refurbishment—sell for upwards of $400,000. Several of these upscale remnants can be seen on Jefferson Street—at Nos. 1069, 1067, and 1063 (with plaster covering the brick of the latter). Constructed by the Irish navvies (construction workers) who built the Chesapeake & Ohio (C & O) Canal, these three red brick Federal houses, just past the *Georgetown Dutch Inn,* have weathered the test of time and the rumbling blight of the Whitehurst Freeway ahead. But before you reach them, note the two-story building at No. 1083, which was built around the time of the Civil War as a stable for the horses and hearses of an undertaker who lived nearby. A hoist to lift hay, wood, and other supplies to the second floor can be seen above a window to the far right. Part of the building is now occupied by a frame shop.

Walk down Jefferson Street to where it crosses the C & O Canal. The bridge crossing this trickling artifact of a bygone mode of transportation is a good place from which to view the locks of the canal.

Completed in 1850, the C & O Canal kept Washington accessible to shipping after the Potomac filled with silt. The *C & O* was the brainchild of George Washington, who first advanced the idea of water traffic moving between the Potomac and Ohio rivers and crossing the Appalachians. Georgetown represents the eastern end of this canal, which extends 184 miles to Cumberland, Maryland—a little short of its destination. By the time this stretch of the canal was completed, the *B & O (Baltimore and Ohio) Railroad* had virtually derailed its usefulness.

The canal consisted of 174 locks and a towpath on both sides for the mules that methodically pulled the barges. Today, the C & O is a historical and aesthetic complement to Georgetown. *Supreme Court* Justice William O. Douglas saved it from the concrete madness of the 1950s, preventing it from being turned into a four-lane highway. From early spring to late autumn, mule-drawn canal barges carry passengers down the waterway. (See *Boating* in DIVERSIONS.) For now, complete the trip on foot down Jefferson Street, crossing K Street under the Whitehurst Freeway.

The riverfront commercial haven that opens before you is *Washington Harbour,* built by Arthur Cotton Moore in 1986. Though it certainly makes no contribution to environmental purity, the fact that it replaced an ugly, foul-smelling foundry makes this ritzy complex an improvement to the area. Top floors house office buildings and luxury apartments. The first floor is monopolized by a column of rather pricey restaurants; a few of the better ones include *Sequoia,* with American fare (on the right overlooking the Potomac; phone: 202-944-4881); *Tony and Joe's Seafood Place* (on the left overlooking the Potomac; phone: 202-944-4200), featuring fresh seafood with an unbeatable view of the river, especially from the vantage point of outdoor seating; *Hisago* (on the right; phone: 202-944-4181), an authentic Japanese restaurant—with such authentic prices you may conclude it's priced in yen; and *Jaimalito's* (on the left; phone: 202-944-4400), a reasonably priced eatery with an unmistakable Santa Fe feel and delicious enchiladas with blue corn tortillas, black bean soup, and mesquite-grilled dishes. If you're not lured by the restaurants, walk around the fountains out to the promenade that runs along the Potomac and enjoy the splendid view of the *Kennedy Center* and the *Watergate* down the river to the left. On the way out of *Washington Harbour,* tip your cap to the statue by J. Seward Johnson, Jr., of a workman on his lunch break.

Once out of *Washington Harbour,* cross K Street and walk back up Jefferson Street; cross over the C & O Canal, and follow a path on the left which leads parallel to the canal and past a jumble of inexpensive eateries. When you reach 31st Street, turn left and cross the canal again. On the left, toward the end of the block and the intersection with K Street, is *Café La Ruche* (1039 31st St.; phone: 202-965-2684), a cozy French eatery that serves excellent desserts and various coffees.

Though it might take some snooping to find it—with the current construction going on in this area—there is a plaque commemorating the spot on which *Suter's Tavern* stood, on the left side at the corner of 31st and K Streets. The tavern was the watering hole where, in 1791, George Washington convinced the men who owned the tobacco farms and marshes east of Georgetown to sell their land to the federal government so that work could begin on forging the capital city. If not for the consent of this tough crowd (George must have won them over with one too many beers), Washington, DC, as we know it might never have been.

It was also because *Suter's Tavern* had the market cornered on libations at the turn of the 19th century that many senators and congressmen settled in Georgetown after the federal government moved from Philadelphia to Washington. One particularly cranky member of Congress wrote that "there was only one good tavern within a day's march" of Congress. Thus, many members lived nearby and were driven to and from the daily sessions of Congress in a rickety coach.

The buildings along K Street—which, along with the Whitehurst Freeway, cast this whole area in perpetual shade—are the domain of many advertising, public relations, and architecture firms. Walk right, down K Street, and stop at the corner of K Street and Wisconsin Avenue. The three buildings on the west side were built in 1830 by Francis Dodge, a local merchant who had a booming grocery business.

Walk up Wisconsin Avenue. Perched on higher ground and beyond a wrought-iron fence on the right is the stone Gothic Revival Grace Episcopal Church. This was the house of worship for those who built and worked on the C & O Canal. At that time this was the poor section of town; but the collection plate is probably a little less barren these days.

Continue along Wisconsin Avenue, over the only bridge crossing the C & O Canal that remains from the 19th century. An obelisk on the north side honors the people who worked on the canal. A more intriguing plaque is embedded in the wall of the *Vigilant Firehouse* (1066 Wisconsin Ave.), built in 1840. Scant on the sordid details, it reads: "Bush, the Old Fire Dog, died of Poison, July 5th, 1869, R.I.P." Return to the intersection of Wisconsin Avenue and M Street, and turn left.

Tastefully hidden behind the reconstructed 19th-century façades of Georgetown's commercial district is *Georgetown Park*, a lovely mélange of tony shops in a Victorian decor which proves that all indoor shopping malls need not be characterless temples to consumerism. It is the type of place in which Queen Victoria would have felt comfortable if she'd been given to mall-cruising in a climate-controlled environment. The mall comprises over 100 shops with names such as *Caché*, the ritzy Miami boutique, *Godiva Chocolatier, FAO Schwarz,* and *Polo/Ralph Lauren* (see *Shopping* in THE CITY). Even if you're not in an acquisitive mood, visit the atrium and indoor garden, which is encircled by three tiers of shops. After returning to the street, continue down M Street away from Wisconsin Avenue.

This stretch of M Street is a chain of shops, broken only by the occasional restaurant, marketing everything from antiques and jewelry to bicycle accessories and records. Of particular interest, in the way of food, is *Clyde's* (3236 M St. NW; phone: 202-333-9180), on the left. Noted for its dark pub atmosphere, its thick burgers and brunch have kept it in business for over 25 years (with some help from its excellent location). There are also some good Ethiopian, Indian, and Thai restaurants along here. And don't overlook *Dean & Deluca* (next to *Georgetown Park* at 3276 M St. NW; phone: 202-342-2500); this branch of the justly celebrated New York food emporium offers a fabulous array of prepared foods, fresh fruits, vegetables, meat, seafood, and deli items. There's also a coffee bar—a pleasant place to enjoy a light snack. The prices aren't for the faint of heart, but there are some (relative) bargains to be had.

Continue west on M Street to the Key Bridge, which leads into Rosslyn, Virginia. Primarily a jumble of office buildings that house consulting firms of one sort or another, Rosslyn is a classic example of the "edge cities" for which Washington is becoming increasingly noted. A house owned by Francis Scott Key, author of the national anthem, once stood on the site where you are now standing. Though his house was cleared from this area to make way for the bridge, the bridge was named after him. (Always swamped with traffic, it's not much of a legacy.) A memorial park to Key has taken root on the plot of ground just east of the bridge.

Now begins the ascent to higher ground. Just past the old brick *Streetcar Barn* (now housing a row of offices), on the right, are the so-called "Exorcist Steps," a favorite site where locals congregate on *Halloween* or after yet another viewing of the eponymous movie that was filmed in and around the red brick *Georgetown University* building at the top and to the left of the stairs (3600 Prospect St.). The exorcist, as you may recall, met an unpleasant, head-over-heels fate on these 75 steps in the movie's final scene. Watch your step. The *Georgetown University* crew team runs up and down these stairs several times daily for a rigorous workout.

After climbing the steps and taking a breather, walk up 36th Street. On the left in a nondescript 18th-century house is *1789* (1226 36th St.; phone: 202-965-1789), a restaurant that features game, salmon, caviar, oysters, and other well-prepared American dishes. With its working fireplace, etchings, and solemn atmosphere, the dining room would have been an ideal setting for FDR's fireside chats. Indeed, after you see the check you may wish the well-heeled late president was here to pick up the tab. Down a flight of steps is *The Tombs* (1226 36th St.; phone: 202-337-6668), a markedly more informal dining experience that is a favorite among *Georgetown University* students and their professors.

At N Street, turn left and walk the short distance to the campus of *Georgetown University* (main entrance is at 37th and O Sts.; phone: 202-687-5055), a world-caliber institution of higher learning that includes President Clinton among its distinguished alums. It's known for its preponderance of international students (they come from more than 90 countries), the nation's only foreign-service program, excellent graduate programs in law and medicine, and an often near-legendary basketball team. Founded in 1789 by John Carroll, the first American bishop, the university is the oldest Jesuit school in the US. Take some time to walk about the campus and experience its old world, scholarly charm. Most notable are the *Old North Building,* the school's original edifice built in 1792, and the *Healy Building* (built in 1879), a brooding yet redoubtable German Gothic structure with a spire that seems to puncture the heavens.

Now, retrace your steps down N Street to the corner of 34th and turn right. At the end of the block, across the street and on the right, is the majestic *Halcyon House,* built in 1783 and named by Benjamin Stoddert, the first secretary of the Navy. Though the interior today features nothing of interest, there is a gorgeous view of the Potomac from here. Appropriately, the street that runs east-west, parallel to M Street, was named Prospect Street because of its mesmerizing vista—especially at sundown.

Return to N Street and turn right. Halfway down the next block on the left is *Cox's Row,* a row of Federal houses built in 1817 by John Cox, a former mayor of Georgetown. In the late 1950s, the simple, red brick house at 3307 N Street was the home of then-Senator John F. Kennedy and his family before they moved into the more spacious quarters at 1600 Pennsylvania Avenue.

The next block is the intersection with 33rd Street. Walk up 33rd almost to the next block. On the left is an intriguing, barn-red stone house with a tiny white steeple on top of it; it was once the stable of the statelier house on the corner. More than 150 years old, the house still has the wooden gable that was used to hoist hay to the second-floor loft. The stained glass windows are said to have come from the *Persian Embassy.*

Continue up 33rd Street to O Street and take a little time to ramble up and down this street. The Federal and Victorian architecture on O Street are some of Washington's most endearing. The brilliantly colored townhouses (tasteful light yellows next to distasteful fluorescent greens next to bright red houses with bright blue trim, and the like) seem to instill ebullience in the spirit and a spring in one's step. Also, notice the trolley tracks and the cobblestones in O Street.

Several blocks east of 33rd Street on O Street is *St. John's Episcopal Church* (3240 O St. NW; phone: 202-338-1796), built in 1809 by Dr. William Thornton, the same architect who built the *Capitol* building. Though the church was altered drastically in 1870 to appear more Victorian than Federal, the *Capitol* resemblance lingers ever-so-slightly in the dome-shape structure, with its extending wings on either side.

Return to 33rd Street and turn right. This thoroughfare cuts through the location of some of Georgetown's nicer homes. The residences become increasingly sprawling as you walk north. Follow 33rd Street five blocks to the intersection with Wisconsin Avenue. Though we will be crossing Wisconsin and swinging around the imposing *Georgetown Library* on R Street, there are several shops that might pique your curiosity on Wisconsin.

For sheer shock value, slink into *Commander Salamander* (1420 Wisconsin Ave.; phone: 202-337-2265), which attracts the "leather-and-attitude" crowd along with some customers who are content to stare at the shop's unabashed weirdness. If in need of leather, chains, leopard skin garments, or rhinestone sunglasses, this shop is pay dirt. (It's open until midnight on Fridays and Saturdays.) Another entertaining clothing store is *Up Against the Wall* (3219 M St. NW; phone: 202-337-9316). *Urban Outfitters* (3111 M St. NW; phone: 342-1012) also offers offbeat clothing and accessories. After browsing, walk up Wisconsin to R Street and turn right.

Pass the library, and continue to 32nd Street and turn north (left). Though it's not immediately apparent, over the brick wall is *Dumbarton Oaks* (1703 32nd St.; phone: 202-342-3200 or 202-338-8278). A painstakingly preserved 19th-century estate, it is one of Washington's truly special places. The badly dilapidated mansion and grounds were bought in the 1920s by Robert Woods Bliss, former Ambassador to Argentina, and his wife. They quickly set about creating the present museum and gardens. *Dumbarton Oaks* also gave its name to a crucial, groundbreaking series of meetings to form the United Nations charter; held in the estate's lavish mansion in 1944, the meetings were attended by representatives of the US, Great Britain, China, and the Soviet Union. Franklin Roosevelt's strategy for holding the talks at *Dumbarton Oaks* was made plain when he said during one of the meeting's press conferences: "If you can get the parties into a room with a big table and make them take their coats off and put their feet up on the table, and give them a good cigar, you can always make them agree." *Dumbarton Oaks* laid the groundwork for the *San Francisco Conference* the following year at which the United Nations was formally founded.

The surrounding gardens are a foliage fanatic's nirvana, and a walk among the intricate network of arbors, gardens, pools, fountains, and terraces is one of Washington's most delightful outdoor experiences. Access to the garden is through the R Street entrance (31st and R Sts.). The museum, which the Bliss family sold to *Harvard University,* contains a world-renowned collection of pre-Columbian and Byzantine art, displayed in nine glass cylinders. The mansion is closed Mondays, and doesn't open until 2 PM the rest of the week. Donations are requested. The lush gardens are open daily, and there is a small admission charge to see them.

Return to R Street and turn left. North of R Street are town parks, *Dumbarton Oaks,* and *Montrose Park,* which lie east of the Bliss estate and were formerly part of the Blisses' holdings. Farther east on R Street, where it turns sharply right, is the private *Evermay* (1623 28th St.), long considered one of Washington's most elegant homes. Now occupied by heirs to the DuPont fortune, this Georgian manor has been restored to its former opulence; the grounds are open to the public once a year during *Garden Week,* sponsored by *St. John's Episcopal Church* in April (see above for phone number).

R Street angles right and intersects with Q Street. A few paces left on Q Street is *Dumbarton House* (2715 Q St.; phone: 202-337-2288), not to be confused with *Dumbarton Oaks*. This 19th-century Georgian home was built by the *Capitol* architect Dr. William Thornton, and features oval rooms and Federal furnishings that are maintained by the *National Society of the Colonial Dames of America*. Fine collections of silver and china are on display. Many famous figures have stayed here, including First Lady Dolley Madison, who is said to have lodged here while fleeing Washington and its sacking by the British in 1814. It's worth a look for its representation of period style, and is open daily; there's an admission charge.

From here, take a right to walk west on Q Street, toward Wisconsin Avenue. Between 31st and 32nd Streets, note *Tudor Place* (1644 31st St.; phone: 202-965-0400) which, despite its name, is a neo-classical mansion; built in 1816, it was first occupied by Martha Washington's granddaughter and her husband, Thomas Peter, son of Georgetown's first mayor. Because of the link with the nation's first First Family, *Tudor Place* contains many furnishings and items from Mount Vernon. The house remained in the same family until 1983, when, after the death of its last Peter family occupant, a foundation was established to refurbish the house and open it to the public. House tours are available Tuesdays through Saturdays; gardens are open daily. There is an admission charge. It is recommended that you call ahead to reserve a place in a tour.

Turn left onto Wisconsin Avenue and walk (downhill, thankfully) four blocks to the corner of Wisconsin Avenue and M Street, where our tour began.

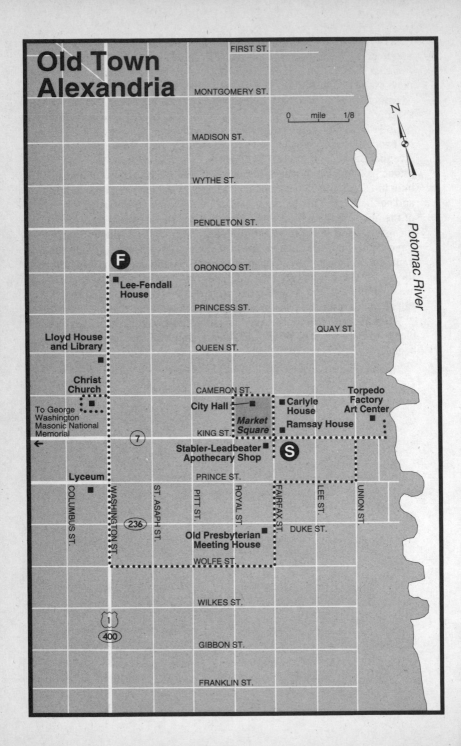

Old Town Alexandria

FIRST ST.

MONTGOMERY ST.

0   mile   1/8

N

Potomac River

MADISON ST.

WYTHE ST.

PENDLETON ST.

F

ORONOCO ST.

■ **Lee-Fendall House**

PRINCESS ST.

QUAY ST.

Lloyd House and Library

QUEEN ST.

■

Christ Church

CAMERON ST.

Torpedo Factory Art Center

To George Washington Masonic National Memorial

■ **City Hall**

■ **Carlyle House**

Market Square

■ **Ramsay House**

■

←

⑦

KING ST.

Stabler-Leadbeater Apothecary Shop ■

S

Lyceum

PRINCE ST.

■

COLUMBUS ST.

WASHINGTON ST.

ST. ASAPH ST.

PITT ST.

ROYAL ST.

FAIRFAX ST.

LEE ST.

UNION ST.

②③⑥

Old Presbyterian Meeting House ■

DUKE ST.

WOLFE ST.

WILKES ST.

① 400

GIBBON ST.

FRANKLIN ST.

Walk 7: Old Town Alexandria

Virginia's rich colonial history is carefully sustained in *Old Town* Alexandria, the heart and soul of a sprawling suburban city just south of the District of Columbia. *Old Town,* as Washingtonians affectionately call it, has masterfully harmonized its cobblestoned streets, historic public buildings, and painstakingly preserved private residences with the neighborhood's newer—and livelier—additions: chic restaurants, pubs, clubs, and shops.

Old Town was founded in 1749 by a spirited band of Scottish merchants, on land purchased by Scotsman John Alexander in 1699. Still represented by shops selling tartans, bagpipes, and kilts, and by a restaurant called *Scotland Yard* (see below), Alexandria's Scottish forefathers are not forgotten by the city's modern-day residents. Their spirits return to life in early December, when the Scottish *Christmas March* down King Street heralds the *Christmas* season.

In the late 18th century, when tobacco was Virginia's cash crop, Alexandria's Potomac port was a center of colonial commerce. In exchange for the hogsheads of tobacco shipped to England from Virginia's burgeoning plantations, schooners returned to Alexandria laden with the fashionable clothing, musical instruments, tea, books, exotic spices, and other trappings of European culture coveted by the wealthy tobacco merchants who constituted the colonial aristocracy. Consequently, stately mansions were built, sophisticated shops were opened, and luxurious inns were established.

Like the ancient Egyptian city after which it was named, Alexandria attracted the area's best and brightest. It was a popular meeting place for the likes of an ambitious land surveyor named George Washington and "Light Horse" Harry Lee, whose son, Robert E. Lee, led the Confederate army during the Civil War. Pervaded by the history of both families, Alexandria is home to more than one venue in which the claim "George Washington slept here" is not just an idle boast. The same can be said about Presidents Thomas Jefferson and John Adams, not to mention George Mason, who was renowned for his efforts in drafting the *Bill of Rights.*

Perhaps to its advantage, Alexandria narrowly avoided becoming the nation's capital in the late 18th century. That idea, promoted for a short time by Thomas Jefferson and others, was vetoed by George Washington. His *Mount Vernon* home dangerously near, Washington probably wanted to maintain his distance from the fragile new federal capital, which was in fact overtaken and sacked by the British less than two decades later. Nevertheless, because of its charm and proximity to Washington, Alexandria has inherited a teeming population of that barnacle on the US ship of state:

the lobbyist. Over 170 associations, ranging from the *Snack Food Association of America* to the *National Helicopter Association,* are headquartered here.

Everything worth seeing in *Old Town* Alexandria can be seen on foot. The historical buildings, quaint shops, and cobblestone streets are concentrated in a manageable, three-hour walk. The *Old Town* tour begins at *Ramsay House* (221 King St.; phone: 703-838-4200), also known as the *Alexandria Convention and Visitors' Bureau.*

Alexandria's oldest building (1724), *Ramsay House* was shipped upriver by barge from Dumfries, Virginia, around 1750, off-loaded, and dragged to its present location. The house now contains a few family letters that belonged to its owner, William Ramsay, a founder of Alexandria, its first postmaster, and lord mayor. The *Visitors' Bureau* on the first floor offers a bounty of brochures on the city, as well as a film about the town that, though generally uninspiring, contains a cameo appearance by Lt. Col. Francis Slate, Alexandria's official town crier. A distinguished Alexandrian who belts out the news in public, Slate once captured the title of world's loudest town crier at a competition in Nova Scotia. The house is open daily and there is no admission charge. After parking, request a pass from the house—and be sure to place it on your windshield. Meter attendants in the Washington area are renowned for their precision timing and lightning-fast ticket writing.

Walking north from King Street, turn the corner on Fairfax Street to *Carlyle House* (121 N. Fairfax St.; phone: 703-549-2997), another remnant of Alexandria's Scottish heritage. Designed to resemble a Scottish stone manor house, it was one of the first homes built in the fledgling town. This grand, mid-Georgian dwelling—home of Scottish merchant John Carlyle—dates from 1752. Perhaps its finest hour, though, was when it was chosen by General Edward Braddock and five colonial governors as their headquarters for planning the early campaign strategy and funding for the French and Indian War. Some of the Carlyle family's personal belongings are on display, rescued from dormant privy shafts and trash chutes by an unflappable band of archaeologists during the building's restoration in the 1970s. Though the contents are what one would expect to find in a flea market, the house is impressive and is best seen on guided tours, scheduled every half hour. Closed Mondays. There is an admission charge, except for children under 10.

Turn right out of *Carlyle House,* then left on Cameron Street, and walk one block to Royal Street.

On the corner is *Gadsby's Tavern* (138 N. Royal St.; phone: 703-548-1288). This was once the *City Tavern and Hotel,* a crossroads of 18th-century political, business, and social life, and a favorite haunt of George Washington. At nearly 200 years old, the restaurant offers historic ambience—plenty of pewter, an original Hogarth painting in one of the three dining rooms (the first room entered was originally the tavern), and waiters and waitresses in colonial garb—and a menu that features game, prime ribs, and some of the finest pecan pie this side of Georgia. A note to patrons from the "Tavern Keeper" explains why it's all right to have left home without your American Express card: "The tax upon this establishment by American Express was more repressive than the tax on tea imposed by the King. We therefore have thrown American Express over the side with the tea. We apologize if any of our customers get wet because of this, but we are sure you applaud this act against tyranny."

Next door to the tavern is *Gadsby's Tavern Museum* (134 N. Royal St.; phone: 703-838-4242). Built in 1770, it contains the second-floor ballroom in which George Washington attended gala birthday celebrations. The room is actually a reproduction, since the original (in its entirety) is now housed in the *American Wing* of New York's *Metropolitan Museum of Art.* A celebration of George Washington's birthday, called the *Night Ball,* is held here annually the weekend of or before Washington's birthday. Around the back are several original outbuildings, including a brick coffeehouse, a stable, a kitchen, and outdoor seating for the restaurant during the warm months.

Return one block to King Street, Alexandria's leading thoroughfare, and turn left. The block on the left is *Market Square/City Hall.* Two half-acre parcels of land were reserved in 1749 for the city marketplace, *Town Hall,* and the courthouse. George Washington became a trustee of the market in 1766 and encouraged its growth by sending wagons of produce from Mt. Vernon to be sold here every week. With all that has come, gone, or burned down over the years—including schools, jails, whipping posts, and a clock and bell tower—this block's service to the city remains unchanged. Here you'll find the *Alexandria Farmers' Market,* the longest continuously operating market of its kind in the US, open every Saturday from 5 to 9 AM, with a mixed bag of stallkeepers peddling produce, meats, baked goods, and handmade crafts from the arcades on the south plaza of *City Hall.* Early visitors (those who arrive before 7 AM) are rewarded with free hot coffee and ham biscuits (phone: 703-370-8723).

A right turn on Fairfax Street leads to the doorstep of the historic *Stabler-Leadbeater Apothecary Shop* (107 S. Fairfax St.; phone: 703-836-3713), a charming remedy to the sanitized, impersonal feel of today's mega-drug-stores. This unassuming little shop is the second-oldest apothecary in the country; it once contributed to the health of the Washington and Lee families, and distributed its own medicines and cosmetics to customers in seven states. Now a museum, it offers a dose of history that includes an impressive collection of antique drugstore furnishings and apothecary bottles (some still filled with their original contents), a note from Martha Washington for a quart bottle of the proprietor's "best castor oil and the bill for it," and an 1861 entry in a logbook by an excited shop clerk reading: "Alexandria taken by US forces this morning at 5 o'clock; Ellsworth killed, great excitement, stores generally closed." It was here, in 1859, that Lt. Col. Robert E. Lee received orders to move to Harper's Ferry to head off John Brown's insurrection. The spot where Lee stood upon hearing the fateful news is marked by a plaque. There is a small admission charge, except for children under 10 and members of the *Mortar and Pestle Society;* it's closed Sunday mornings.

Return to King Street and walk east toward the Potomac. The blocks past *Ramsay House* are dense with restaurants, bookstores, boutiques, and more. There are more than 200 shops within walking distance of *Ramsay House;* most are individually owned and operated, featuring all manner of unique and specialty merchandise. There are art galleries, fancy food stores, and shops selling jewelry, cookware, pipes and cigars, and more. The French Quarter meets the Scottish Quarter at *219* (219 King St.; phone: 703-549-1141), a better-than-average creole restaurant with cool, traditional jazz played upstairs in the *Basin Street Lounge.* Next door is the *Scottish Merchant* (215 King St.; phone: 703-739-2302), an emporium selling kilts, tartans, bagpipes, and the best (and only) collection of Scottish music cassettes in the Washington area. The shop still does some business among the local clans.

Across the street is a collection of shops that feature Civil War books and memorabilia, foods and wines, and a café with excellent coffees. Farther along is the *Small Mall* (118 King St.; no phone), with shops offering American craftworks by artists from across the country. Back across the street is the *Fish Market* (105 King St.; phone: 703-836-5676), located in an 18th-century warehouse used to store ships' cargo. This is one of *Old Town*'s most bustling watering holes, and an ideal location to savor a plate of oysters, chowder, broiled scallops, or crabs prepared in any conceivable style. The place is also known for its "schooners" of beer, the swimming pool–like glasses in which they serve up the froth.

At the corner of King Street (at the top) is Union Street, which runs parallel to the Potomac, whose waters are visible beyond the pier straight ahead. On the northeast corner is one of Alexandria's treasures, the *Torpedo Factory Art Center* (105 N. Union St.; phone: 703-838-4565). Formerly a munitions plant where naval torpedoes were manufactured for World Wars I and II, this spacious, restored building is now devoted to a rather more docile effort. Though it remains as industrious as it was when serving the war effort, it now serves the muse as the studio and gallery for more than 175 professional artists, including painters, jewelers, photographers, sculptors, and textile designers. All the workshops are open to visitors, and most of the work can be purchased at reasonable prices; it's open daily, and there is no admission charge. In the same building is the museum and laboratory of *Alexandria Archaeology,* an organization that conducts explorations around Alexandria and displays objects that have been uncovered from as far back as 3000 BC. It's closed Mondays; no admission charge (phone: 703-838-4399).

For a better view of the Potomac, walk around behind the art center to a recently constructed waterfront area that includes—jutting out over the river—the *Chart House* restaurant (1 Cameron St.; phone: 703-684-5080), with its solid menu of prime ribs, fresh seafood dishes, and the always boda-cious 67-item salad bar for which this chain is famous. The restaurant's *Capitol Room* affords a view of the *Capitol Building* up the river, in Washington. This area is also home to numerous fast-food eateries, in case you don't have the time or the budget for a real sit-down meal.

Now, walk south, back across King Street, on Union Street. Between King and Prince Streets in a brick building on the right is the *Union Street Public House* (121 S. Union St.; phone: 703-548-1785), a pub/restaurant usually well-stocked with patrons and good cheer. It is one of the Washington area's finest settings for swilling brewery beer (try the *Virginia Native,* brewed by the *Virginia Brewing Company* exclusively for the pub), and features a mishmash of good American food with a southern flair.

Follow Union Street south one block to Prince Street. Turn right and begin climbing this picturesque cobblestone street. The first block is known as Captain's Row because of the charming homes built by old sea captains in the late 18th century. Though the homes occupy the same block, their different sizes, building materials, and façade decorations bear witness to the fierce independence of the salty dogs who built them.

The cobblestones in the street, according to legend, were laid by Hessian mercenaries who fought for the British during the Revolutionary War and were later imprisoned in Alexandria. Watch your step; it's easy to twist an ankle here. The Greek Revival *Athenaeum* (201 Prince St.; phone: 703-548-0035) sits solidly at the corner of Prince and Lee Streets. Built in the mid-19th century to house the *Bank of Old Dominion,* it served its fiscal purpose for over a century. In the 1950s, this reddish-brown building was purchased by the city of Alexandria for use as an art museum and cultural-activities cen-ter. The *Athenaeum* frequently features original exhibitions of contemporary art; it's closed Mondays and Tuesdays and there is no admission charge.

The string of townhouses from Lee to Fairfax Streets beyond the *Athenaeum,* known as Gentry Row, is a series of private residences built in the mid-18th century. The houses are all in the colonial style, but their bricks are painted in wildly varying colors. It's fun to walk down this cob-blestone street of museum-like homes at night, too, where, surprisingly often, the curtains are left open.

At Fairfax Street, turn left. Less than two blocks down Fairfax on the right, just beyond Duke Street, is the *Old Presbyterian Meeting House* (321 S. Fairfax St.; phone: 703-549-6670), a popular meeting place built by and for the Scottish patriots in the Revolutionary War. Built in 1774 and still a functioning church, this somber-looking building was the site of George Washington's funeral service. A weathered tombstone in a small cemetery in the back honors the *Unknown Soldier* of the American Revolution. Sunday services are held at 8:30 and 11 AM.

Walk south one block from the meeting house to Wolfe Street. At Wolfe, make a right and stroll the several blocks to Washington Street, one of *Old Town's* main thoroughfares; turn right again into Washington Street.

Just over a block down Washington Street on the left is the *Lyceum* (201 S. Washington St.; phone: 703-838-4994), an early-19th-century building that is yet another repository of this city's treasured past. In this Grecian-style building, Alexandria's history unfolds in the form of etchings, photographs, original documents, and video presentations. It's closed Sunday mornings, and there is no admission charge.

If hunger strikes, walk a bit farther down Washington Street and turn left on King Street where you'll find *Geranio* (722 King St.; phone 703-548-0088) and *Terrazza* (710 King St.; phone: 703-683-6900), a pair of tantalizing Italian dining spots featuring northern Italian dishes. At the corner of King and Washington Streets is *Scotland Yard* (728 King St.; phone: 703-683-1742), a restaurant that features finnan haddie, quail, venison, and other Caledonian favorites. Its bar stocks the area's best selection of single malt Scotch whisky. Actual British bobbies, usually in plainclothes, may be seen hanging around here; they're in town because of an officers' exchange program between London's *Scotland Yard* and the *FBI.*

Return to Washington Street. Just past King Street is *Christ Church* (118 N. Washington St.; phone: 703-549-1450), an English country-style church that was once the house of worship of George Washington and, later, Robert E. Lee. Washington plunked down over £36—a good chunk of change at the time—for a pew (salvation wasn't cheap, even in colonial times). His pew (No. 60) is marked with a plaque, as is the pew of the Confederate general (No. 46), who grew up just down the street. The current US president is invited each year to attend services on the Sunday closest to Washington's birthday. The interior features a dazzling chandelier that was imported from England at George Washington's expense. Services are held Sunday mornings, and the church's offices are open weekdays for inquiries. Before returning to Washington Street, circle the church to see the surrounding cemetery, which contains some of the earliest sculptured gravestones in the area.

Continue north on Washington Street past the *Lloyd House and Library* (220 N. Washington St.; phone: 703-838-4577) on the left. Built in 1779, this excellent example of late-Georgian architecture was saved from demolition at the 11th hour by Alexandria's feisty preservationists. Today it houses a wealth of documents and books on Virginian history. Closed Sundays, it's part of the public library system, so there is no admission charge.

Forge ahead, noticing cobblestone Princess Street on the right, with its collection of 18th-century buildings. Two blocks from *Lloyd House* is Lee Corner, at the intersection of Washington and Oronoco Streets. At one time, a Lee family house stood on each of the four corners of this intersection. The well-marked residence on the immediate right, the *Lee-Fendall House* (614 Oronoco St.; phone: 703-548-1789), is one of only two Lee houses remaining. It was the home of Richard Henry Lee, whose moniker graces the *Declaration of Independence,* and "Light Horse" Harry Lee, a cavalry commander and father of Robert E. Lee. The 19th-century town-house across Oronoco Street (607 Oronoco St.; phone: 703-548-8454) is the boyhood home of Robert E., where he lived until decamping to West Point in 1825. His first glorious steed, a prized rocking horse, is on display here. Both homes welcome visitors, are closed Sunday mornings, and charge small admission fees.

This completes the walking tour of *Old Town* Alexandria, but a three-quarters-of-a-mile jaunt up King Street to the *George Washington Masonic National Memorial* (King St. at Callahan Dr.; phone: 703-683-2007) is recommended. This tower, based on the design of the *Pharaoh's Lighthouse* in ancient Egypt's Alexandria, is as much a temple of Masonic lore as it is a tribute to George Washington, one of the society's most prominent members. Though there are many who think it's an eyesore, it undeniably makes for a distinctive landmark, and the tower's observatory yields a splendid view of Alexandria and the Potomac. It is open daily, and there is no admission charge.

Index

Index